T0323812

Technological Innovation and Economic Development in Modern Japan

This book analyzes the relationship between technological innovation and economic development in Japan before World War II.

Guan Quan deploys econometric analysis, multivariate statistical analysis and case studies from different industries to shed light on technological innovation in the Japanese context with particular emphasis on the importance of the patent system. A great deal of new inventions and patents in this period led to fast economic growth in Japan characterized by the simultaneous development of both traditional and modern industries. These insights help reshape the understanding of Japan's economic development and industrial advancement at an early stage and provide pointers to developing countries as to how human capital, social capabilities and thereby technological innovation can figure in economic growth.

The book will appeal to academics of the East Asian economy, development economics and modern economic history as well as general readers interested in the miracle of the Japanese economy as the first to achieve economic development and modernization among non-Western countries.

Guan Quan is a professor at Renmin University of China. He has majored in Development Economics, and his research interests include China's economy and Japan's economy.

China Perspectives

The *China Perspectives* series focuses on translating and publishing works by leading Chinese scholars, writing about both global topics and China-related themes. It covers Humanities & Social Sciences, Education, Media and Psychology, as well as many interdisciplinary themes.

This is the first time any of these books have been published in English for international readers. The series aims to put forward a Chinese perspective, give insights into cutting-edge academic thinking in China, and inspire researchers globally.

Titles in economics partly include:

Demographic Perspective of China's Economic Development
Cai Fang

Inflation in China
Microfoundations, Macroeconomic Dynamics and Monetary Policy
Chengsi Zhang

China's Economic Reform and Development during the 13th Five-Year Plan Period
Lin Gang, Wang Yiming, Ma Xiaohe, Gao Debu

Cultural Economics
Li Yining

Technological Innovation and Economic Development in Modern Japan
Guan Quan

Resources, Power and Economic Interest Distribution in China
Zhang Yishan

For more information, please visit www.routledge.com/China-Perspectives/book-series/CPH

Technological Innovation and Economic Development in Modern Japan

Guan Quan

Routledge
Taylor & Francis Group

LONDON AND NEW YORK

First published in English 2021
by Routledge
2 Park Square, Milton Park, Abingdon, Oxon OX14 4RN

and by Routledge
52 Vanderbilt Avenue, New York, NY 10017

Routledge is an imprint of the Taylor & Francis Group, an informa business

© 2021 Guan Quan

English version by permission of China Renmin University Press.

British Library Cataloguing-in-Publication Data
A catalogue record for this book is available from the British Library

Library of Congress Cataloging-in-Publication Data
Names: Guan, Quan, 1955– author.
Title: Technological innovation and economic development
in modern Japan / Quan Guan.
Other titles: Kindai Nihon no inobēshon. English
Description: Abingdon, Oxon; New York, NY: Routledge, 2020. |
Series: China perspectives | Includes bibliographical references and index. |
Identifiers: LCCN 2020027661 (print) | LCCN 2020027662 (ebook) |
ISBN 9780367619831 (hardback) | ISBN 9780367635091 (paperback) |
ISBN 9781003109839 (ebook)
Subjects: LCSH: Technological innovations–Economic aspects–Japan. |
Industries–Technological innovations–Japan. | Japan–Economic conditions–1868–
Classification: LCC HC465.T4 G8413 2020 (print) |
LCC HC465.T4 (ebook) | DDC 338.952–dc23
LC record available at https://lccn.loc.gov/2020027661
LC ebook record available at https://lccn.loc.gov/2020027662

ISBN: 978-0-367-61983-1 (hbk)
ISBN: 978-1-003-10983-9 (ebk)

Typeset in Times New Roman
by Newgen Publishing UK

Contents

Figures

Tables

Foreword

I. Purpose and significance of this book

An economic powerhouse, Japan is also a technologically advanced country. The relationship between the two is inseparable. In other words, economic development is attributed in large measure to technological development or technological advance, as evidenced by a host of studies. Whether before or after World War II, the rate of technological advance or total factor productivity of the industrial and mining industries in Japan was higher than that of many developed countries today, and this figure was higher than that before World War II. A high technological advance rate or high total factor productivity does not indicate that technological levels in Japan are higher than those in other developed countries because, on the one hand, technological level is also affected by factors other than technological advances, such as the overall educational level of society; while, on the other hand, it is due to the Japan's national conditions, such as the early popularity of basic education, and industrial manufacturing skills. However, what is certain is that technological innovation activities were launched early, and that the rapid improvement in the social capabilities promoting technological innovation was a critical catalyst.

The two points are, of course, the research topics of this book. The information obtained from the technological advance rate does not exceed the level based on purely numerical estimates. The question as to whether technological innovation indeed exists, what are the characteristics if so, and how this has contributed to economic development in Japan remain unanswered. Moreover, Japan lags behind European countries and the U.S., and has abundant existing technologies available for use. At the same time, it has a high or increasing social capability to digest and absorb modern technologies. The improvement in social capabilities increases the rate of technological advance and spurs economic growth. However, social capabilities are more broadly defined than technological advances, making it hard to conduct quantitative demonstration.

Bearing this in mind, I focus on studying the relationship between Japan's economic development and technological innovation before World War II, and hopes to study the role of technological innovation in Japan's economic development. Notwithstanding that This cannot directly prove that Japan's social capabilities have improved, but it reveals the intimate link between economic development and technological innovation and shows that technological innovation underpins economic development. It also shows that social capabilities improve in tandem with the economic development, or the two are complementary, in that technological innovation is a crucial component of social capability.

This book also hopes to give some insight for developing countries. When Japan began to see economic development (or from then on), today's developing countries were chiefly colonies or semi-colonies. For example, while China was not a colony of any country, it was invaded by many countries, who set up foreign settlements, and divided up it Chinese territories. Some Asian regions became Japanese colonies, such as the Korean Peninsula, Taiwan of China, and Northeast China. In other words, when Japan initiated modern economic growth, the majority of developing countries could not develop their economies independently, and did not see any development until after World War II. Given the differences of era and historical facts, it may be rash and unreasonable to directly link Japan's development experience with other Asian countries. However, notwithstanding the different periods of economic development, the opportunities for developing countries to develop economies are not nonexistent. This varies from country to country. After World War II, some countries rapidly got back on track and saw an early economic takeoff, such as the "Four Asian Dragons". Some countries, such as those in Africa and some in Central Asia, were mired in internal strife and chaos for a long time, and did not see normal economic development. China's economic development sustained many setbacks, and did not see obvious improvement until nearly 40 years ago.

A host of factors are involved in economic development. It is not just down to abundant natural resources, a large population, or a long history. Some countries have a vast land, but cannot harness these resources to develop their economies. They can only export resources (primary products) in exchange for finished industrial products. There is still a wealth of such countries today. Other countries have a large population, but the caliber is low. Wealth generated is chiefly spent by this population, making accumulation impossible. Some countries have been subject to an unstable political environment for a long time, where the populace live in misery, while the few ruling people abuse their power and feather their own nests without any regard for the interests of the country and its populace. In this sense, Japan's experience is worthy of emulation as it has neither abundant natural resources nor a unique geographical advantage. It has seen rapid development by relying on its human resources. As these exist in every country, the key to success lies in improving and harnessing these resources.

Since the reform and opening up, China has made full use of its own natural and human resources, and mobilized the whole population to achieve rapid and globally impressive economic development. China has already reached the middle-income level, with GDP per capita in excess of US$10,000 in 2019, which is no mean achievement. As China progressed slowly in modern times, it could not hold a candle to Japan's rapid progress. For some 30 years after 1949, China made tremendous efforts and made significant progress, but could not narrow the gap with Japan. It was not until 1978, when China implemented the reform and fully mobilized its domestic resources to achieve rapid growth with the aid of external resources, that it gradually caught up with Japan. Despite a large gap (Japan's GDP per capita is about US$40,000), its current status is not what it once was. In the past, Japan saw rapid growth while China was beset by difficulties. Now Japan is slowing down while China is progressing apace.

Whether it be Japan's development over the last 150 years or China's catch-up efforts since 1949 (especially 1978), it shows the "late-mover advantage," or verifies the existence of such advantage. In other words, while making full use of domestic resources, these countries harness external resources as much as possible, especially by importing technology, to achieve rapid growth. It is noteworthy that the import of technology requires certain capacity in the importing country, including visionary entrepreneurs, and studious skilled workers who master the principles of technology. Furthermore, as far as Japan and China are concerned, government impetus and support are indispensable; the governments of both countries have made an important contribution to long-term economic development.

II. Features and composition of this book

This book studies the technological advances and technological development issues in modern Japan, with an emphasis on technological innovation. Previous studies made many observations with regard to technological advances in modern Japan, but the vast majority were concerned with the diffusion and dissemination of Western technologies and their popularization in Japan. Research on technological innovation issues is few and far between, because people generally think that in modern times, Japan did not have its own technological and innovation capability, instead achieving economic development by importing, imitating, absorbing, or making slight improvements to Western European technology. This book is geared towards technological innovation issues for two reasons: First, it is held that the improvement in Western European technology after it was exported to Japan is also a type of technological innovation, because any technology imported by Japan by its very nature was state-of-the-art. Japan could only approach or catch up with Western Europe in this way. This approach requires certain technical know-how, as well as constant exploration. These efforts are a type of innovation for Japan. Second, Japan set up the patent system in the late nineteenth century, and granted over 160,000 invention patents in 1885–1945. Moreover, the *Utility Model Act* was enacted in 1905, and a total of

340,000 utility models were registered from 1905 to 1945. Although not all of these were applied to actual purposes, they played a vital role in technological development. Moreover, some important inventions have brought benefits to Japan and even the world as a whole.

Given the above, this book attempts to find the relationship between technological innovation and economic development by looking at data on invention patents during this period, treating patents as the important part of technological innovation, and combining them with data on economic activity. Previously, only Tadashi Ishii of Japan's Patent Office collected and sorted out data on patents and compared these with data on economic activity, but he did not carry out a comprehensive economic study. In this sense, this book is original and pioneering to a certain degree, because if the data on patents that existed before World War II remained untapped, it is impossible to gain a real understanding of technological innovation in Japan during this period, nor understand whether there is an interrelationship between Japan's economic development and its technological advance. Through the research in this book, it can be said with certainty that there is an intimate relationship between the two. This is of great significance for learning about Japan's economic development and the progress of industrialization in the early stages. In other words, Japan made great efforts in technological innovation and amassed rich experience in the early days of industrialization. Furthermore, Japan evolved into a developed country because of its solid technical basis. This is not possible in many developing countries today. China promulgated regulations on incentives for inventions under the Beiyang government in the early years of the Republic of China, but to little avail. Fewer than 200 registrations were made during the entire Republic of China period (1912–1949). That is to say, technological advancement and technological innovation require not only clear provisions in laws and regulations and government support, but also a social basis. Since the founding of the People's Republic of China, there was no relevant law until 1985 when the *Patent Law* was enacted. Since then, activities became increasingly active in China, with an upward trend year on year. In the twenty-first century, China gradually became a world power in terms of annual patent applications, ranking first in the world. Despite certain quality problems, there is no denying that this achievement is highly related to the laws and knowledge awareness in society.

This book consists of five parts. Part One "Preliminary investigation" has only one chapter: "Topic and outlook" (first published as "Technology Development in Modern Japan: Topic and Outlook", *Business Studies* 42, Hitotsubashi University, September 2001). This summarizes research on technological innovation and economic development in modern Japan, and proposes the research direction of this book. Parts Two, Three, and Four each comprise three chapters studying the process and characteristics of industrial development in modern Japan from different perspectives, with emphasis on the technological innovation issues in modern Japan, especially patents. The role of technological innovation and technological advance is studied via case studies in several industries. The main content of this book was published in relevant Japanese journals, and the monograph (Quan: *Technological Innovation in Modern Japan: Patents and Economic Development*, Japan: Fuko, 2003) was published in Japan.

Part Two, "Characteristics of Innovation and Development" comprises three chapters that focus on the classification of traditional industries and modern industries, and the research into the basic relationship between technological innovation and economic development. Chapter 2, "Structural changes in industrial development: Tradition and modernity" (first published in *Economy and Economics*, Tokyo Metropolitan University, Issue 82, February 1997) focuses on the development of the industrial development in Japan from 1909– 1945. This chapter first divides the entire manufacturing sector into traditional and modern sectors based on the dual structure theory, and analyzes the similarities and differences between the two;, it then uses multivariate statistical methods such as cluster and discriminant analysis for more rigorous analysis.

Chapter 3 "Industrial development and innovation: Technology impetus and demand driver" (first published as "Technology and Civilization", 9(2) *Japan Institute of Industrial Technology History*, January 1995) completes Part Two. This chapter analyzes the nine categories including textiles, food, chemicals, and machinery. It also discusses the debate on the technology impetus and demand-driver theories in industrial development. The basic conclusion is that modern industries are driven by technology while the traditional industries are chiefly driven by demand. This chapter adopts the regression analysis approach of econometrics for demonstration.

Chapter 4, "The regional nature of the power revolution: Technological advance and regional disparity" (first published in *Economy and Economics*, Tokyo Metropolitan University, Issue 84, July 1997) uses the approach of Japanese scholar Ryoushin Minami to investigate the changes in power in various regions of Japan from the late nineteenth- to the mid-twentieth centuries, confirming Minami's view that Japan has experienced two power revolutions in modern times, and that the gap between the regions has narrowed thanks to the power revolution (popularization). In other words, the advancement and popularization of power technology has spurred industrialization, and narrowed regional disparities.

Part Three, "Conditions for innovation and development" includes three chapters, which study the role of human resources, market structure, and technology policies in promoting technological innovation and economic development. Chapter 5, "Human resources: Analysis of inventors" (51(3) *Economic Research*, Hitotsubashi University, July 2000) is the statistical analysis of the data on 860 inventors, revealing the prominent characteristics among inventors in traditional industries and modern industries, such as educational background, job title, level of invention. At the same time, it studies the educational background of inventors from an overall perspective, such as the substitution and complementary relationship between secondary and primary education, and higher education. This chapter adopts the principal component analysis, one of multivariate statistical analysis approaches, for analysis.

Chapter 6 "Market structure: TheSchumpeter Hypothesis" ("Innovation and Market Structure in Prewar Japan", first published in 35(1) *Hitotsubashi Journal of Commerce and Management*, 2000) tests the so-called Schumpeter hypothesis through research into the history of Japanese manufacturing enterprises at that time. The Schumpeter hypothesis means that large monopolistic enterprises hold more advantages in technological innovation compared to competitive SMEs. This led to different conclusions based on different empirical analysis results in the Western academic community, but no research has been conducted on Japan before World War II. Through statistical analysis (correlation analysis) and a case study, this chapter basically negates this hypothesis, holding that it is not suited to modern Japan.

Chapter 7 "Industrial policy: Analysis of the patent system" (first published as "Technological Innovation and Patent System in Prewar Japan", in 36(1) *Hitotsubashi Journal of Commerce and Management*, 2001 ("*Nankai Studies of Japan 2011*," Beijing, World Affairs Press, 2011) chiefly studies the special technology policies or mechanism closely related to technological innovation, namely the significance of the patent system. Drawing on K.J. Arrow's economics theories on major and minor inventions, it was applied to Japan's *Utility Model Act* (the law to protect minor inventions), which was introduced from Germany and developed. Data analysis proves that minor inventions played a crucial role in Japan at that time. In the absence of laws to protect this type of invention, they would have come to nothing, and the efforts of their inventors would not have been recognized. Imitation would inevitable have followed. Therefore, I hold that this institutional innovation is of crucial importance to developing countries.

Part Four "Cases of innovation and development" comprises three chapters, analyzing industrial upgrading issues in industrial development using three cases in transportation machinery. Chapter 8 "Traditional industries: The Rise and Fall of the Rickshaw Industry" (first published in *Economy and Economics*, Tokyo Metropolitan University, Issue 87, July 1998) studies the positive role of this mode of transportation invented in Japan during the Meiji period as well as the subsequent decline. Rickshaws were invented by the Japanese before and after the Meiji Restoration (1868). Thanks to the simple technology and demand in society, rickshaws quickly caught on in Japan and became an important export product, which had wide influence in China and Southeast Asia. The emerging bicycles and automobiles replaced the rickshaw industry, which is a typical transition sector.

Chapter 9 "Intermediate industry: The development of the bicycle industry" (first published as "Science of Socioeconomic History" in 62(5) *Japan Society of Socioeconomic History*, January 1997) studies the process of bicycles in Japan that emerged in the late nineteenth century and became an important machinery industry in the 1930s. Bicycles were invented by the

Germans in the early nineteenth century. After several decades of innovation, bicycles had became a safe mode of transport by the end of the century. When it was exported to Japan, a blacksmith-turned-craftsman quickly imitated and manufactured the bicycle, which caught on in Japan. In 1937, it became the top export in the Japanese machinery industry.

Chapter 10 "Modern Industries: The Rise of the Automotive Industry" (first published in "Hitotsubashi Books", Hitotsubashi University, Vol. 125, Issue 5, 2001) discusses the development of the automobile sector from scratch in Japan in the first half of the twentieth century. Cars were invented in Europe in the nineteenth century. Due to their complicated technology, they took a long time to reach mass production and popularity in Japan. Nissan and Toyota, which came into being in 1936, symbolized the emergence of the Japanese automobile industry, but the market was still dominated by trucks. Limousines did not become popular until after World War II.

Part Five, "Concluding Remarks and Implications" contains Chapter 11. This sums up the main research of this book in the hope of obtaining some patterns. It supplements the study of economic development in modern Japan and also provides inspiration for future technological advances. The conclusion summarizes three aspects of industrial development, technological innovation, and flying geese paradigm. Three aspects of industrial development, technological innovation, and the role of government, are summarized in the hope of offering reference for the study of economic development and technological innovation issues in other countries.

III. Research process and acknowledgments

I developed an interest in the subject of economic development and technological innovation in Japan chiefly for two reasons. One is the follow-up thoughts before going to Japan for overseas studies. At the end of the 1970s, China began to institute reform and open up policies following the Cultural Revolution, but at this time China was one of the least developed countries with a low GDP per capita in the world (less than $200, lower than sub-Saharan Africa). In 1972, China normalized diplomatic relations with Japan. After the reform, Japan offered economic assistance to China. Japanese products, especially home appliances, were popular in China: as the vast majority of Chinese people were unable to go abroad, clear TV images and practical refrigerators were extremely popular. As a result, the Chinese began to take a new look at Japan. For a long time, the majority of Chinese people had generally viewed Japan in a negative light due to the Cold War between the East and West, coupled with a lingering hatred from Japan's aggression toward China in the past. The Chinese had no idea what Japan was like after a gap of several decades.

In the 1980s, when China initiated reform, the Chinese began to care about foreign development. The thinking public, cultural circles, and intelligentsia took the lead in translating a wealth of new Western ideas, trends, schools, and developments, including many books on Japan's economic development.

A graduate student at that time, I majored in the world economy, and studied the Japanese economy taking a great interest in the success story of Japanese economic development. How did Japan, a country poor in natural resources, become a developed country? Through reading, I have learned that Japan attributes its success in large measure to the use of its human resources. From a micro perspective, this chiefly lies in corporate management and mastering technology. During the Cultural Revolution, I worked in agriculture in the countryside, and developed interest in agricultural production technology, but had little idea of business management.

Another reason is that many of the teachers and classmates I met at Hitotsubashi University in Japan studied technological advancement issues. My supervisor, Ryoushin Minami, published a monograph *Power Revolution and Technological Advance* (1976, English edition 1987) and other studies of technological advance in modern Japan. My associate supervisor, Yukihiko Kiyokawa, published a monograph *Economic Development and Technology Popularization in Japan* (1995) and a slew of papers related to technological advancement. Another tutor, Konosuke Odaka, published a monograph *The World of Craftsmen and the World of Factories* (1993), which studied "soft technology" issues such as worker proficiency. My senior schoolmate, Husao Makino, published studies on technological advancement including the monograph *Prometheus Summoned: Technological Development in Modern Japan* (1996). Murakami Maoki, with whom I cooperated while working as a research assistant at Tokyo Metropolitan University's Economics Department, studied post-war technological innovation issues in Japan from the perspective of industrial organization. In the context of this research environment, I resolved to study this topic.

Nonetheless, the research process has not been smooth sailing. The problems of scientific research cannot be resolved by means of enthusiasm alone. For starters, this topic is heavy going for me. On the one hand, I have limited knowledge about economics and science and technology, especially technology. Research on technological advancement, especially empirical analysis, requires a knowledge of economics theories and approaches, and also an understanding of the technical characteristics of industries for the research objects. In addition to gleaning information in the study of technical issues, teachers also consult technical experts, and sometimes visited enterprises and factories for investigation. Secondly, it is difficult for a foreigner to study the issues of technological advance and innovation in Japan before World War II. Since Japan was the first to become a developed country outside Europe and America, the fact that I was from a developing country and had no direct experience in many respects, the concept was hard to grasp. Thirdly, I spent a great deal of time studying the issues before World War II, including the Meiji period, because Japanese was a difficult language at that time, especially that used in the more obscure memoirs.

Some unrelated details must be mentioned, as this book is about to be published. As observant readers will note, some chapters in this book were published in related magazines, as far back early as 1995. It never occurred to me that such a book would be published over 20 years later. In 1996, my supervisor, Ryoushin Minami, published *Economic Development and Income Distribution in Japan* (Iwanami Shoten, Japan), a monograph that studies the issue of income distribution in modern Japan. In his foreword he said: "It took a total of 20 years to write this book since the collection of materials. I was doubtful at that time: Does it take 20 years to write a book? My doubt is now dispelled. Sometimes it takes longer, and 20 years seems to be a short span of time."

This book includes both my master's and doctoral theses, the results of my participation in the key research project on long-term economic statistics in Asia at Hitotsubashi University's Institute of Economic Research, as well as my experience after returning to China. The Japanese edition of this book was published in 2003. When in China, I thought about publishing the Chinese edition, but it was not published for at least three reasons. First, there were few readers in China for the issues of economic development and technological advance in Japan before World War II. Second, due to daily chores, I could not stick to this undertaking. Third, as it is not a popular subject, it is hard to obtain funding for publication.

If this book contributes to the academic community in China, thanks are due to many teachers, classmates and friends who have given me guidance and help over the years. For starters, Professor Song Shaoying, my tutor for my master's degree at the Institute of Japanese Studies of Northeast Normal University, initiated me into the field of research on the Japanese economy, enabling me to gain some insight into research on Japanese economy. He also recommended that I study abroad so that I could acquire knowledge on advanced economics theories and methods in Japan. I am eternally grateful to him. Secondly, in 1988, I studied economics and the Japanese economy under the tutelage of Professor Ryoushin Minami of the Institute of Economic Research of Hitotsubashi University. I benefited tremendously from his direct and indirect tutoring; he suggested the title of my master's thesis and directed my thesis writing, as well as providing inspiration from participating in daily seminars and reading my tutor's books. A prolific scholar, my tutor is involved in many fields. He studied population and labor in his early years, was involved in the compilation of long-term economic statistics on Japan led by Kazushi Okawa, studied technological advance and income distribution, and studied China's economy by using empirical research for the Japanese economy. There were two professors at a seminar I attended at postgraduate level: one is Yukihiko Kiyokawa, who has had a great influence on my studies and research; the professor left a deep impression on me due to his unique perspective on problems, rigorous attitude to academic studies, and excellent analytical skills. In addition to the Japanese economy, he also studied the Indian and Chinese economies, and has rich knowledge on related disciplines such as statistics and sociology. He is a rare scholar. The other professor involved in the seminar was Konosuke Odaka, who is of noble ancestry and who once studied in the U.S. Of a gentle disposition, he has many achievements in such fields as labor economics, development economics, and Japanese economy.

Fumio Makino (Hosei University), my senior schoolmate, has given me great help and guidance since my postgraduate years. With a nimble mind, he is always bursting with new ideas. When studying technological innovation in Japan, I consulted Professor Hoshimi Uchida of Tokyo Keizai University, who patiently gave me new ideas and shared research experience. Murakami Maoki (Nihon University) was my advising professor when I was a teaching assistant at Tokyo Metropolitan University and studying industrial organizations and the Japanese economy in the early days, and later, the Chinese economy. I benefited greatly from our communication. Moreover, I received guidance at various seminars from Hitotsubashi University professors such as Osamu Saito, Yoshiro Matsuda, Masahiro Sato, Hiroyuki Itami, Takaoki Shimizu, Akimitsu Sakuma, Hiroshi Kataoka, and Shiro Kurihara. My senior schoolmate Liu Deqiang (Kyoto University) was one of the first to study in Japan after the reform. With a solid foundation and perseverance, he mainly studies the Chinese economy, setting a good example for me in academic studies and research. Luo Huanzhen (Tokyo Keizai University) and Hao Renping (Toyo University) are my junior schoolmates. Both graduates from prestigious Chinese universities, they have given me a great deal of encouragement and help in our long-term exchanges. Tomoko Hashino is my junior schoolmate. She did a good job in studying economic history in modern Japan, and offered helpful suggestions for my research. When the Japanese edition was published in 2003, Yasuko Kataoka, an assistant to the School of Business Administration (SBA) at Hitotsubashi University, helped me revise the book in Japanese. When I was collecting materials in Japan, the staff of the Patent Office's data division were very helpful me. While I was writing my doctoral, I received funding from Fuji Xerox Consortium and was strongly supported by Mr Michiru Inuduka, the president of Fuko Publisher, when the Japanese edition was published. When the Chinese edition was published, I received support from the Renmin University of China Press and funding from the National Social Science Fund of China. Here, I would like to express sincere gratitude to the all these people and organizations.

September, 2020

Part I
Preliminary investigation

1 Topic and outlook

Section 1 Introduction

Nowadays, it is recognized that technological advance and technological innovation are the driving force for the long-term economic development of a country. The first and second industrial revolutions in the eighteenth and nineteenth centuries, as well as technological advances in scientific fields, for example, the semiconductor revolution in the late twentieth century, have spurred on economic development. People also eagerly await the great scientific and technological advances in the near future, and the resulting economic growth. This expectation can be explained by the fact that the economic development in major countries to date has indeed benefited from legions of scientific and technological advances that have occurred. Western Europe, North America, Japan, and even China have seen rapid economic growth in recent years have benefited tremendously from the great strides in technology such as IT and the internet.

Economic research on the role of technological advance and innovation in economic development can be traced to the 1950s.[1] It has became more colorful since the 1970s and includes groundbreaking theoretical research, and a wealth of empirical analysis; it is geared to developed countries in Europe and the U.S., and has produced huge results in developing countries. It covers the current short-term changes, and also provides research on historical changes. It can be said that there is a cornucopia of literature on the subject.[2]

Nevertheless, the study theme of this book is Japan before World War II. There are achievements galore regarding Japanese economic development in this period, but studies on technological innovation are few and far between. Japan at that time was the first country with a non-Western culture to learn from the West and it made significant achievements. If we say Western European and North American countries adopted similar Christian cultures, Japan is part of the East Asian Confucian cultural circle and has its unique features. In the early days of economic development, it lagged far behind the West. Despite the "advantage of backwardness," it would be hard to catch up if there was too large a gap, as evidenced by the reality in many developing countries today. There is a huge gap between developing and developed countries. Even if there is the "advantage of backwardness," few countries can now catch up with the developed countries. The reasons for this are myriad: political, economic, social and cultural. However, the lack of "social capability" is an indisputable fact. Social capability embraces many aspects, such as natural resources, human resources, science and technology, the education system, and government competence. This book studies the relationship between technological innovation and economic development in modern Japan, while technological innovation and advance is also part of social capability.

Section 2 Topic, perspective, materials, methods, scope

I. Topic and perspective

(1) Research topics

Except for industrial technology policies, the research on technological advance in Japan before World War II have probably been conducted using the following two methods: the calculation of total-factor productivity (TFP) or the rate of technological advance, and case studies. The former studies the whole country or the major industrial categories, while the latter is geared towards individual industries, individual periods, and individual enterprises. Based on the results of these two kinds of research, it can be said that technological advances in Japan before World War II can largely be explained. However, the former shows the "surplus" after the contribution of factor inputs to output growth is eliminated. It is, in a sense, a black box and cannot account for the specific content of technological advances. In other words, it does not explain what specific factors constitute the TFP, although it is generally recognized that it includes technological advance, economies of scale, improved management, and improved proficiency. The endogenous growth theory that emerged after the 1980s gets rid of this weakness of using technological advance as an exogenous variable, while human resources, research and development (R&D) and other factors become endogenous. Considerable progress has been made in this regard. However, this endogenous growth model may be applicable to developed countries or middle-income countries, but not to countries that have yet to see economic take-off or are just seeing the start of modern economic growth, because good education resources and technology, a mature market, pioneering entrepreneurs, and a promising government are absent in these countries. Compared to this type of research, the accumulation of case studies is vital, but a drawback of this kind of research is that it is hard to produce a universally applicable theory. Therefore, the combination of theory and practice, and macro and micro perspectives offer the best solution. Nevertheless, due to a lack of data, this is extremely difficult. This is also the top subject in the research in this field, namely how to overcome these difficulties and the approach truth as far as possible.

The second subject is that previous research on technological advances before World War II concerned technology choice rather than technological innovation, and comprehensive studies were few and far between. The reasons are twofold: first, Japan achieved technological development before World War II mostly by importing technology from advanced countries, studying it, then making some improvements. All in all, this is imitation. Because the overall technological level in Japan at that time was low, it was hard to produce high-level innovation and, as a result, research had a low value. However, compared to technological innovations, the import or the popularization of technology is more closely related to economic activity, and is therefore more appropriate for economics research. Second, in comparison to the technology choice and the popularization of technology, the data on technological innovations is scarcer. For instance, data on R&D expenditures and R&D personnel at the industries and enterprises are practically nonexistent, and information on new products and processes is also few and far between.

This book attempts to study the two topics above. It is an analysis of the relationship between industrial development and technological innovation in Japan before World War II, in the hope of figuring out the type of relationship between economic development on the one hand and industrialization and technological innovations on the other hand, as well as the underlying reasons and conditions. We believe that economic development in Japan before World War II was, in large measure, linked to technological advances and technological innovation. We hope to perform studies from the perspective of the entire industry and specific sectors.

(2) Research perspective

Economic development always follows on the heels of changes in the industrial structure. The most basic logic and empirical rule about changes in the industrial structure is Petty-Clark's law,[3] which is verified by the fact of economic development in the vast majority of countries.[4] Moreover, W.G. Hoffmann divided the manufacturing sector, a main sector of the second industry, into consumer goods and investment goods. Through the measurement of added value, it has been concluded that the higher the proportion of investment in the goods sector, the lower the consumer goods sector. This is called the "Hoffmann ratio."[5]. Moreover, the approach of dividing the manufacturing industry into light industry and heavy industry is similar to Hoffmann's idea. This classification was popular in the early days, especially in socialist countries and Japan.[6] Nowadays, the manufacturing sector is often classified using labor-intensive and capital-intensive approaches, but this is not absolutely accurate, in that some industries have a dual character and are both capital- and labor-intensive, such as the electronics sector. Some industries have a high technology content, resulting in a technology-intensive category.

"Dual structure" is often mentioned in development economics, especially when studying the developing countries in the early days and the present developing countries. The so-called "dual-structure" theory divides the economy into traditional and modern sectors. Traditional sectors include those which have low productivity without using modern machinery and equipment such as agriculture and handicraft. Modern sectors are those which have high productivity by using machinery and equipment. It is generally recognized that as the share of modern sectors increases in economic development, the share of traditional sectors will dwindle.[7] In addition, the concept of dual structure is sometimes applied to other sectors, such as large enterprises and SMEs in manufacturing, and traditional and modern industries.

Furthermore, research on traditional industrial theory emerged in Japan after the 1970s. These scholars chiefly researched the issues of traditional industries in the early days of economic development. These scholars including Takeshi Abe (1989), Takafusa Nakamura (1997), and Masayuki Tanimoto (1998) mainly researched the issues of traditional industries in the early days of economic development as far back as the Edp period?

(3) Insights

This book conducts analysis from the viewpoint of dual structure. This is chiefly based on the reality in modern Japan, which had been pressing ahead with modernization and industrialization since the Meiji period. On the one hand, it imported modern industries and technologies from Western Europe. On the other hand, traditional sectors played an important role. The two coexisted for a long time. Research results are abundant from this perspective, but most of these are attributed to the field of labor economics.[8] There were also some studies from the angle of technological advance, albeit they are small in number. Closely related to this book are those by Susumu Hondai (1992), Yukihiko Kiyokawa (1995), and Husao Makino (1996). The research by Susumu Hondai is geared to the manufacturing sector, which is divided into large enterprises and small and medium enterprises (SMEs). Analysis was conducted using the data contained in the *Statistics Table of Factories*, especially the problem of organizational innovation issues caused by the division of labor among enterprises. Yukihiko Kiyokawa's research chiefly concerns the issue of technology popularization in traditional industries, including the agricultural sector. The research of Husao Makino selected some representative industries from traditional sectors and modern sectors for comparison. The analysis focuses on technology choice and technology popularization.

As distinct from the perspectives of the above researches, this book mainly divides the manufacturing industry into traditional and modern industries, and carried out quantitative analysis of the manufacturing industry. It is concluded that this plays a greater role in traditional industries in modern Japan. On this basis, by gleaning and analyzing patent data, the author analyzed industrial development and technological innovation, and concluded that technological innovation has played an important role in industrial development.

II. Data, methods and scope

(1) Data used

As the quantitative data on the intensity and speed of technological innovations, the R&D expenditure and the number of researchers (sometimes technicians) are usually used as input indicators. New products and processes, as well as the number of papers and patents are used as indicators of output. However, in Japan before World War II, there were no other types of data, especially data on the manufacturing sector except for patent statistics. There are barely any statistics for individual companies and industries, much less data that can be pieced together over a long time. This book chiefly collects and uses material on patents, so that it can be used to measure the output of R&D activities as far as possible.

There are a few results in which patent materials are used to study industrial and economic development in Japan before World War II. Tadashi Ishii (1980–1982) analyzed the data on patents, but this was limited general observations and explanations, and did not provide comprehensive in-depth analysis of industrial development. Keijiro Otsuka (1987) and Yukihiko Kiyokawa (1995) analyzed the fiber industry from different perspectives. In the case of the cotton industry, the former used relevant investigations as indicators of adaptive technological innovation, and studied how imported technologies induced domestic technological innovation. The latter cited technological innovations in six different aspects of the fiber industry, and compared their characteristics with others from the perspective of entrepreneurship. Further, Tadashi Ishii (1979) specifically analyzed individual inventors.

In the six decades from the establishment of the patent system in 1885 to the defeat of Japan in 1945, Japan granted some 160,000 (490,000 applications) invention patents. In forty years from the promulgation of the *Utility Model Act* in 1905 to 1945, a total of 340,000 (950,000 applications) utility models were granted. This mass of patent data was not valued by scholars in the past and was rarely used. Of course, in addition to a poor understanding of technological innovation at the time, there are also problems with the patent materials. For example, technology and industry classifications are different, and many adjustments are required before these can be used.

The material on patents used includes statistical data and data from literature. The statistical data are chiefly based on official publications such as the *Annual Report (Table) of Japan's Patent Office*,[9] the *Japanese Statistical Yearbook*, and the *Statistics Table of Agriculture and Commerce*, as well as statistical data from Japan's Patent Office. Document literature includes the *Detailed List of Inventions* and biographies of inventors, as well as literature featuring the commendations and evaluations of inventors. The specific literature is explained in detail in each chapter. The basic data is explained according to the purpose of this book, and any problems and limitations are pointed out.

For example, there are concerns about the data on quantity. Continuous data on the number of invention patents and utility models by category and country mainly stem from the *Annual Report (Table) of Japan's Patent Office*, the *Japanese Statistical Yearbook*, and the *Statistics Table of Agriculture and Commerce*. These data are used in this book. For example, by studying the proportion of Japanese and foreign inventions, it is possible to observe and analyze the gap between Japan and foreign countries in terms of technological level. Likewise, the gap in technological level among industries can be seen from the respective proportions of utility models and invention patents.

However, the information mentioned above leaves something to be desired. The classification data of the *Annual Report (Table) of Japan's Patent Office* began in 1899; the data for 14 years from the promulgation of the Patent Act in 1885 to 1898 are missing. Besides, data on the inventions by foreigners are only available for 11 years from 1899–1909. There are also problems with the data in the *Statistical Yearbook* and the *Statistics Table of Agriculture and Commerce*. They do not publish harmonized data every year, and in some years, data are missing. More importantly, this yearbook ceased publication in 1920. There is a common problem in the aforesaid statistics, namely technology classification changed in 1920. There were 136 categories before 1920, and 207 after 1921. To join the dots of these data, they must correspond to the appropriate years. This is a complex and difficult task as we are not technical experts and can only make an analysis according to the rough criteria of classification before and after the change.

What is most useful for this book is that Japan's Patent Office recalculated the number of invention patents in the original *Detailed List of Inventions* to commemorate the centennial of the establishment of the patent system. The data made a distinction between categories, countries, individuals, and legal persons. Thus, indicators of assistance to this book could be calculated. For example, the technological gap among industries can be judged from the proportion of Japanese inventions (proportion of Japanese inventions in all inventions) and the proportion of individual inventions (proportion of individual inventions in all Japanese inventions). The proportion of invention patents (proportion of invention patents to the sum of invention patents and utility models) can also be calculated. As we know, invention patents were superior to utility models, and foreign inventions were better than Japanese inventions, and inventions by legal persons were better than inventions by individuals.

The literature mainly included the *Detailed List of Inventions* held by Japan's Patent Office, as well as the biographies of inventors including Shigetaro Nara

(1930), Kentaro Matsuhara (1952), *Japanese Invention Dictionary* (1939), Japanese Institute of Invention and Innovation Osaka (1936), as well as related records and dictionaries.

(2) Research Methods

As mentioned above, as regards the role of technological innovation or technological advance in economic development, the methods used include the calculation of the "residual" other than the contribution of factors to growth on the basis of production function, or the calculation of R&D function, among others. These methods can clearly study the causal relationship among an array of variables, but these require better statistics, such as the number of labor and capital stock, and factor payments (such as salary), especially continuous data with time series. However, as far as Japan before World War II is concerned, only the data on the manufacturing industry as a whole are available, there are no detailed data by industry. It is even harder to obtain the data required by R&D function, such as the number of researchers, amount of R&D expenditure, new products, and new processes. The missing data is also one of the reasons there has not been much research into this aspect of Japan before World War II.

Due to these constraints, this book focuses on three aspects. First, discussion is carried out within the framework of economics theory as far as possible. Second, although formal economics theory is not used, technological innovation and production activities are combined for analysis wherever possible. Econometric method is used for analysis, such as regression and correlation analysis. Third, it can be said that it is a common problem in the early days of economic development. Various variables do not necessarily have a causal relationship, as a mass of materials are scattered and independent of one another, and are not quantitative. Therefore, the data needed to be re-sorted, improved and, wherever possible, quantified. The method of multivariate statistics was used for this purpose.[10]

(3) Research scope

This book mainly focuses on the manufacturing sector mainly for the following reasons. First, manufacturing is the central sector in a country's industrialization. A study of this industry can largely explain the overall development of the economy. Second, the data on patents used herein are mainly geared to the manufacturing sector, as there is hardly any data on agriculture, and much less on the service industry. Third, it is relatively easy to obtain data on manufacturing production activities, such as the *Statistics Table of Factories*, and compare these to the data on patents.

The period for study in this book is basically the Meiji period (1868–1912) until the end of World War II in 1945. However, due to the availability of data, the main period for study occurred after the late nineteenth century, especially the promulgation of the *Patent Act* in 1885. Nevertheless, some content can be backdated to the early Meiji period (e.g. the rickshaw sector).

Section 3 Process and characteristics of technological development

As mentioned earlier, quite a few studies have been conducted on technological innovation and technological advance in modern Japan, but most of these focus on technology import and popularization, and studies on technological innovation itself are few and far between,[11] because modern Japan was generally in the process of catching up with Western countries. During this process, Japan mainly learned from Western countries, specifically, importing and popularizing technology. In fact, as far as developing countries are concerned, the process of technology import and popularization also necessitates innovation, in that it is hard to physically use a great deal of technology. This requires modifications to some extent, or a wealth of capital and fund investment, but these resources are not often available.

The purpose of this chapter is to provide an overview of the subsequent detailed analysis in this book by combining previous research results on technological advances and technological innovation in modern Japan.[12] Some previous literature, including works by Yukihiko Kiyokawa (1984), Tetsuo Nakaoka (1992), and Yukihiko Kiyokawa (1995), have focused on the technology itself, or have emphasized technology import and popularization. This chapter focuses on technological innovation. Below is a discussion in two parts. The first part is the process and features of technological development, including the three stages of technology import, technology popularization, and technological innovation. The second part studies the causes and conditions of technological development, including human resources, market conditions, the role of governments, and other aspects, including information network, rules and regulations, and culture. The discussion in this chapter is chiefly consistent with the overall structure of the book.

Technological development in developing countries generally begins with the import of technology from advanced or developed countries, and gradually reaches technological innovation through popularization in the whole country. Successful countries first export technologies to countries with a lower level of development, and as they progress, to developed countries. This is similar to the flying geese paradigm of the industrial development, namely import → domestic production (import substitution) → export. Given that the scope of research in this book is modern Japan, technological output by economically advanced Japan after World War II is not discussed here. In this sense, Japan was the first country to achieve catch-up development. Some industries and technologies began to be exported to neighboring economies before World War II, such as Taiwan, Northeast China, and the Korean Peninsula.[13]

I. Importing technology

Generally speaking, technological development in developing countries calls for stimulus from more advanced or developed countries. This usually manifests in the importing of technology through all manner of forms. This path is adopted, whether it be pre-war Japan or many developing countries after World War II. Some countries pulled off technological advance and economic development, such as the "Four Asian Tigers" and China after World War II. Of course, many countries have been unsuccessful, including the majority of African countries, and some countries in Central, South, and Southeast Asia. How are some countries successful while others come to grief? To answer this question, consideration will be given to at least two factors. One is the choice of technology. The other is whether there is the capability to digest and absorb imported technology.

(1) Advantage of backwardness and social capabilities

The "advantage of backwardness hypothesis" advanced by Gerschenkron must be mentioned when studying the technology import by developing countries. He advanced a hypothesis about the economic development of these countries after studying the history of countries less advanced than Britain, such as France, Germany, and Russia. According to the hypothesis, the greater the gap between developing and advanced countries, the faster the rate of subsequent economic growth, mainly because developing countries have more opportunities to import advanced technology from advanced countries.[14] In this regard, Japanese scholar Ryoushin Minami holds that Japan's early economic development was made possible by the introduction of technology from Western countries. This is a typical case of the "advantage of backwardness hypothesis." He demonstrated Japan's advantage of backwardness from two perspectives: first, the gap between Japan and advanced nations when began to see economic growth in modern times. Second, the gap between Japan and advanced nations when various countries began to see economic growth in modern times. He reached this conclusion by using historical data from over ten developed countries. Ryoushin Minami also imposed additional conditions that gaps in the existence of technology are not a sufficient condition for technology transfer. To make use of imported technologies, it is necessary for the importer to have the "social capability" that absorb the new technology. He pointed out that countries such as the U.S. and Japan, which initiated industrialization later than Britain and continental Europe, achieved success by virtue of this capability. However, this is not now available to many developing countries today. Japan possessed these capabilities at the time. Moreover, he cited several aspects that have become social capabilities, including the modernization of human resources, management organizations, information networks, and capital goods industries. He also holds that Japan bolstered social capabilities through industrialization. Better social capabilities make it easier to import technology, thereby increasing the rate of technological advance (TFP) and spurring economic development.[15]

Keiitiro Nakakawa (1981) mentioned the relationship with entrepreneurship. Husao Makino (1996) made a positive evaluation of Gerschenkron's hypothesis through analyzing technology choice and technology popularization. However, some scholars take a cautious attitude to this hypothesis, while others are opposed to it. Hoshimi Uchida (1990) holds that even though this hypothesis is recognized in Western Europe, the so-called "advantage of backwardness" is actually discounted due to a slew of obstacles in terms of race, culture, language, and others in Japan. Yukihiko Kiyokawa (1995) is also of the opinion that there is no empirical analysis as a sufficient basis for this hypothesis, and further demonstration is required. Since Japan was the first non-Western country to achieve economic development, Japanese scholars often mention the advantage of the backwardness hypothesis when exploring the reasons for economic development. Shunsaku Nishikawa (1985) also discussed this hypothesis.

As mentioned earlier, there have been many discussions about the advantage of backwardness hypothesis, including both positive evaluations and skeptical or even negative views. We hold it is a hypothesis worthy of confirmation. It is more appropriate to explain the economic catch-up of the developing countries if Kuznets' concept of "social capability" is added. In other words, when launching its economic development, a country, in addition to considering the advantages of backwardness, should also endeavor to improve its own social capabilities to ensure it can utilize it.. Furthermore, there is a negative correlation between the advantage of backwardness and social capabilities. Generally speaking, the larger the gap with advanced countries, the lower the social capabilities. Conversely, a country with higher social capabilities has a smaller gap with advanced countries. However, the gap among countries is indeed huge, and it may not be easily explained through a harmonized standard. For instance, some countries lag far behind advanced countries, but have relatively high social capabilities; conversely, some countries have a smaller gap, but have low social capabilities. For example, after the industrial revolution, both China and Japan lagged far behind Western European countries, or both had advantages of backwardness, but the social capabilities of China and Japan were not the same at that time. More importantly, their respective developments diverged. Japan improved social capabilities through modernization and narrowed the gap with Western countries. Conversely, China did not see economic growth for a long time, and was unable to improve social capabilities. It is only in the past forty years that China has achieved rapid growth through reform and opening up; it has narrowed the gap with Western countries, although this still persists.[16]

(2) Types of technology imported

This book mainly introduces the experience gained by Japan as a country catching up with advanced countries. In early modern times, the import of modern technology was well-nigh impossible due to Japan's long-term selection from the world. As a consequence, it had a huge technological gap with advanced countries in the early days of modern economic growth. From another perspective, however, developed countries had a wealth of technologies that Japan could use at the time, especially when Britain lifted export restrictions. The technology gap between Japan and developed countries narrowed, but the technological level in developed countries was also on the rise, so it did not completely vanish.

Japanese scholar Akira Ono divided technology import into three types, and Ryoushin Minami made improvements to this.[17] The first type is the state-of-the-art machinery and equipment imported in its entirety that was developed and being used in advanced countries. The production function (relationship between labor productivity and capital–labor ratio) in developed countries is the blend of potential production methods made possible by certain technical knowledge. When this technology is exported to a developing country, the production function there becomes the so-called "limitational production" function as there is no scope for technology choice.[18] Wages are low in developing countries, and technology with low capital-labor ratio is more practical under this wage system. In other words, judging from factor endowment in developing countries (abundant labor, low wages; scarce capital, high prices), developed countries are excessively capital-intensive. However, the import of state-of-the-art technology is also often seen in developing countries for several reasons. As regards some industrial technologies, it may be hard to make physical modifications, or much as it is physically feasible, there is no actual capability to make the modification. Perhaps, extreme nationalism pursues the cutting-edge technology without the need for modification.

The second type is to modify the technology of developed countries according to the factor endowment in developing countries. In other words, developing countries recombine the imported capital equipment. Through a combination of materials and institutions, developing countries maximize profits in the context of their wages by developing other potential parts on production function. Compared to advanced technology, modified technologies have a lower capital-labor ratio and also lower productivity. However, abundant cheap labor can save expensive capital, yielding a high profit margin. This is the reason why developing countries develop modified technologies rather than directly importing advanced technology. The development of modified technology is often conditional upon the existence of inherent technology that has been passed down over the years. Inherent technology is developing technology. Nevertheless, developing countries can develop new technologies by incorporating the structural elements of modified technologies and creating more advanced technology. In other words, modified technologies are often the result of the compromise between advanced technology and developing technology. Moreover, the development of modified technologies is conditional on the existence of entrepreneurs who pursue high profits, and technicians and mechanics who can digest advanced technology and make the appropriate improvements.

The third type is the import of second-hand technology from advanced countries. Developed countries have a full array of technologies with a potential production function, from which suitable technologies can be chosen. Some SMEs in in developed countries use cheap machinery and equipment with a low capital–labor ratio. Developing countries can choose to achieve the same effect as developing modified technologies. The second and third types fall between advanced technology and developing technology, and meet the conditions for the import of factor endowments. Thus, they are often called "intermediate" or "suitable."

Ryoushin Minami also cited examples of various descriptions. He holds that a case in point for the first type, namely the import of technology without any modification or improvements, is railway and electric power. Both industries are capital- and technology-intensive, and it was hard for Japan to make modifications at the time (the early Meiji period). Ironically, in the case of electric power, power plants in Tokyo and Osaka imported technology from Germany and the U.S., respectively, while power generation technologies varied in the two countries: one adopted 50 Hz, and the other 60 Hz. This situation still remains today, resulting in enormous economic losses. The second type is the modification to imported technology. A typical example is the mechanical silk reeling industry. Japan first imported the well-known Tomioka Silk Mill from France, but its operation failed. However, this technology was combined with local Japanese technology by a company in the Nagano prefecture with tremendous success. The third type is outdated technology imported from the West. A case in point is the loom. The imported technology at that time was not the most advanced in Europe, but slightly outdated. This type of technology was more suited to Japan, which quickly made improvements.[19]

(3) Technological gap theory

Yukihiko Kiyokawa (1984) did not agree. In his view, these were individual cases and more comprehensive data was required. He held that the opportunity for adaptation of imported technologies required the separation of production functions and the factor–price ratio. It is difficult to explain the above model when the adaptation of imported technology was not carried out due to the large gap in technology. Moreover, in the absence of a fully developed market, the discussion on technology choice based on production function is hardly tenable, and its shape and concept are arbitrary. It can therefore be called into question.[20] Based on this, Yukihiko Kiyokawa proposed his own hypothesis – the "technological gap theory."[21] He divided the gap between imported technology and local technology into large and small gaps, holding that this gap determined localization. From this perspective, he pointed out three aspects of the characteristics of technology development in Japan.

First, there is huge difference in the establishment of imported technology in a new economy. In other words, imported technology greatly different

from local technology and needs to undergo three stages: Import period →
popularization period → efficient use period. By comparison, technology with
a small gap can be popularized early, and the popularization and efficient use
periods take place almost simultaneously, with no clear boundary. Second, the
localization of imported technology should be gauged by fostering market
competitiveness. There are distinct differences in the form of adjustment and
adaptation toward efficient use brought by technology and the market. In other
words, for technologies with a large technological gap, the efficient use will be
reorganized in the market with the highest relevancy, and the market will adapt
to the technology; for the imported technology with a small technological gap,
there is a strong tendency of technology adapting to the market. Third, the
issue of differences in the impact on the local inherent technology and related
technologies. Generally speaking, technologies with a large technological gap
have large differences in productivity. Once localization is successful, it will
drive the local inherent technologies out of the market. At the same time, as
this technology contains a wealth of technical know-how and information,
there is a large correlation effect with related technologies. By comparison,
if the technological gap is small, the imported technology will adapt to the
local technology. At the same time, thanks to modifications and improvements,
the two have a small gap in productivity and technology, and coexist in the
market. However, as the market develops, inherent technologies with lower
productivity will gradually be knocked out. He regarded the modern industries
such as iron and steel, cotton textiles, shipbuilding, transportation machinery,
and chemical fiber as the former cases (large technological gap), and regarded
silk reeling, weaving, wood, papermaking, teamaking, and brewing as the
latter (small technological gap). However, Ryoushin Minami (2002) holds that
there is no essential difference between the classification methods of Yukihiko
Kiyokawa and Akira Ono. The former classification by Yukihiko Kiyokawa
is equivalent to the first type by Akira Ono, and the latter is equivalent to the
second type. The two have a lot in common.

Furthermore, there has been a great deal of empirical analysis on technology import and technology choice. For example, Masahiko Shintani (1987)
on teamaking, Ryoushin Minami and Husao Makino (1983) on the textile
industry, Yukihiko Kiyokawa (1985) on cotton textiles, Ryoushin Minami
and Husao Makino (1987) on the silk reeling industry, Keijiro Otsuka (1990)
on shipbuilding, and Husao Makino (1996) on shipping, milling, and household sectors carried out verification and analysis of the hypothesis through
detailed data. Akira Ono (1986) conducted a comparative analysis of Brazil,
India, and Japan, and Otsuka et al. (1988) conducted a comparative analysis
of Japan and India.

II. Technology popularization

As a complex process, technological advance not only requires R&D, but also
extensive application. It locates the drawbacks and weaknesses of a certain

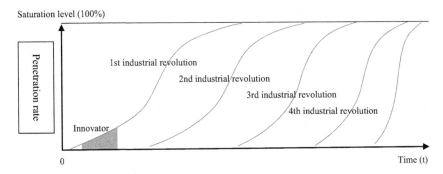

Figure 1.1 Scientific and technological innovation and forms of penetration.
Source: Guan Quan (2013, 2014).

technology through application, providing a basis for subsequent improvement. Technology application is also a process, ranging from the initial laboratory to production workshop at enterprises, and then propagation to other enterprises. This is commonly called "technical diffusion." In a nutshell, this refers to the wide application and promotion of a new piece of technology. In addition to the simple acquisition of production technology, it also stresses the construction of technical capabilities for technology importers. From the perspective of human history, technical diffusion has played a crucial role in technological advances. Technological innovation will not contribute to the economy in any material form unless it is widely used and applied.

Technology can be diffused in many ways. The best-known is the "epidemic model," which is summed up in Figure 1.1. The S-shaped curve in the figure has several names: "epidemic curve," "growth curve," "popularization curve," "innovation curve" and so on. The "epidemic curve" indicates that an epidemic emerges, spreads, and weakens in the S-shape. In other words, few people are infected at the beginning, but more people are infected after a period of time, leading to a state of diffusion or "outbreak." Next, due to the emergence of "antibodies" and progress in treatments means, the number of infected people begins to fall and the epidemic eventually ends. The "growth curve" indicates that economic growth is akin to the growth process of living things. To begin with, the growth rate is low due to a dearth of available resources. After a period of accumulation, the growth rate picks up, even soars, before declining. The "popularity curve" generally refers to a process in which the commodity consumption and the technology spread starts slowly, increases rapidly, and then wanes, because it takes time for people to learn about it. This is the reason for the Chinese saying "information spreads from one person to ten persons, and from ten to one hundred." The "innovation curve" means that the development and research of technology will hit many difficulties to begin with, with little progress. Repeated "trial and error" is required. Once a breakthrough is made, it will be smooth sailing, which may then be followed by new "bottlenecks." In other words, the technology matures but its development may be constrained.[22]

This is the first process. In terms of the research, development or spread of science and technology, it is the development process of single technology. From the angle of the entirety and continuity of technology, the first "decline" will be followed by the second and third wave. Thus, we call it the "band" or "staged" rule of science and technology development. In this way, technological development has a continuous and staged process. It explains why science and technology sometimes develops rapidly, and sometimes slowly, or there is a "wavy" development pattern. In some periods, concentrated explosive growth will occur, while in other periods there is stagnant development, with no groundbreaking results like the "darkness before dawn." In fact, this process is one of knowledge accumulation. This period is more important, in that before there is a technology breakthrough, everyone is at the same starting line. The question is whether everyone can remain at the starting line.[23] Besides, as can be seen in the figure, the S-shaped curve shows an increasingly steep line from left to right, because as science and technology and economic development advance, and the information age dawns, there is increasingly fast technology R&D and spread. It used to take years or even decades to develop a vehicle. Now this period is usually one or two years. This can be proved by the upgrading of household appliances, PCs, cameras, and mobile phones, among others.

At the national level, the popularization and spread of technology is of great significance. Imported advanced technology can only have an economic effect if it is adopted and mastered by more producers. In many cases, technology can be absorbed through popularization and diffusion. In developing countries, especially in the early days of development, traditional industries had a large market share. The improvement and popularity of these technologies has had the same effect as the import of modern technologies. While any as these industries and technologies will be replaced in the long run, they are of great significance in the short term. Generally speaking, the traditional industries have a more competitive market due to the involvement of SMEs; they are different from modern industries composed of a few large companies with powerful capital and equipment. The technological popularization in these traditional industries is of particular importance. In other words, the modern industries' market was dominated a small number of companies. If one of them succeeds, the others will soon follow, and the entire industry will be successful. Traditional industries can only get off the ground if what they develop becomes popular. As traditional industries had a larger market share in the early days of economic development, technological popularization in traditional industries was critical.[24]

Many theoretical and empirical studies exist on technology popularization, the most typical of which is the aforesaid "epidemic model." Other models emerged later. More details in this regard can be seen in Coombs et al.

(1987), Stoneman (1995), and Yukihiko Kiyokawa (1995). This book chiefly introduces the model that can reflect the characteristics of developing countries, especially Japan in the early days.

(1) The Davies model

Davies (1979) divides technology into two types. The first type (A) is simple and can be imported without much cost. This type of technology has a strong learning curve and can catch on rapidly. The second type (B) is high cost, technologically complicated and requires a good foundation. A good foundation is required for the import and popularization of this technology. It also takes a long time to use this technology. Few companies introduce this technology, and the learning effect is not as fast. Nevertheless, since this technology has greater room for improvement than the first type of technology, its popularity rate and scope will eventually exceed the first type in the subsequent stages. Davis regards consumer durables such as televisions and washing machines as belonging to Type A, and capital goods such as chemical plants and steel mills as belonging to Type B.

If Davies' classification method is applied to Japan before World War II, Type A refers to the traditional industries, and Type B to modern industries. Generally speaking, the technical system of traditional industries is simple and not much cost is involved. In contrast, modern industries have relatively complicated technology and require major investment. Therefore, technology in traditional industries can be popularized easily and rapidly, but it will soon hit the upper limit of their technology. Conversely, technology popularization in the modern industries takes time to begin with, but the speed will soon pick up, and new technologies will be longer in duration.

The above discussion is confirmed and explained here through the cases of road transport machinery in Japan before World War II. Figure 1.2 shows the popularization of three types of transportation: the rickshaw, the bicycle, and the car. Just like many other industries in modern Japan, technological "alternation" also occurred in these industries. The Meiji period was the era of rickshaws, possibly with some imported bicycles. The bicycle industry took shape at the end of the nineteenth century but was still not mature enough. The same is true of cars. At that time, Japan only had a few imported cars. Only in the early twentieth century did a few individuals attempt to make locally developed cars. However, rickshaws were gradually superseded by bicycles in the 1920s due to their simple technology, convenience and flexibility. At that time, bicycle technology was mature, met domestic demand and also saw a wealth of exports. Notwithstanding some attempts in the early twentieth century, cars were in large measure unsuccessful. After the 1920s, the car industry gradually took shape, but was still not mature enough. The market was cornered by American companies Ford and General Motors. After the 1930s, it gradually matured thanks to the strong government protection policies. However, industry development left a lot to be desired due to restrictions such as the levels of national income.

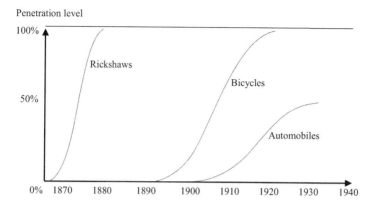

Figure 1.2 Process of technology penetration of rickshaws, bikes and cars.

Source: Rickshaws based on Guan Quan (1998), bicycles based on Guan Quan (1996), cars based on Guan Quan (2001).

Like other industries, these three modes of transportation had a product lifecycle. The process from import to popularization to innovation can be observed technically.[25] Of course, as the rickshaw was invented by the Japanese, there was the problem of technology output without the problem of technology import. As can be seen in Figure 2.1, the more traditional the industry, the faster the technology spread, and the more widespread its popularization. By comparison, the more modern the industry, the slower the technology spread, and the narrower the technology diffusion. For example, cars did not achieve complete popularization before the end of World War II.[26] For rickshaws, the process from invention (around 1870) to nationwide popularity took just a few years. On the one hand, the technology was relatively simple, so it could be imitated by many carpenters, especially those who repaired large carts. At the same time, the patent system was lacking at the time, so there was no mechanism to protect inventors. By contrast, the bicycle and automobile industries came into being based on the imported introduction. The popularization of technology took more time, especially for cars. Bicycle technology belongs to intermediate technology, with a technical system which is not complicated as that of cars. Therefore, traditional technologies can be used instead in some areas, or some traditional technologies can be improved. Thus, localization can be accepted and realized more easily.

(2) Hypothesis of information content gap

Yukihiko Kiyokawa proposed the information content gap hypothesis of technology popularization in developing countries based on popularization experience in Japan before World War II.[27] According to this hypothesis, when new technologies or new technological innovations begin to be popularized, a gap emerges in the information content of this technology between the requiring party and the supplier. There are different popularization forms between technology with a large gap and technology with a small gap. As the requiring party better understands the technology and as the demand curve gradually moves, the technology with a large gap (such as biotechnology in agriculture) is gradually popularized. If this information content gap is large enough, the price elasticity of the supply curve is large due to the overwhelming supply capacity. Therefore, the beginning and speed of popularization are chiefly determined by factors on the part of the requiring party. Conversely, in the case of a small information content gap (such as reeling machine and power loom), the demand curve approaches the horizontal due to the unlimited potential demand. Improvements in new technologies made by many companies and inventors result in competitive development. Its popularization is brought about by supply factors.

Empirical studies on technology popularization are legion. For example, Husao Makino (1996) on plowing with cattle and horses technology, Yukihiko Kiyokawa (1995) on silk reeling and textile, Seiji Sakiura (1984) on rice variety improvement, Tikihisa Doi (1983) on sericulture, Ryoushin Minami (1976) on prime motors at plants, Ryoushin Minami et al. (1982) on power loom, Tadashi Ishii (1986) on loom, textile machinery, and reeling machine, and Yoshio Sugiura (1987) on electric lights carried out analysis using their unique perspectives and methods.

III. Technological innovation

We cannot speak of technological innovation without mentioning J. A. Schumpeter. He advanced the theory of innovation, thinking that "innovation" is "to establish a new production function," namely introducing the "new combination" of production factors and production conditions into production system. These new combinations have five types: (1) introduce new products, (2) adopt new production methods, (3) tap new markets, (4) control new sources of supply of raw materials, and (5) introduce new forms of production and organization. An invention is an idea, drawing, or model that is made to improve a design, product, process, or system. Innovation refers to new products, processes, systems or equipment that are introduced into commercial activities for the first time. Invention is both a technological and an economic concept. Studies reveal that the average time lag between invention and innovation in developed countries is 10–15 years.[28] By analyzing the five types of innovation proposed by Schumpeter, we can make the judgments as follows: the first and the second belong to technical innovations; the third and the fourth belong to market innovations; the fifth belongs to organizational innovation. These five innovations complement each other and are indispensable. The two innovations are fundamental and central, in that application of science and technology is indispensable for modern economic growth.

However, advances in science and technology need to be digested in the market to see whether they have any economic value. As we know, a wealth of scientific inventions and historical technological innovations have not played a major part in spurring economic development. Only technological advances that are put to the test by the market and consumers can become the driver for economic development.

It has been 100 years since Schumpeter advanced these five kinds of innovations. In an era of IT application and globalization, this must be expanded appropriately. The author attempts to propose the following new types of innovation. First, the acquisition of new sources of information. In the information era, the quantity and accuracy of information often holds the key to the survival of an enterprise. How to acquire information, such as the direction of technological advances, market trends, consumer preferences, and government policies, is vital for enterprises. Second, the development of new financing channels. As financing plays an extremely important role today, securing funding may be more important for an innovative company than technology per se. Technology is public in many cases, and can be inquired and traded (such as patents for inventions), but it is not easy to obtain funds, and a variety of challenges are needed. Third, the acquisition of new human resources. Human resources are the lifeblood of a modern enterprise. It is hard to achieve success without sufficient human resources. There are different ways to acquire human resources, through the market or in-house training. This depends on the corporate and social culture, as well as the development of the labor market. Fourth, the expansion of new corporate boundaries. In reality, some enterprises specialize in certain products or services, while others operate more diverse business, covering multiple industries. It involves the characteristics of an industry and the will of an entrepreneur or manager, as well as the stages of economic development and social and cultural differences. Fifth, the introduction of new strategies and new thinking. This is a rapidly changing era. Models of cars are frequently updated as are mobile phones. The innovative results of new concepts and new thinking are highlighted in the transition from cathode-ray tube TV sets to digital display TV sets, from film cameras to digital cameras, and from traditional mobile phones to 5G mobile phones.[29]

As regards the source of innovation, Schumpeter holds that innovation activities are chiefly carried out by entrepreneurs. Entrepreneurs are a cohort of people with "creative destruction" dispositions and entrepreneurial spirit. This so-called "entrepreneurial spirit" is summed up in the following five aspects: (1) The pioneering spirit of entrepreneurs, (2) The entrepreneurs' desire for success, (3) Risk-taking and calmly handling setbacks, (4) Acumen, reason and agility, and (5) Dedication. It is noteworthy that Schumpeter refers to entrepreneurs as being different from the general "economic man," namely business managers seeking short-term gain. This expression sounds hollow, but it provides a principle basis for our study of entrepreneurs. In a word, entrepreneurs are people endowed with a spirit of innovation.

John Richard Hicks, an honoree of the Nobel Prize in Economic Sciences, holds that a change in the relative prices of production factors will inspire inventions that can make more economical use of factors that have become expensive, and the factors with expensive prices are relatively scarce. In other words, the relative scarcity of production factors and changes in their relative price determines the direction of technological inventions and innovations. According to this idea, Japanese economist Yujiro Hayami and American economist V. W. Ruttan proposed the "induced innovation" model.[30]

The factors that impact technological innovation are observed from the following perspectives: market structure, the internal characteristics of enterprises, organizational forms, forms of property rights, as well as national technology policies. As regards market structure, the best-known is "Schumpeter's Hypotheses." There is a view that a monopoly market is one of the preconditions for innovative activities,[31] because in this kind of market, the surplus funds resulting from monopoly profits can be used for technological innovation. Conversely, another view stresses the benefits of competitive markets. There are legions of empirical studies on this point, but the jury is still out on which one is better.[32] Of course, there is a third view, namely a compromise between the first two: The market structure of monopolistic competition is most conducive to technological innovation. Furthermore, regarding the forms of property rights, it is generally held that solely owned enterprises have strong innovation motorization because innovation profits are owned by individuals. However, with limited funds, low risk tolerance, and low technology development capabilities, this is more suitable for innovations on a smaller scale. As a legal person with limited responsibilities that can raise a wealth of capital, a limited liability company has a strong innovation capability suitable for innovations on a larger scale. Of course, the national policies on technology are also very important. In particular, because developing countries lag behind developed countries in terms of technology, it is hard to compete with developed countries without state support. However, a state's technology policy cannot be directly involved in R&D activities, but should help enterprises to carry out innovation activities.

As mentioned above, if technological development goes smoothly in developing countries, it will progress from technology import to technology popularization to technological innovation. The technology imported in the early stages is digested to a certain extent through popularization in a country, and technology innovation such as imitation and modification can be carried out on imported technology. This can be seen in Japan before World War II. However, compared to the import and popularization of technology, technological innovation does not play a big role in the early stage of economic development, so research on technological innovation in this period is sparse.

After World War II, economics research on technological advance gradually emerged. For starters, neoclassical economics that focused on production functions adopted theoretical and empirical analysis of technological advance, laying a good foundation for further research. The work in this area can be divided into two parts: One is the reason for economic growth or productivity increase. This is hard to measure using the earlier input scale as there is surplus that cannot be explained. The other is to analyze the nature of technological changes and the accumulation of technological knowledge in economic activities, namely the so-called "endogenous attempts." Simply put, the former regards the factors of technological advance as exogenous variables, while the latter regards it as an endogenous variable for analysis.

There is epoch-making technological innovation, some of which is carried out in fits and starts. In reality, the latter prevails. Some scholars regard this as "learning by using." Accumulation and exploration in production practices often make a great contribution to economic activities.[33] This technological innovation can also be explained by the experience or learning effect. David (1975) explains this based on the two hypotheses below: The first is the locality of technological advance, and the second is its neutrality.[34] He used the changes in the isoquant curve represented by the labor coefficient (L/Y) and the capital coefficient (K/Y) to illustrate the course of technological advance. Two types of technologies can be chosen: α and β. Under the current wage-capital price ratio, β with the lowest unit cost is selected. If technological advance is supposed to be local and the market selects technology β, technological advance will take place nearby. As technology α is not selected, there is no progress. In this case, the production frontier (isoquant curve) that can lead to new technological advance occurs under the technology β system. At this time, even if the price ratio between wage and capital falls, technology β will still be selected from the perspective of the lowest cost. That is to say, technology is local. When the experience effect is large, the same technology is still selected, regardless of the changes in factor-price ratio. Where such technological advance is local, technology β will be improved through the experience effect.

The David model was perhaps used in Japan before and after World War II. In the pre-war period, the conversion from rickshaw to bicycle, and from carriage to cars is all in line with this model. Akimitsu Sakuma (1998) conducted an empirical analysis of several industries in Japan after World War II, and reached conclusions on the industrial development stage or the maturity of the technology system. Technological advance in the pre-war period featured technology import and popularization, but there was much empirical analysis of technological innovation. For example, Yukihiko Kiyokawa (1995) on modern hybrids of silkworm, Keijiro Otsuka(1987) on the cotton industry, Toshiyuki Kako(1986) on automatic tillers, Tadashi Ishii(1987) on the power loom, Yukihiko Kiyokawa and Husao Makino (1998) on mats, Guan Quan (1996) on bicycles, and Guan Quan (1998) on rickshaws made a great effort towards data mining and method development.

Section 4 Reasons and conditions of technological development

As mentioned above, technological development in developing countries usually began with the import of technology, followed by technology popularization and technological innovation. However, this does not occur naturally and many conditions must be met. The process requires a certain amount of human resources as well as a developed market, and support policies. Of course, it also includes the so-called "social capabilities" such as moderate development of the capital goods sector, the modernization of organizations and systems, and the ability to acquire information. Given the reality in modern Japan, this book studies several important conditions and influencing factors in technological development.

I. Human resources

Ryoushin Minami (1987) points out two pieces of requirements for talent training. First, there are entrepreneurs who can select and import foreign technology and achieve localization. At the same time, technicians who can understand foreign technology and have the ability to improve it are also important. This is also of the essence for the popularization of domestic technology. Secondly, workers are also indispensable for technological innovation, as they have to operate the new equipment. More workers master skills through in-house training. This highlights the importance of the national education system, which produces a skilled workforce.

(1) Entrepreneurs

The most crucial human resources in private economic activities should be the decision-makers and managers of enterprises, who are also called entrepreneurs. Of course, this type of entrepreneur is not necessarily the same as one with an innovative spirit, referred to by Schumpeter as being capable of "creative destruction" and "new combination." They can apply to use products and new processes, tap new markets, and improve organizations. Research on entrepreneurs has mainly focused on the field of management science. According to the summary by the Institute of Business History (1985), research on entrepreneurs and managers can be divided into three areas. First, some research focused on the social attributes of entrepreneurs and managers such as their class, birthplace, and educational background, thereby studying issues such as social background and consciousness as well as focusing on the reality of social mobility. Second, the specific business operations and entrepreneurs and operators as decision makers were linked in order to study the role of entrepreneurs and managers. Third, their behavior and thoughts were studied, based on the biographies of individual entrepreneurs and managers, to explore the historical characteristics of Japanese entrepreneurs and managers.

Different from the approach to the history of management science mentioned above, Yukihiko Kiyokawa (1995) offers another possibility for the study of entrepreneurs. He points out that the drawback of past research is that the basic attributes of entrepreneurship cannot be selected through specific and objective methods to become measurable concepts. He argues that Schumpeter's definition of entrepreneurs should be expanded, and put forward two amendments. He holds that, when developing countries introduce advanced technology, there is a greater need to introduce the ability to localize imported technology compared to creative entrepreneurship. At that time, Japan's invention patents and utility models were essentially copying foreign technology, rather than original inventions. Second, attempts were made to capture the concept of traditional entrepreneurship. Small-scale technological innovations and accumulation of technological improvements form the basis of major technological innovations. At the same time, these can act as a catalyst for more small-scale technological innovations. The collection of technological innovations of all descriptions brings about the movement of production functions. Therefore, adaptive innovators and imitative followers are equally important for moving production functions.

(2) Technicians

Hoshimi Uchida (1988, 1990) divides the roles of technicians into two categories. One is the static function of directing workers in routine production activities or in charge of the operation of equipment. The other is the dynamic function that designs new products or equipment, studies the improvement in production methods, introduces new imported technologies, and prepares for diversification of new businesses. Before the Industrial Revolution, a class of technicians emerged from the artisan class in Europe, and subsequently engineering education institutions emerged, which gradually superseded the earlier artisan class. This is a continuous process. By contrast, in the course of industrialization in Japan, professional modern technicians appeared because the technology system in the Edo period differed from the imported Western European technology. This is a discontinuous process. In the early Meiji period, foreign technicians were only hired for a short time. At the same time, engineering education institutions were established in Japan, and their graduates became mainstream professionals who introduced European and American technologies and achieved technological advances in Japan. Through the Meiji period, Japanese technicians reached new heights in terms of quantity and quality, which is the most important reason for localization of imported technology. From 1880 to 1920, Japan saw the fastest increase in the number of technicians among the five countries of Britain, France, Germany, the U.S., and Japan. From the perspective of human resources of technicians, it can be said that Gerschenkron's "advantage of backwardness hypothesis" is in line with reality in Japan. There are few researches on Japanese technicians before World War II. Those by Ryoichi Iwauchi (1973,

1977), Hidemasa Morikawa (1975), Kenji Imatsu (1989), and Minoru Sawai (1995) are worthy of reference.

(3) Craftsmen

Technicians play a big large in modern industries, while craftsmen made a greater contribution to traditional industries. Craftsmen often bear the dual identities and responsibilities of technicians and workers. Kounosuke Odaka (1993) raised views worthy of note by examining the role of craftsmen in indus-trialization in Japan. He holds that the craftsmanship occupation in Japan was destroyed earlier compared to Western European countries such as Britain and Germany. The influence of craftsmen still existed until recently in Britain, while the U.S. was in between Britain and Japan. Developing countries after World War II had weak craftsmanship or no such occupation in the early stage. This proposition actually implies that there is a negative correlation between the time when modern economic growth started and the role of craftsmen. The role of craftsmen is greater in countries which had earlier modern economic growth, while craftsmen had a smaller contribution in countries which indus-trialization began later. Modern economic growth in European and American countries occurred spontaneously based on the original technology, and this original technology is essentially craftsmanship. Compared to the Western European model, Japan saw the coexistence of imported technology and ori-ginal technology for some time. However, as the original technology in today's developing countries is not developed, advanced technologies with a high capital-labor ratio were imported during this period. There are few opportun-ities to cultivate craftsmen or give full play to the role of craftsmen.

(4) Workers

It is the workers who operate machinery and equipment, regardless of the number of excellent entrepreneurs, technicians, or managers. Speaking of workers, the quantity and qualifications are crucial. In terms of quantity, there was no shortage in modern Japan. The problem is the qualifications of workers. Of course, it is not easy to make accurate measurement, because human qualifications refer not only to physical strength (nutrition and health) and intelligence (education and proficiency), but also cultural and individual aspects such as carefulness, rules and perception.

Kounosuke Odaka (1993) makes the following statement about workers: The recruitment of factory workers in the course of modern economic growth is far more difficult than what is supposed in economic theory. In order to establish the supply system of factory workers, it is not enough to ensure the freedom of occupation and mobility. The following three new conditions needed to be met. One is the discipline and obedience required for collective work in the long term. The second is the minimum basic literacy (reading, writing, abacus use). The third is skill training; factory workers are not only required to abide by collective management, but also work proactively and efficiently, go to work without absenteeism or tardiness. The due work must be done as well as possible even without supervision.

Further, Kounosuke Odaka (1990) divides manufacturing factories into four types, and points out their respective main players. It consists of traditional and modern types according to production technology. It consists of a large and small scale depending on the size of a factory. Manufacturing can be combined into four forms via these four types. Type I, which are traditional and small factories, feature traditional small scale production technology, but survived after the Meiji period. By contrast, type M, which are modern and large enterprises, feature chiefly imported products and production methods after the Meiji period. The remaining two combinations belong to the mixed type: Type I* which combines traditional technology and imported large-scale technology; and Type M* in which technology is imported for development in small-scale enterprises, albeit on a small scale, are applied to traditional commodity production. Type I is traditional skill passed on from the Tokugawa Shogunate era. These skills basically survive in the original form through appropriate modifications. In principle, this situation is preserved as it is in accordance with the skills and work organization of "craftsmen." Type I* is a way of working that harnesses traditional skills, and the scale of factories is also expanded. Here, new technicians are needed for the accumulation of new skilled labor, and the original skills and organizational methods had gradually changed. For Type M, foreign technologies are imported to cultivate a wealth of production process workers who can master new skills. Under the guidance of supervisors and technicians, they play a role in modern large-scale factories. In this case, due to a lack of previous industrial activity, they are almost all novices who start from scratch. Type M* refers to small-scale factories for independent operations on the basis of skilled workers borrowed from Europe and the U.S. These skilled people include those who have studied overseas, and many new workers who have worked at the aforesaid type I* factories, thus gaining new skills and knowledge.

II. Market conditions

From the perspective of technological development, market conditions have two aspects: one is the degree of market development, a factor of the demand side in economic development or technological development; the other is the market structure, namely whether it is monopolistic or competitive. Although the first point is an indirect cause of technological development, it should never be ignored. Ryoushin Minami (1987) cited these five points as reasons for technology absorption capacity in modern Japan: (1) the development of the capital goods sector, (2) cultivation of talents, (3) development degree of operating organizations, (4) development degree of information networks, and (5) the government's role. The first point is explained as follows: If the domestic capital goods sector develops, it will be easier to use new technologies for mechanized production, and the modification of imported technologies corresponding to Japan's factor endowment and preferences of demand will become easier. The precondition for the development of the domestic capital goods sector is that there is a huge market demand for capital goods. Besides, this market depends to a large extent on the level of development of the consumer goods sector. Japan's economic development began with the production of consumer goods as the center, which became the basis for the subsequent expansion of capital goods production. In other words, the development pattern of the Japanese economy is the shift of its focus from consumer goods to capital goods.

With respect to the relationship between market structure and technological innovation, Schumpeter hypothesis is the best known. He points out that, compared to competitive SMEs, monopolistic large enterprises are more conducive to technological innovation. Much empirical analysis has been conducted on this hypothesis, with Europe and the U.S. as the center, but no consensus has been reached. There have been a few studies on Japan after World War II, but most of these do not support Schumpeter hypothesis.[35] This may be due to the special nature of Japan. In other words, SMEs in Japan have a greater role in technological innovation than those in European and American countries. There is no in-depth research due to lack of sufficient statistical data prior to World War II. Chapter 7 of this book and Guan (2000) made some attempt, albeit insufficiently. We adopted industrial survey data on major cities around 1933 to investigate the relationship between the scale of several industries and the technology characteristics. The survey reveals that there is a substitution relationship between the production technology in large enterprises and SMEs in the same sector. In other words, large enterprises prefer to adopt capital-intensive technologies, whereas SMEs adopt labor-intensive technologies. The number of invention patents and utility models was calculated based on the historical records of some enterprises and the correlation analysis was carried out on the size of enterprises (number of employees), showing that SMEs carried out technological innovation activities more actively than larger enterprises. Moreover, given the role of zaibatsu enterprises in the economy before World War II, the number of invention patents held by zaibatsu enterprises in several industries was investigated. The results revealed that zaibatsu had distinct advantages in the modern industries, but not in the traditional industries. In other words, the advantages of zaibatsu in technological innovation were basically limited to the modern industries.

III. Role of government

Ryoushin Minami (1987) gives some views on the role of government. In the early Meiji period, the government built and operated modern factories in the military-related metallurgy and machinery fields in the name of policy of the shokusan kogyo (Increase Production and Promote Industry). Moreover, in the light industry field, model factories were built to cut imports and step up exports. However, these factories performed poorly, and were eventually sold to private enterprises at a low cost. Of course, this is actually a process of trial and error attendant upon the transfer of new technologies. It can be seen that the cost of this technology transplant was borne by the government. At the same time, however, due attention should be paid to private enterprises who imitated the government's efforts. Industrialization may not have been successful without them. The role of the government was greatly weakened after the early Meiji period, because practically all the factories were private. Except in the munitions sector and monopoly business, only Yawata Steel Works was government run. This was privatized in 1933. During this period, the government's role was chiefly to support private enterprises and build infrastructure, to cultivate professionals, to help the import and popularization of non-governmental technologies, and set up state and public universities and research institutes.

Hoshimi Uchida (1986) examined the various influential means adopted by the government for the development and popularization of industrial technology from the end of the Shogunate period to 1930. He divided the government's activities into the industrial sector and the non-industrial sector. The former includes such fields as the military, state-owned factories, state-owned railways, communications organizations, and public universities whose technical activities directly mirrored the impact of government policies; the latter exerted an indirect impact on the private sector through policy measures such as supervision, guidance, reward, and prohibition.

Guan (2001) analyzed the patent system of representative technology policies, and pointed out that one of the major characteristics of Japan's patent system was the enactment of the *Utility Model Act*, which provided a legal basis for the emergence of a wealth of minor inventions and innovations in Japan. The *Act* protected small technological innovations. Without this law, legions of minor inventions would not have been protected, and it would have been difficult for them to contribute to the development of traditional industries at that time. Given that Japan was dominated by traditional industries at the time, this protection for small technological innovations was even more important. Moreover, Minoru Sawai (1991) and Juro Hashimoto (1994) analyzed technical policies while Masaki Kobayashi (1977) examined government-run undertakings.

IV. Other conditions

(1) Information networks

Ryoushin Minami (1987) made two points regarding the relationship between technological development and the developed information network. The first point concerns technology transfer. The existence and development of an overseas information network is a vital condition. The early days of industrialization in large part relied on the government collecting information from overseas by participating in international fairs and conducting surveys through consulates; for domestic technology popularization, it includes research activities at national and regional levels, domestic fairs, and Competitive Exhibition, among others. Second, as industrialization intensified, enterprises were more able to collect information. For example, through worldwide commodity trading or by using information networks around the world, a corporate commune can capture newly developed products and technologies, putting it into production as soon as possible, or providing relevant information to enterprises with whom they have their own business relationship. As regards the popularization of technology domestically, industrial organizations also play a big role.

Sakae Tsunoyama (1986, 1988) studied Japanese consulates around the world from the end of the shogunate and the Meiji period. Based on this, the Meiji government collected information on overseas markets, laying the groundwork for the establishment of an information system network which integrated the public and private sectors, as well as domestic and overseas markets. Additional efforts were made in systematic information collection and processing. This network surpassed that of Britain, at that time a world hegemonic country, in terms of comprehensiveness and successfully tapped into their overseas markets.

According to Kaoru Suguhara (1996), the Ministry of Foreign Affairs set up a consulate in Shanghai in 1870. Thereafter, consulate numbers increased from 24 in 1884, to 59 in 1900, and to 92 in 1911. The consular reports provide a vital source of information on the business activities of Japanese businessmen from the 1880s to the 1990s. This is high-quality information about the end of the Meiji period, and is also the most comprehensive source on information on overseas trade. It is widely published and has been reprinted in major economic magazines and other government journals.

During the same period, China also set up consulates in other countries, but they did not use the consular reporting system to carry out organized information collection. In a sense, the differences between the two countries also determined their subsequent development direction in economy, trade, and technology.[36]

Japan actively participated in a slew of international expositions, including the Vienna World's Fair in 1873. It often held industrial expositions and Competitive Exhibitions.[37] Yukihiko Kiyokawa (1995) held that Expos and Competitive Exhibitions were essential to promote the popularization of technical know how and information, and their activities promoted quality and technological improvements in the traditional industries through a competitive market.

This industrial combination also made an important contribution to popular domestic technology. For example, a public experiment was carried out on the performance of tea-making machinery. The tea combination played an important role in the spread of the experimental results.[38] The Japanese

Textile Federation set up a "seminar of textile technicians" made up of the engineering directors of participating members who exchanged technical information. This organization promoted the rapid conversion of the textile technology from the outdated to new spinning frame.[39] Takanori Matsumoto (1993) summed up the following six functions of the trade combinations: viz. (1) product inspection, (2) market survey, (3) evaluation formula, (4) publicity and advertising, (5) improvement in infrastructure through the establishment of industrial test sites, educational institutions, and (6)common business.

(2) Institutions, habits, and culture

According to Kazushi Okawa and H. Rosovsky (1973), two systems that emerged in the twentieth century also improved social capabilities: One is zaibatsu, and the other the permanent employment system. Zaibatsu makes effective use of capital and entrepreneurship by integrating industries. The permanent employment system promotes the cultivation of skilled labor, prevents employee turnover, and also avoid employees' opposition when labor-saving technologies are adopted. Moreover, Kazushi Okawa and Hirohisa Kohama (1993) cited capital investment, organizations, systems, and human capabilities as the components of social capabilities, with a particular emphasis on the role of human capabilities, and used these growth accounting methods to analyze the effect of education.

Yukihiko Kiyokawa (1995) examined the role of the modern factory system, particularly the Tomioka Silk Mill, pointing out that its significance and role are immense. For example, many women were trained at the mill, and new methods were adopted for both quality and labor management. It played a key role in the construction of subsequent mechanical silk mills. Inspired by the experience of Tomioka Silk Mill, Kiyokawa proposed the "neutral value hypothesis" and explained the technology popularization and its reasons from a cultural perspective. He held that, generally speaking, according to the order of culture → organization → technology → commodity, demand will become easier and the popularization course will be faster.

Section 5 Concluding remarks

I. Japan's experience

Individual projects are studied separately above. This is a summary of the overall technology development in modern Japan. Yukihiko Kiyokawa (1995) cited two characteristics of the socio-economic structure in Japan: the competitiveness of the economy as a whole, and the developed socio-economic systems and organizations that complement and spur market economy activities. He pointed out the following: First, during technological development in Japan, there was a mutually supportive relationship between the level of technology and the degree of market development. He held that in developing countries, it is not so much the lack of ability to absorb technology as the lack of market adaptation. Second, the rapid spread of technology is in large measure linked to the characteristics of a small country, because the economies of small countries are usually conditional upon competition in the international market, while large countries with their vast lands and population are easily prone to import-substitute industrialization. Third, the issue of value systems in modernization, namely cultural issues, such as differences in religion (India) and socioeconomic systems (China).

Husao Makino (1996) believed that R&D in Japan shows these two trends: There was greater emphasis on applied R&D compared to basic research; and there was greater emphasis on process innovation compared to product innovation. Regarding the technology development in Japan as a whole, he also proposed the following three points: First, technology choice and popularization are basically realized through rational economic activities of entrepreneurs and the household sector. Second, due to reasonable technology choices, the technologies adopted by entrepreneurs are not necessarily the most state-of-the-art, and those with intermediate attributes combining traditional technologies are often adopted. Third, the adaptation of advanced technology in Japan has been achieved through imported capital goods and so-called "reverse engineering (RE)" and "learning by using (LU)" or "Learning by failing (LF)" on this basis.

II. An evaluation of this book

Here are the views about this book. First, there has been some excellent research on the development of technology in modern Japan, and convincing explanations have been made in many fields. For example, as regards the technology introduction and selection of types, the Akira Ono = Ryoushin Minami model (factor endowment hypothesis) mirrors the reality of Japan as a developing country. Yukihiko Kiyokawa's hypothesis about the information content gap was a huge step forward for the research on the technology popularization in developing countries with a dual structure. These research results are convincing for Japan before World War II, and are also worthy of reference for today's developing countries.

Second, although there is not much introduction, this book has many original results in empirical analysis and case studies. It shows the application of new research methods, the mining and improvement of new data, and the new possibilities of empirical analysis from a new perspective. It is also of great significance for constructing theories. For example, the factory model designed by Ryoushin Minami and Husao Makino (1987), the multivariate analysis method used by Yukihiko Kiyokawa (1985), the use and development of patent materials by Keijiro Otsuka (1987) and Tadashi Ishii (1980–1982) and the estimates by Husao Makino (1996) on capital profit rate and wheat flour supply are important outcomes.

That is not to say that these studies are at the pinnacle and have no need of further improvement. A legion of studies to date have mainly been based on the theory of neoclassical economics and the methodology of quantitative economic history. Of course, the study of the history of institutions and business is included. In the future, there will be research on institutional economics and comparative economic history, as well as new methods and perspectives on current aspects. It is expected that more research results on Japan's economic and technological development will emerge.

Notes

1 Robert Merton Solow first advanced the concept of technological advance or total factor productivity, see Solow (1956, 1957).
2 The literature on technological advance is legion, see Stoneman (1995).
3 On this law, see Clark (1940).
4 See Kuznets (1966).
5 See Hoffmann (1958). See, Yuichi Shionoya (1987) for a critical discussion on this issue
6 For a discussion of Japan, see Miyohe Shinohara (1976).
7 There is much discussion on this point, including the "dual structure of society" and the "dual structure" of technology. For details, see the textbooks on development economics, such as those by Guan Quan (2014, 2018). Japanese textbooks include those by Yasuhiko Torii (1979), Yasuoki Takagi (1992), Toshio Watanabe (1996), Yonosuke Hara (1996), Yujiro Hayami (1995).
8 For example, Akira Ono, Ryoushin Minami (1973, 1975), and Kounosuke Odaka (1984, 1989).
9 Japan's Patent Office is equivalent to China's Patent Office, and is a government agency in charge of patents.
10 For the use of multivariate statistical analysis, see Yukihiko Kiyokawa (1985, 1995).
11 There are legions of research results about technological advance in modern Japan, such as Ryoushin Minami, Yukihiko Kiyokawa (1987), Minami et al. (1995).
12 The discussion in this chapter is chiefly by Guan Quan (2001, 2003).
13 This technology export is mainly achieved through foreign investment; see the relevant chapters for industries like the rickshaw and bicycle industries.
14 Kuznets denied the "advantage of backwardness", see Kuznets (1971). In addition, there are many studies on this hypothesis in the field of economic growth theory, namely phenomenon of convergence. Some hold that some developing countries indeed caught up and narrowed the gap with developed countries, but not all developing countries can achieve this. See Baumol (1986), De Long (1988), Mankiw et al. (1992), Barro and Martin (1992, 1995), Jones (1998), et al.
15 For the above discussion, see Ryoushin Minami (1981).
16 Although a simple introduction to China's development course is given, it can basically be said that the hypothesis of advantage of backwardness is established. For the long-term development of the Chinese economy, see Guan Quan (2019); for the development of industries in modern China, see Guan Quan (2018).
17 For Akira Ono's views, see Shozaburo Fujino et al. (1979) and Ono (1986), Ryoushin Minami (1981).

18 There is no substitution between production factors and the production function in which the ratio of factors of production is fixed.

19 For the cases of imported technologies, see Ryoushin Minami (1981) pp. 117–121.

20 For the above views, see Yukihiko Kiyokawa (1984).

21 See Yukihiko Kiyokawa (1975, 1987).

22 On the penetration curve and the issue of technology penetration, see Yukihiko Kiyokawa (1995).

23 Digital technology was still in its infancy in the late 1980s. The electronics market around the world was basically dominated by major Japanese manufacturers. South Korea's Samsung Group, decided to step up its investment in digital technology. In the twenty-first century, it even surpassed Japanese companies to become the world's largest electronics manufacturer.

24 Yukihiko Kiyokawa also acknowledges this point; see (1995).

25 Guan Quan (1996, 1998, 2001) examined the long-term development and technological innovation in the rickshaw, bicycle, and car industries before World War II. See also the subsequent chapters in this book.

26 In this regard, it is exactly the same as model by Davies. One reason is that the vertical axis in his model is not the penetration rate.

27 Yukihiko Kiyokawa (1995) p. 8.

28 Schumpeter (1990).

29 For the content of this part, see Guan Quan (2014). Moreover, Chinese entrepreneur Ma Yun also proposed a new marketing approach, which deserves reference.

30 The following introduction is from Hayami Y., and V.W. Ruttan (2000), Yujiro Hayami (1995).

31 Schumpeter (1999).

32 Guan Quan (2003) (and see Chapter 6 of this book) confirmed the situation in Japan before World War II, and the results did not support Schumpeter hypothesis.

33 For "learning by doing," see Arrow (1962).

34 The discussion here is based on David (1975) p. 66, Sakuma (1998) p. 199, and Guan Quan (2003) p. 40.

35 On this point, see Kenichi Imai (1970), Noriyuki Doi (1977, 1993), Masu Uekusa (1982), Naoki Murakami (1986, 1988), and Ryuhe Wakasugi et al. (1996).

36 Sakae Tsunoyama (1986).

37 For information on expos held in Japan at that time, see Mitsuo Yamamoto (1973).

38 Masahiko Shintani (1987).

39 Yukihiko Kiyokawa (1987).

Part II
Characteristics of innovation and development

2 Structural changes in industrial development

Tradition and modernity

Section 1 Introduction

The chief purpose of this chapter is to study the industrial development and structural changes in modern Japan, especially its relationship with technological innovation. The period for examination is from 1909 to 1940, mainly due to the following two considerations: First, in this period, Japan saw rapid economic development, and the country's industrial structure also underwent major changes. From the perspective of the entire economy, great strides were made in the transition from agriculture to industry. The industrial structure of the real GDP is as follows: in 1900, the primary industry accounted for 34.6%, the secondary industry 17.9%, and the tertiary industry 47.5%. By 1938, the proportions stood at 15.9%, 51.8%, and 32.3%.[1] While both primary and tertiary industries experienced a decline, the secondary industry saw a substantial expansion. This indicates that during this period, Japan was basically at the first stage of the so-called Petty-Clark Law, or it can be said that industrialization had initially been achieved. Second, from the perspective of employment structure, the primary industry accounted for 65% in 1900, 52.9% in 1920, and 43.9% in 1938. The non-primary industry accounted for 35.% in 1900, 47.1% in 1920, and 56.1% in 1938. In this, the secondary industry jumped from 24.4% in 1920 to 28.7%, and the tertiary industry increased from 22.7% in 1920 to 27.4%.[2] The change in employment is not as large as that in GDP, and the employment structure relatively lags behind. This is a common empirical feature in various countries. In view of this, we consider that it was preliminary industrialization. If the employment structure is completely reversed like the GDP structure, it should be considered complete industrialization.[3]

This is a brief introduction to the situation in China. The GDP structure and employment structure in 1952 were as follows: The primary industry accounted for 50.5% and 83.5%, the secondary industry 21.0% and 7.4%, and the tertiary industry 28.6% and 9.1%, respectively. In 2005, the structure was as follows: The primary industry accounted for 12.5% and 44.7%, the secondary industry 47.3% and 23.9%, and the tertiary industry 40.2% and 31.4%, respectively.[4] On the whole, it can be judged that the structure in China in 1952 was not as good as that in Japan in 1900 (mainly the high proportion of the primary industry). The structure in 2005 was roughly equivalent to the best period in Japan before World War II.[5] However, an explanation is necessary. The figures in Japan in 1938 may correspond to a period of a general war in China against the Japanese aggression at that time. Therefore, the industrial structure was in an abnormal state, but it does not have a major impact overall.

The statistical data during this period is comprehensive, ensuring our analysis. For example, the *Statistics Table of Factories* introduced hereunder is the only reliable data that comprehensively reflects industrial production at that time. By contrast, there was no comprehensive and continuous statistical survey in China at the time. For example, the *Statistics Table of Agriculture and Commerce* in the 1910s was equivalent to *Statistics Table of Agriculture and Commerce* in Japan, but it was poorly formulated; the *Statistics of Factories in Manchuria* for Northeast China in the 1930s was an imitation of Japan's *Statistics Table of Factories*. Since the 1920s, no continuous national factory surveys were carried out. There is only the 1933 *Industrial Survey Report of China* and the occasional one-time survey in some regions or periods and these reports have limitations in quality and comprehensiveness.[6]

Section 2 Definitions and distinction

I. Previous research

Manufacturing industries are usually classified by attribute, such as chemicals, textiles industry, and machinery. In fact, they can be divided according to different division methods, such as light and heavy industry, or traditional and modern. Due to the different periods and perspectives of research, it is sometimes necessary to have traditional and modern industries. In this section, the traditional and modern industries in this period will be divided. Some previous studies have been conducted on this issue, see Kazushi Okawa (1962), Takafusa Nakamura (1976, 1985, 1997), and Yoshiro Matsuda et al. (1984). These research outcomes are discussed below.

Before the analysis, it is necessary to define what is meant by traditional and modern industries. Kazushi Okawa held that traditional industries refer to "sectors that have the local or inherent origin or such characteristics in the Japanese economy." At the same time, he also acknowledged that "it is very hard to differentiate local or inherent elements from foreign elements when studying an economy," while "differentiating these elements in Japan is both necessary and possible." The economic components in 1955 are distinguished on the basis of this view.[7] Takafusa Nakamura held that

> traditional industries in principle refer to the industries that include agriculture, forestry, and aquaculture in a broad sense, but exclude these in a narrow sense, and that result from the small operations that provide

traditional goods and services in the pre-modern times, chiefly household labor, with a few by hired labor.

However, he also pointed out that "many industries introduced from overseas after the Meiji period had characteristics similar to the operations of traditional industries" and called this "assimilation." He also pointed out that some traditional industries formed so-called "new traditional industries" after importing "foreign materials and technologies." According to this view, he used the data from the 1920 census to classify all industries, including the manufacturing sector.[8] Moreover, when studying factory production at the end of the Meiji period, Yoshiro Matsuda et al. used, in the case of the manufacturing sector, materials such as the *Statistics Table of Factories 1909* and a *General Overview of Factories* to calculate the motorization rate, the average number of employees in a factory, per capita production volume, and the proportion of joint-stock companies, and classified the four indicators. Their analysis considers both business forms and production technology factors.[9]

Inspiration in three aspects can be gained from the above research. First, it is neither easy nor clear how traditional and modern industries have been divided. Further exploration is required as many industries blended into one another later in the development process. Second, data from different periods may lead to very different classification results, because some industries saw great changes with the development of the economy (e.g., there were few modern industries in Japan in the late nineteenth century). At that time, the majority of industries were traditional industries. If the data after World War II were to be used, the results would be entirely different. Third, the types of statistical data are also important. Harmonized data should be preferred, and multiple indicators should be used instead of single.

II. Our view

Through the above discussion, we hold that, except in some typical industries, most industries at that time had elements of both traditional and modern industries. It is therefore hard to distinguish these by a certain period or definition. Specific classification is required. The question is what methods should be used. In the final analysis, the differences between the two were chiefly as follows: (1) whether factory production or a family business; (2) large-scale or small-scale production; (3) whether power was used; (4) capital-intensive or labor-intensive; (5) whether labor productivity was high or low. If the above characteristics are sufficiently reflected, the outcome may be closest to the reality. In principle, we are of the opinion that the two sectors should have the following characteristics: Traditional industries (manufacturing) are chiefly small labor-intensive factories that do not use power, whereas modern industries chiefly feature capital-intensive large-scale factories that use power. Even this has its limitations: it can be difficult to distinguish between large- and small-scale operations.

In line with this idea, multivariate statistical methods are used for the relativization of various industries, and (relative) traditional industries and modern industries are distinguished. Specifically, using 1909 as the benchmark year, the analysis also covered the years 1920, 1930, and 1940. The year 1909 is used as the benchmark for two reasons: First, This is the first year that comprehensive data on factory statistics was available For the years before this the only data available was in the *Statistics Table of Agriculture and Commerce*. Second, it is easy to compare previous studies, such as the 1909 study by Matsuda et al.

The indicators for distinction are all selected from the *Statistics Table of Factories*, which mainly takes into account two factors: factory scale and technical level. The following six indicators are selected: (1) Motorization rate (X_1); (2) employee-factory ratio with more than 30 people (X_2); (3) average horsepower at factories (X_3); (4) average number of factory employees (X_4); (5) intensity of horsepower (X_5); and (6) actual production volume per capita (X_6). Of the six indicators, X_1, X_3, and X_5 represent technical variables; X_2 and X_4 represent scale variables; and X_6 represents the efficiency indicator, reflecting comprehensive capabilities and levels. For example, the motorization rate is the proportion of factories using power in a particular industry. The use of power obviously affects labor productivity, because the use of power by humans represents a significant technological advance, which cuts labor intensity and bolsters production efficiency.[10] X_3 and X_5 are proxy variables of capital intensity, because machinery and equipment in factories using power must be driven by the prime motors. The horsepower of prime motors indirectly represents the capacity of machinery and equipment. As regards X_2 and X_4, large factories generally have a scale effect, with a high level of modernization and much machinery and equipment. X_2 chooses a factory with over 30 people as an indicator. While this is a little arbitrary, we think that the number is suitable, given the specific circumstances at the time. A factory with 30 employees was no longer regarded as a small factory at that time; factories with over 30 employees accounted for some 16% (see Table 3.3), which is an appropriate ratio. On the whole, the proportion of modern factories at that time was relatively small, which tallies with the actual situation.[11]

As regards the choice of industry, consideration is given to the following: First, in order to distinguish their respective characteristics, the industries will be differentiated slightly. Second, we will follow the rough classification contained in the *Statistics Table of Factories* from 1909. We have no choice but to choose the year 1909 as the benchmark, because if a more detailed classification was used, we could not analyze the situation in 1909. If the year 1909 is used as the base line, certain industries in the years with more detailed classification can be combined. Third, in order to make a comparative analysis with other studies, mutual correspondence is maintained as much as possible. In the end, 60 industries were selected for analysis, as shown in Table 2.1.

Table 2.1 Names, abbreviations, and characteristics of industries for analysis

Industry number	Industry name	Abbreviation	Characteristics	Industry number	Industry name	Abbreviation	Characteristics
1	Silk reeling		B	31	Lacquerware		A
2	Textile		B	32	Tanning		A
3	Raw silk		B	33	Matches		B
4	Cotton		B	34	Gunpowder		B
5	Fabrics		A	35	Oil and wax		B
6	Dyeing		A	36	Pharmaceuticals		A
7	Weaving		A	37	Industrial medicine		B
8	Tailoring		A	38	Rubber		B
9	Embroidery		A	39	Soap, candles, cosmetics		A
10	Netting		A	40	Dyes, coatings, pigments		A
11	Hat		A	41	Fertilizers		B
12	Textile miscellaneous		B	42	Chemical miscellaneous		B
13	Prime motor		B	43	Brewing		A
14	Machine-made		B	44	Sugar-making		B
15	Ship		B	45	Tea		A
16	Railway vehicle		B	46	Milling		B
17	Other vehicles		A	47	Beverages		B
18	Appliance		A	48	Dessert		A
19	Battery and bulb		B	49	Can		A
20	Weaponry		B	50	Animal products		B
21	Mechanical miscellaneous		A	51	Aquatic products		A
22	Metal refining		B	52	Food miscellaneous		A
23	Casting		B	53	Printing and binding		A

(*continued*)

Table 2.1 Cont.

Industry number	Industry name	Abbreviation	Characteristics	Industry number	Industry name	Abbreviation	Characteristics
24	Metal products		A	54	Paper products		A
25	Electroplated products		A	55	Timber, wood products		A
26	Pottery and porcelain		A	56	Leather		A
27	Glass		A	57	Feather products		A
28	Cement		B	58	Bamboo and willow products		A
29	Tile		A	59	Handicraft		A
30	Papermaking		B	60	Other miscellaneous		A

Notes: The results herein come from cluster analysis; A refers to traditional industries, and B refers to modern industries.

Next, the industries in 1909 are judged. We conducted a statistical analysis of 60 industries according to the above indicators using the cluster analysis method. The cluster analysis method is a multivariate statistical method for the quantitative study of classification issues. The basic idea is as follows: Individuals in the same category have great similarities, and individuals in different categories have great differences. According to multiple indicators in the sample, the statistics that can measure the similarity between samples (or variables) can be found, and a clustering method is adopted to cluster all the samples (or variables) in different categories. The clustering method used here is Ward's method (minimum incremental agglomerative clustering of the sum of squares of distances between categories), and the measurement method for distance or similarity is Squared Euclidean Distance ($D = (x_1-y_1)^2 + (x_2-y_2)^2 + \ldots$). The results of the analysis are shown in Table 2.1 (represented by A and B, respectively).[12]

Another characteristic of cluster analysis is that the results are displayed in a dendrogram so that they can be observed clearly. Due to its large size, a dendrogram is not shown here. The horizontal number is the scale of the cluster, namely the distance of mutual combination of each sample (industry). This chapter looks at Squared Euclidean Distance. The vertical figure shows a combination of various industries. It can be clearly seen that it is divided into two groups: The upper group belongs to the traditional industries, the lower group the modern industries. From the top to the bottom, traditional industries are: other vehicle miscellaneous, miscellaneous machinery, other miscellaneous, fabrics, weaving, dyeing, metal products, netting, hats, glass, feather products, lacquerware, tea, handicrafts, aquatic products, tiles, paper products, tailoring, ceramics, bamboo and willow products, embroidery, brewing, leather products, snacks, tanning, food miscellaneous, pharmaceuticals, utensils, canned food, soap, printing, gold plating, dyes, wood, and animal products. The remaining industries belong to modern industries, such as weaponry, ships, machinery manufacturing, prime motors, railway vehicles, metal refining, cement, papermaking, gunpowder, oil making, industrial drugs, rubber, chemical fertilizers, and so on. The results shown in Table 2.1 are not greatly different from what people expect, and are similar to the results of previous studies. This indicates that the results of this classification are credible. As mentioned earlier, silk reeling, papermaking, matches, flour milling, beverages, animal products, printing, binding, wood, wood products and other industries have dual characteristics, containing elements of traditional and modern industries. Of course, as mentioned earlier, our classification is inevitably subject to certain data and methods as it is based on the selection indicators in the *Statistics Table of Factories 1909*.

Is the result of this classification accurate? In order to verify the quality of classification, another multivariate statistical analysis method, namely discriminant analysis, is adopted. Very similar to cluster analysis, discriminant analysis is also a statistical method that can classify samples, but the two have important differences. The categories are unknown for the cluster analysis in

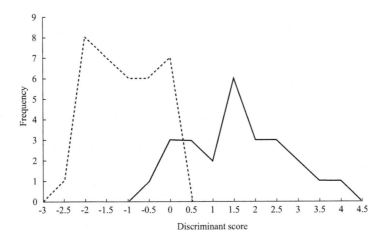

Figure 2.1 Results of the discriminant analysis (1909).

advance, while the discriminant analysis derives a discriminant function or a set of discriminant functions based on the sample data under the condition of known categories, and also formulates discriminative rules to determine the category to which the sample to be discriminated belongs. Due to this feature, the discriminant analysis is also a method for testing the quality of the cluster analysis results. Based on this principle, the discriminant function is as follows:

$$Z = 0.733X_1 + 0.419X_2 - 2.525X_3 + 2.215X_4 + 1.502X_5 + 0.032X_6$$

Correct discrimination rate: 93.33%.

Judging from the coefficients of the discriminant function, the degree of interpretation of the discriminant function is shown in the order of X_3, X_4, X_5, X_1, X_2, indicating that the 3rd, 4th, and 5th variables play a greater role in interpreting the discriminant function. It also means that they are important factors for determining the nature of an industry. Figure 2.1 shows the graph results of the discriminant analysis. It can be seen that there is a certain gap between the two industry groups, and their distribution is not very close (little overlapping). This shows that there is a large difference between the two, and that the previous cluster analysis has good and significant results.

Section 3 Structural changes

I. Overview of two industry groups

The changes in the two industry groups are studied here based on the results of analysis in the preceding section. We first take a look at the basic situation of the two industry groups. Table 2.2 shows the number of factories, horsepower

Table 2.2 Basic situation of traditional industry groups and modern industry groups

Industry groups	Number of factories (10,000)	Horsepower of prime motors (10,000)	Number of employees (10,000 people)	Actual production volume (10m yen)
1909				
Entire manufacturing sector	3.20(100.00)	31.15(100.00)	78.05(100.00)	104.89(100.00)
Traditional industry group	2.41(75.08)	7.93(25.46)	37.22(47.69)	53.03(50.56)
Modern industry group	0.80(24.92)	23.22(74.54)	40.83(52.31)	51.85(49.44)
1920				
Entire manufacturing sector	4.56(100.00)	144.12(100.00)	147.90(100.00)	309.83(100.00)
Traditional industry group	3.33(73.19)	34.69(24.07)	64.75(43.78)	139.73(45.10)
Modern industry group	1.22(26.81)	109.43(75.93)	83.15(56.22)	170.09(54.90)
1930				
Entire manufacturing sector	6.18(100.00)	427.61(100.00)	167.56(100.00)	619.05(100.00)
Traditional industry group	4.66(75.40)	115.26(26.95)	77.50(46.25)	288.10(46.54)
Modern industry group	1.52(24.60)	312.35(73.05)	90.06(53.75)	330.95(53.46)
1940				
Entire manufacturing sector	13.72(100.00)	1 063.38(100.00)	419.63(100.00)	1 810.49(100.00)
Traditional industry group	9.85(71.79)	209.64(19.71)	237.06(56.49)	826.28(45.64)
Modern industry group	3.87(28.21)	853.74(80.29)	182.57(43.51)	984.21(54.36)

Source: *Statistics Table of Factories* over the years by (Japan's) Ministry of Agriculture and Commerce/Ministry of Commerce and Industry.

Note:
1 The entire manufacturing industry is the total of 60 industries, rather than the manufacturing sector in the *Statistics Table of Factories*.
2 The figures in brackets are calculated based on the entire manufacturing industry as 100.
3 For the propose of rounding, the totals in the table and subtotals are slightly different. The remaining is the same.

of prime motors, employees, and actual production volume at four time points from 1909 to 1940. Judging from the manufacturing industry as a whole, the number of factories was 32,000 in 1909, 61,800 in 1930, and more than doubled in 1940, showing accelerated development. The horsepower of prime motors soared from 311,500 in 1909 to 14.412 million in 1920, 4.2761 million in 1930, and 10.6338 million in 1940. Its staggering growth rate exceeded that of factories by a considerable way. This means that there was a quantum leap in technological advances during this period, or that capital equipment had greatly improved. The number of employees increased from 780,500 in 1909, to 1.497 million in 1920, 1.6756 million in 1930, and 4.1963 million in 1940. Although the increase is slower than that of horsepower, it far exceeded that of factories. This also shows that the scale of factories was expanding, which was bound to have a certain scale effect, thus reflecting the modernization of factories as a whole. The actual production volume jumped from 1.0489 billion yen in 1909 to 3.0983 billion in 1920, to 6.1905 billion in 1930, and to 18.1049 billion in 1940, up by over 16 times in 30 years.

Next, traditional industries and modern industries are compared. Judging from the number of factories, the ratio of the modern industry group to the traditional industry group was about 75:25 from 1909 to 1930, and the proportion of the traditional industry group declined slightly in 1940 (figures within brackets in the table). This shows that the main composition of factories before World War II was traditional industries, while modern industries only accounted for a small portion. This situation basically remains unchanged, which also confirms our proposition: Japan achieved preliminary industrialization rather than full industrialization before World War II. The proportion of the horsepower of prime motors is exactly the opposite of the number of factories. From 1909 to 1930, the ratio of the two stood at 25:75. In 1940, the proportion of traditional industry groups fell further. The proportion of the horsepower of prime motors indicates that traditional and modern industries had a large technical gap in areas such as machinery and equipment and power capacity before World War II, and there was no significant change. The number of employees was basically 50:50. In other words, traditional and modern industries were on a par in terms of employment during this period. This also demonstrates that traditional industries with more factories were smaller in scale and did not hire more workers, whereas modern industries with fewer factories employed many more. The proportion and change as regards the actual production volume are similar to that of employees, although there are slight differences. The proportion of employees was lower than 50 in 1909 and higher than 50 in 1940 in traditional industries. The reverse is true for actual production volume. The proportion of traditional industries had remained at around 45 since 1920.

II. The characteristics of the two industry groups

Comparative analysis of the two industry groups is carried out based on the indicator variables stated earlier. Table 2.3 shows the mean (figures outside

Table 2.3 Basic characteristics of traditional industries and modern industries

Industries	(X₁) Motorization rate (%)	(X₂) Proportion of factories with over 30 employees (%)	(X₃) Average horsepower of factories	(X₄) Average number of factory employees	(X₅) Intensity of horsepower	(X₆) Actual production value per capita
1909						
Manufacturing sector as a whole	34.52(27.09)	15.18(15.45)	34.25(95.70)	37.02(93.80)	0.69(1.05)	24.46(41.91)
Traditional industries	18.57(14.94)	8.93(5.87)	2.91(2.61)	15.78(5.99)	0.19(0.19)	17.47(17.70)
Modern industries	56.86(24.42)	23.93(20.03)	78.13(138.08)	66.74(141.43)	1.39(1.34)	34.25(60.85)
1920						
Manufacturing sector as a whole	63.24(24.77)	18.66(14.93)	70.10(148.37)	45.39(83.63)	1.15(1.52)	33.97(62.60)
Traditional industries	51.53(22.16)	11.78(6.00)	8.80(7.22)	18.59(7.00)	0.47(0.39)	25.16(25.51)
Modern industries	79.51(18.45)	28.30(18.21)	155.92(202.22)	82.91(120.87)	2.11(1.97)	46.30(91.87)
1930						
Manufacturing sector as a whole	77.73(20.12)	17.54(15.46)	171.96(379.67)	37.09(62.80)	3.46(5.62)	63.89(79.65)
Traditional industries	72.67(20.27)	12.47(12.05)	22.54(17.36)	16.63(5.99)	1.32(0.97)	46.62(41.93)
Modern industries	84.83(17.97)	24.63(17.08)	381.16(525.16)	65.73(90.44)	6.46(7.76)	88.08(109.83)

(*continued*)

Table 2.3 Cont.

Industries	(X_1) Motorization rate (%)	(X_2) Proportion of factories with over 30 employees (%)	(X_3) Average horsepower of factories	(X_4) Average number of factory employees	(X_5) Intensity of horsepower	(X_6) Actual production value per capita
1940						
Manufacturing sector as a whole	79.89(22.00)	17.19(15.80)	141.92(310.77)	43.94(64.21)	2.89(4.62)	53.36(44.17)
Traditional industries	77.27(20.39)	11.55(8.44)	23.60(30.01)	21.13(18.97)	1.11(1.04)	44.15(32.46)
Modern industries	83.56(24.02)	25.09(20.03)	307.56(432.61)	75.86(88.35)	5.38(6.31)	66.26(54.84)

Source: *Statistics Table of Factories* over the years by (Japan's) Ministry of Agriculture and Commerce/ Ministry of Commerce and Industry.

Notes:
1 Motorization rate = number of power-driven factories ÷ number of all factories X 100.
2 Intensity of horsepower = horsepower of prime motors ÷ number of employees.
3 The unit of actual production value per capita is 100 yuan per person.
4 The figures are the average means of various industries. Figures inside the brackets are standard deviation.

brackets) and standard deviation (figures inside brackets) of each variable. We first take a look at the change in the mean. The overall change in the first variable, motorization rate (X_1), saw an increase from 34.2% in 1909 to 79.89% in 1940. During the same period, the figure rose from 56.86% to 83.56% in modern industries, and from 18.57% to 77.27% in traditional industries. As an absolute value, modern industries still have a large advantage, but the growth rate of traditional industries surpassed that of modern industries, and the two were close in the later stages. The changes in the variables X_3 and X_5 are highly similar to X_1; the two industry groups increased by about three times from 1909 to 1940. Of this, the growth rate of modern industries was roughly the same as the overall sector, while traditional industries saw an even faster increase (7 times for X_3, 5 times for X_5). In general, the number of prime motors increased at a fast clip, and traditional industries grew faster than modern industries. In a sense, this shows that the technological gap between traditional and modern industries was gradually shrinking. For instance, the growth rate of X_3 fell from 27 times in 1909 to 13 times in 1940, and the growth rate of X_5 fell from 7 times to 5 times. As mentioned above, there was still a large gap between traditional and modern industries during this period.

The ratio (X_2) of factory with more than 30 employees – a variable representing the size of factory – saw no significant change from 1909 to 1940 (although there was some increase from 1909 to 1920), and the average number of employees in factory (X_4) was similar. Basically, a certain scale expansion took place from 1909 to 1920, after which point the changes were not obvious. This is largely the case even if traditional and modern industries are viewed in isolation. In other words, whether it be the industry as a whole or the distinction between traditional and modern industries, the proportion of factory scale did not change much in this period. In the end, the actual production volume per capita increased threefold from 1909 to 1940, and traditional and modern industries also increased by a similar factor.

We now take a look at the standard deviation. For starters, the motorization rate (X_1) of the manufacturing sector as a whole continued to decrease from 1909 to 1940, while modern industries saw little change (slight decrease in the middle). Traditional industries expanded somewhat. In other words, the gap between the two industry groups narrowed. Secondly, there were similar changes in the ratio of factories with over 30 employees (X_2) and the average number of employees in factories (X_4). The average horsepower (X_3) and horsepower intensity (X_5) of factories expanded overall, while traditional industries had a larger expansion, indicating that the gap between the two industry groups was narrowing. Finally, in terms of actual production volume per capita (X_6), traditional industries saw a larger expansion than modern industries, showing that the gap between the two was narrowing. We can, therefore, draw the conclusion that much as modern industries still had a great advantage, on the whole, the gap between traditional and modern industries was narrowing.

III. Statistical analysis

For a closer examination of the changes between traditional and modern industries, it is necessary to conduct specific analysis by means of a statistical analysis method. The author uses another multivariate statistical analysis method. In other words, the principal component analysis method extracts the characteristics of various industries, and offers a comprehensive evaluation. Principal component analysis is a multivariate analysis method that examines the correlation among several variables. It studies how to explain the multivariate variance-covariance structure through several principal components (linear combinations of original variables). In other words, several principal components are derived so that the information of original variables is retained as far as possible, and there is no mutual correlation. Principal component analysis is oftentimes used to judge comprehensive indicators of certain things or phenomena, and to offer a proper explanation for the information contained in the comprehensive indicators, so that an in-depth exploration is given for the inherent laws of things.

The above six variables are used for the principal component analysis for the years 1909, 1920, 1930, and 1940. Due to lack of space, Figures 2.2 and 2.3 show the results in the years 1909 and 1940 only. The horizontal axis is the first principal component value (Z_1), and the vertical axis is the second principal component value (Z_2). As the coefficients of each variable of the first principal component value are positive, it can be called comprehensive evaluation axis (contribution rate = 40.7%). According to our purpose and the nature of variables, industries closer to the right better reflect the characteristics of modern industries, and industries closer to the left better reflect the characteristics of traditional industries. There are both positive and negative coefficients of each variable of the second principal component value, which can be viewed as a reference axis or technology and scale axis (contribution rate=23.0%). The results of the linear combinations shown below are obtained through panel analysis at four time points from 1909 to 1940. These are for reference here.

$$Z_1 = 0.499X_1 + 0.697X_2 + 0.847X_3 + 0.769X_4 + 0.553X_5 + 0.301X_6$$

$$Z_2 = 0.031X_1 - 0.480X_2 + 0.147X_3 - 0.490X_4 + 0.675X_5 + 0.659X_6$$

Cumulative contribution rate: 63.7%.

The following two points can be seen from Figure 2.3. First, it is highly consistent with the previous observations and analysis results. Traditional industries and modern industries can be clearly distinguished. In other words, industries closer to the right better reflect the characteristics of modern industries, while industries closer to the left better reflect the characteristics of traditional industries. For example, industries such as textiles, railway

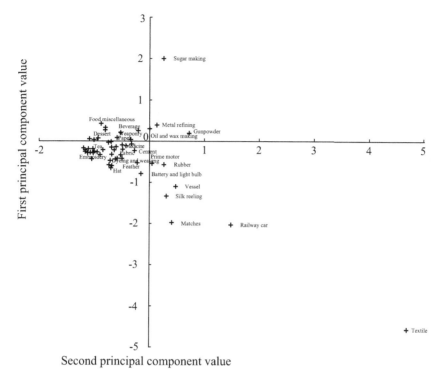

Figure 2.2 Analysis of the characteristics of industries (1909).

vehicles, gunpowder, sugar making, metal refining, fertilizers, oil making, wax making, rubber, weaponry, ships, industrial medicine, prime motors, batteries, light bulbs, cement, and flour milling are closer to the right side, and better reflect the characteristics of modern industries. Industries such as embroidery, crafts, lacquerware, aquatic products, tea, other miscellaneous, paper products, leather products, fabrics, bamboo and willow products, hats, feather products, netting, weaving, metal products, and brew are closer to the left side, and, as we can see at a glance, belong to traditional industries.

Second, the modern industry group has a larger variance than the traditional industry groups. In other words, the various industries in the modern industry group have relatively few similarities. Conversely, the various industries in the traditional industry group have more similar characteristics. This can be explained by the following points. Modern industries have relatively diversified characteristics, some large in scale and others having high technical level. In traditional industries, there is similarity in terms of scale and technology. With a small scale and low technology, it is not easy to make a distinction. However, this changed in 1940, when traditional industries began

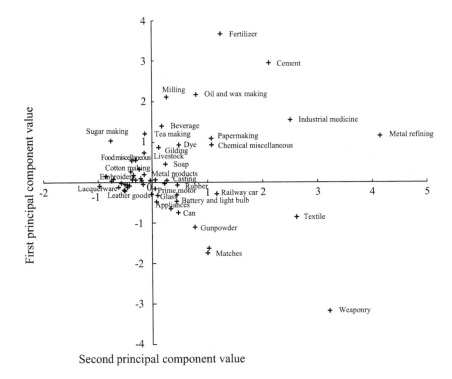

Figure 2.3 Analysis of the characteristics of industries (1940).

to see diversification. It means that many traditional industries incorporated more modern elements, such as power and machinery and equipment.

Section 4 Cause analysis

I. Progress of the power revolution

We hold that the reasons for the structural changes in the manufacturing sector during this period were brought about by the greater strides in the power revolution. According to research by the Japanese scholar Ryoushin Minami, Japan saw two power revolutions from the end of the nineteenth century to the 1930s. The first was the transition from the waterwheel to the steam engine from 1890 to around 1905, and the second is the transition from steam engines to the electric motor (also known as electrification) from 1905 to 1930.[13] The period under discussion in this chapter occurred during the second power revolution. Therefore, analysis is carried out with electrification as its center.

Motors, large and small, can be made, and easily controlled. It is therefore more suitable for various fields. According to the research conducted by Ryoushin Minami, the introduction of electric motors to large factories means motorization did not start with electrification, but with the steam engine. This is different at SMEs, where the introduction of electric motors resulted in the motorization of factories, because the majority of SMEs did not use steam engines or any other form of power. Some enterprises still used traditional Japanese waterwheels.[14] Much as our analysis does not directly study large enterprises and SMEs, enterprises in traditional industries are chiefly SMEs, while those in modern industries are usually larger. Therefore, the two are not contradictory and should even be considered as the same matter (see Table 2.3).

Figure 2.4 describes the progress of motorization from 1909 to 1920. During this period, all industries made great strides (all above the 45-degree line), and the manufacturing sector as a whole rose from about 30% to about 60% (mean value). Another characteristic is that industries with a high motorization rate in 1909 had a high rate thereafter, while industries with a low rate in 1909 also had a low level thereafter. In other words, the

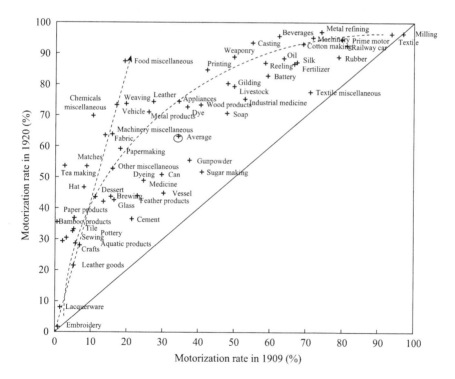

Figure 2.4 Progress of the power revolution (1909–1920).
Source: (Japan) *Statistics Table of Factories* 1909 and 1920.

modernization rate of modern industries was relatively high in 1909 and higher still in 1920, but there was change in the absolute level, while traditional industries still remained at a relatively low level. However, some industries, including some traditional industries, grew rapidly (this can be measured according to the gap with the 45-degree line), such as weapons, printing, casting, beverages, food miscellaneous, vehicles, weaving, chemical miscellaneous, fabrics, machinery miscellaneous, matches, tea making, hats, paper products, and confectionery.

The progress of the power revolution during this period is evident from the transition from steam engines to electric motors, as shown in Figure 2.5. In 1909, judging from the average of the manufacturing sector, the ratio of steam engines was about 60% and the electrification rate was about 20%. By 1920, the former was about 20%, while the latter was about 70%. The ratio of steam engines in modern industries fell from 57.0% to 25.2%, while the electrification rate soared from 25.4% to 65.4%. The ratio of steam engines in traditional industries plunged from 66.2% to 24.4%, while the electrification rate jumped from 15.7% to 68.4%. Traditional industries saw greater changes compared to modern industries. In some industries, such as embroidery and lacquerware, the electrification rate skyrocketed from zero to 100%.

The progress of the power revolution continued in the 1920s, but this cannot be reviewed as the process of electric motors replacing steam engines

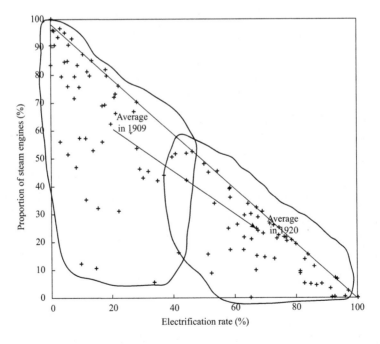

Figure 2.5 Transition from steam engine to motor (1909–1920).

Source: (Japan) *Statistics Table of Factories* 1909 and 1920.

because, by 1930, the average motorization rate of the manufacturing sector had reached 77.73% and the electrification rate had reached 88.4% (see Table 3.3). From 1930 to 1940, there was a slight increase in the motorization rate, and the gap between traditional industries and modern industries was also small. Therefore, the motorization rate during this period is not the principal reason for the structural change in the two industrial groups.

II. Impact of technological advances

The power revolution, as discussed in the preceding section, demonstrates the progress of general technology and this played a vital role in boosting the productivity of the manufacturing sector in the first decade of the twentieth century to the 1920s. However, by the 1930s, the power revolution had basically achieved its aims, and the role of other technological advances and economies of scale we highlighted. As mentioned earlier, the so-called change in scale and structure means that traditional industries adopted large-scale operations and modern industries adopted a dual structure. The large-scale operations of factories does not mean a simple expansion of scale, because it was actually accompanied by the addition of capital equipment and technological advances.

Before World War II, there were 110,000 or so inventions in traditional industries and some 120,000 inventions in modern industries. Traditional industries boasted some 35,000 patents and some 75,000 utility models, while the figures were about 57,000 and 64,000 in modern industries, respectively. The technical gap between the two industry groups is evident from these figures, because patents generally have higher technical level than utility models. The more patents (or the proportion), the higher the technical level.[15] Do the outcomes of these technological innovations have a direct bearing on production activities? Figures 2.6 and 2.7 show the relationship between the number of patents and production volume. It shows a positive correlation between the two in 1909 and 1939. This correlation is increased somewhat (correlation coefficient is increased). Therefore, it can be preliminarily judged that technological innovation has a positive – and close – impact on production activities to some degree.

The technological advance in all industries is shown by the changes in the approximate production function, as shown in Figure 2.8. The horsepower per capita is used instead of the capital stock per capita, and the production volume per capita is used instead of labor productivity (or added value per capita). This constitutes an approximate production function relationship. Theoretically, as capital per capita increases, the output per capita will also increase. The figure shows this state of change. It can be seen that from 1909 until 1937, it moves to the upper right, although there is some stagnation during the middle of the period. However, this is normal, as a consistent rapid increase is impossible. Of course, there is reason for stagnant growth, possibility due to a period of economic adjustment, a lack of technological advance, or a period of greater progress. This occurred twice in Figure 2.8.

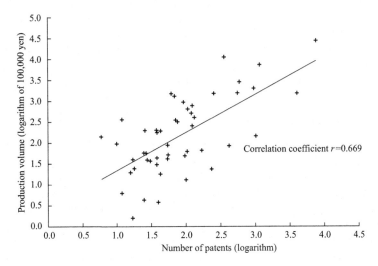

Figure 2.6 Relationship between the number of patents and production volume by industry (1909).

Source: Production volume from (Japan) Ministry of International Trade and Industry (1961), number of patents from Japan Patent Office.

Notes:
1 The number of patents is the total number from 1906 to 1909.
2 The horizontal axis is the logarithm of the number of patents, and the vertical axis is the logarithm of the production volume (100,000 yen).

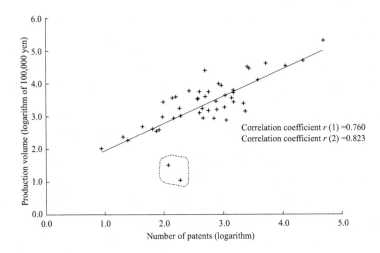

Figure 2.7 Relationship between the number of patents and production volume by industry (1939).

Source: Ministry of International Trade and Industry (Japan) (1961).

Note: The correlation coefficient r(1) includes two points in the circle, and the correlation coefficient r(2) excludes these two points.

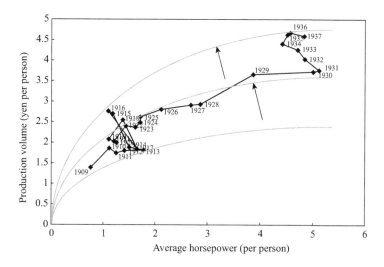

Figure 2.8 Technical changes from 1909 to 1937: All industries.
Source: (Japan) Ministry of International Trade and Industry (1961).

The first time this occurred was from 1914 to 1925. While there is stagnant growth, it is moving to the upper right. It should be said that it is transferred to the combination of another production function. Of course, there is a fall in the middle. It is unsuccessful, and then moves to the upper right along the production function in the middle. This happenend again from 1930 to 1937 and is also adjusted to the production function at a higher level. Although the data in Figure 2.8 do not fully represent the fact, it is commendable that the change over nearly 30 years is so reasonable. This means that the progress of China's manufacturing sector as a whole, including technological advance, is one of industrial upgrading and transformation. For starters, it should be the upgrading of the production function. This form is shown here.

Section 5 Concluding remarks

Through the analysis above, the following conclusions can be drawn: First, although it is hard to define and distinguish traditional industries and modern industries, it can be achieved through a comparative approach, and this may be a feasible approach. This goal may be achieved as long as the indicator variables and data can be selected. In this chapter, six variables are selected from the *Statistics Table of Factories* in 1909 and classified using the statistical analysis method. The results essentially tally with previous studies, and some inspiring results are obtained from these. It should also be pointed out that this method has its drawbacks that different years and variables may result in different results. Therefore, how these data and variables are chosen remains a controversial issue.

Second, in the twentieth century, before World War II, both traditional and modern industries saw a simultaneous increase. Specifically, traditional industries saw a productivity increase through power revolutions and other types of technological improvements. Despite being labor-intensive industries, these achieved economies of scale by expanding the scale, thereby maintaining a high growth rate. For modern industries, investment in new capital equipment and high levels of technological innovation spurred growth. The growth rate of traditional industries in the 1920s even exceeded that of modern industries.

Third, the reasons for the structural changes in traditional industries and modern industries vary from period to period. For example, the power revolution (transition from steam engine to electric motor) from 1909 to 1920 played a big role, but more reliance was placed on other technological advances in the later period. In a broad sense, however, the power revolution is also a kind of technological advance, in that it has a wider use. It is therefore discussed separately.[16]

Fourth, other technological innovations are measured by patents and utility models. They are not necessarily applied to actual production activities. However, technological innovations mentioned here are not exactly the same as Schumpeter's concept.[17] Emphasis is placed on pure technological innovation, namely R&D. Even if a lot of inventions were not used, they might provide inspiration for others as a kind of technological innovation. Furthermore, the emergence and application of these technologies are driven by economic benefits. The phrase "necessity is the mother of invention" illustrates this point. Entrepreneurs have motorization to introduce new inventions and technologies only when they see economic benefits.

Notes

1 Ryoushin Minami (2002), p. 76.
2 Ryoushin Minami (2002), p. 203.
3 On this issue, see Guan Quan (2014).
4 *China Statistical Yearbook* (2006).
5 Ryoushin Minami (1991) studied the gap between China and Japan in the early 1990s.
6 For statistics on industry in modern China, see Guan Quan (2018).
7 Kazushi Okawa (1962).
8 Takafusa Nakamura (1976, 1985).
9 Yoshiro Matsuda et al. (1984).
10 There are well-known researches by Ryoushin Minamion motorization in factories; see Ryoushin Minami (1976) and Minami (1987).
11 In fact, at that time, 30 employees were almost used as the standard at the time. China's factory law, enacted in 1931, also used 30 employees as the standard. The *Industrial Survey Report of China* was also investigated and edited according to this standard.
12 Due to lack of space, no tree diagram is shown here; see Guan Quan (1997).

13 Ryoushin Minami (1976) and Minami (1987).
14 The Japanese waterwheel is a traditional type of waterwheel. It is mostly located near rivers, and its wheels are driven by the drop of water or the weight difference between the side of bowl-shaped boxes filled with water on the waterwheel and another side without water. The force of up and down movement is converted into rotary force, and it can be used for rice or flour milling, and in many other fields.
15 On specific applications and economic analysis of patents and utility models, see Chapter 7 of this book or Guan (2001) and Guan Quan (2011b).
16 Chapter 4 of this book and Guan Quan (1997) examined the power revolution in the region.
17 Schumpeter's *Theory of Innovation* refers to how entrepreneurs introduce new production technologies and management approaches to the corporate production and services.

3 Industrial development and innovation

Technology impetus and demand driver

Section 1 Introduction

The research on Japan's economic development and technological innovation before World War II are chiefly case studies of individual industries or regions, while the analysis of the manufacturing sector as a whole or the number of major industries is few and far between. In other words, if the quantitative relationship between the development of the manufacturing sector and technological innovation is unclear, it will cause a misconception of whether there is a correlation between economic development and technological advances during this period. It is difficult to make a direct linkage. One of the reasons for lack of such research is that there was little research on the quantity and intensity of technological advance at that time. The so-called quantitative indicators refer to R&D expenditure or the number of researchers as well as new products and patents. In fact, few materials represent this content, especially continuous data divided according to industry or enterprise. The so-called intensity is an indicator of the quality of technological advance, such as the difference between great and small technological advances, or the distinction between product and engineering innovation.[1]

Another reason is that people think that Japan was in the early days of economic development at that time, and are doubtful as to whether there was a great deal of technological innovation. Therefore, there is a wealth of research literature on the introduction of technology, its digestion, transfer, and popularization. For example, Ryoushin Minami (1976), Yukihiko Kiyokawa (1995), and Fumio Makino (1996) focus on how technology is popularized in Japan after technology was imported. Of course, these studies are not completely focused on technology popularization, they also cover technological improvement and innovation. It is just that they did not focus on basic innovation as their main research object.[2]

This chapter chiefly analyzes patent data. As this chapter chiefly discusses the level of classification in the industries,[3] patent data must be rearranged according to industry classification. However, as patent classifications differ somewhat from industry classifications, they need to be merged or reorganized before they can be analyzed. Section 3.2 compares industry and patent data through the reorganization of patent data, with a view to finding the correlation and similarities between them. Section 3.3 analyses two opposing hypotheses about the relationship between industry and technological innovation, showing that the study was in line with the reality in Japan.

Section 2 Observation of technological innovation

I. International comparison

Before our analysis, it is necessary to make a simple comparison of the status of patents in major countries in modern times. Table 3.1 shows the growth rate of patents. Japan saw the highest growth rate, followed by Switzerland, Italy, and Germany. It is interesting that these countries were relatively backward at the time. Conversely, developed countries such as Britain, the U.S., and France saw a growth rate below 1%. Looking at this period, the rate is highest in Japan, and it is higher in the earlier period than the later period. Switzerland, Italy, and Germany basically had a similar trajectory to Japan. However, this varies in other countries.

Using this simple comparison, a bold judgment can be made: In the early days of economic development, technological innovation sees an upward trend. As economic development gradually matures, technological innovation

Table 3.1 Growth rate of patent applications and number of grants in major countries (%)

Period	Japan	U.S.	Britain	Italy	Switzerland	Germany	France
(A) Number of patent applications							
All periods	5.3	0.8	0.5	3.5	3.6	3.2	0.7
1889–1900	7.5	1.3	2.6	5.9	6.9*	6.6	2.9*
1901–1910	10.7	4.2	0.8	7.0	6.0	6.6	2.1
1911–1920	4.2	1.8	0.4	2.8	1.1	0.2	0.6
1921–1930	4.3	0.5	2.1	0.8	4.5	4.8	3.4
1931–1942	1.2	−3.2	−3.1	−0.6*	0.2	−2.9*	−4.7
(B) Number of granted patents							
All periods	6.9	0.9	0.2	3.8	3.0	2.8	0.6
1889–1900	9.9	1.1	3.1	4.8	5.8*	6.6	2.8*
1901–1910	13.0	3.4	1.5	8.3	6.2	4.3	1.9
1911–1920	1.6	0.9	−1.2	−2.4	0.9	1.0	−0.4
1921–1930	7.9	2.1	3.2	6.4	4.8	5.0	5.2
1931–1942	2.2	−2.3	−5.0	1.1*	−1.6	−3.5*	−5.8

Source: Japanese Patent Office (1955).

Note:
1 The figure is a moving average over seven years.
2 For those marked with *, Italy is from 1931–1938, Switzerland from 1892–1900, Germany from 1931–1940, and France from 1890– 1900.

slows. In other words, technological innovation activity reflects an inverted U-shaped growth pattern, in line with changes in economic activity. According to the "advantage of backwardness" hypothesis, an important factor for rapid economic development in developing countries is that they can import technology from developed countries without making huge investments in R&D.[4] Imported technology is also a type of innovation for these countries. Of course, it should also be acknowledged that it is precisely due to the huge gap between developing and developed countries that this phenomenon occurs. Moreover, in order to catch up with the developed countries, developing countries need to make unremitting efforts, not only as regards imports, but also by making improvements and innovation. For this reason, as mentioned above, the research on technological advance in Japan before World War II focused more on the import and popularization of technology.

Despite the high growth rate in developing countries such as Japan, the number of patents granted was not necessarily high. For example, in Japan, the number of patent applications from 1885 to 1945 was 493,213, and the number of grants was 158,178, while the corresponding figures in the same period were 3,569,181 and 2,090,558 in the U.S., 1,744,574 and 864,617 in the UK, 400,751 and 354,070 in Italy, 308,529 and 241,051 in Switzerland, 2,287,782 and 714,254 in Germany, and 896,521 and 825,802 in France, respectively. As can be seen the data above, Japan is similar to Switzerland and Italy.[5] This shows that the capitalist countries had advanced science and technology, which was beyond the reach of developing countries in the short term. It also shows that modern developed countries relied, in large measure, on science and technology to develop their economies. This shows the strength of the earlier developed countries, such as Britain, and also the strength of countries such as the U.S., France, and especially Germany who had developed later. It also shows the scientific and technological strength of Germany, as Germans were awarded the largest number of Nobel Prizes before World War II. Japan still lagged behind developed countries in Europe and America at that time, but it was quickly catching up.

II. Data and observations

As mentioned above, statistical data that shows the relationships between the two are indispensable when comparing technological innovation and production activities by industry. Data such as the number of factories, number of employees, production volume, and the horsepower of prime motors can be obtained from the *Statistics Table of Agriculture and Commerce* and the *Statistics Table of Factories*.[6] Data on patents can be obtained from the *Annual Report (Table) of Japan's Patent Office* or the *Japanese Statistical Yearbook* and *Statistics Table of Agriculture and Commerce*. However, the two contain different classifications. Moreover, new standards were issued for patent classification in 1921, so the data on patents in the two periods needs to be recombined.[7] In this chapter, the relevant data from the above materials have been recombined to produce several indicators for classification in the industries, including Japanese patents, individual patents, corporate patents, and utility models.

Next, we observe technological innovation activities exhibited through patents in Japan. Table 3.2 shows the growth rates of various indicators according to industry. Overall, modern industries such as printing, chemical and kiln, metal, and machinery have a relatively high growth rate, while traditional industries such as food, textile, wood, and others have relatively low growth rates. In fact, except in utility models, the earlier the period, the higher the growth rate, but there are some differences among various projects in different industries during different periods. For example, corporate inventions in textiles, chemicals, and kiln sectors showed a very high growth rate in the first decade of the twentieth century.

In addition to the total number of patents, Table 3.2 also shows Japanese patents, foreign patents, individual patents, corporate inventions, and utility models. The *Utility Model Act* was promulgated in 1905, while the patent law was promulgated in 1885. In the early stage of economic development, a great number of patents in advanced technology fields were obtained by foreigners due to a low level of technology in Japan, confirming Japan's developing economy and lack of technology. Furthermore, individual inventors played a leading role in the early stage of economic development, and even became the mainstay of invention activities. As economic development progressed, corporate inventions or inventions by legal persons[8] gradually replaced individual inventions. Corporate inventions had the highest growth rate.

We shift our gaze to the growth of various indicators of production activities (number of factories, number of employees, horsepower of prime motors, production volume). It can be seen from Table 3.3 that these showed similar changes with technological innovation activities. That is to say, the growth rate of modern industries was faster than traditional industries. However, this is not the case for all indicators, such as the growth rate of the number of factories. This indicates that since enterprises in traditional industries are mostly SMEs, which generally do not require much capital and technology, these have an advantage in terms of quantity. Due to this feature, the number of employees hired by them did not increase significantly, and there is no advantage in the increase in production volume. As regards the horsepower of prime motors, practically every sector saw a great growth rate before World War II, indicating that the progress of Japanese manufacturing equipment in this period was significantly faster than other indicators. This also indicates technological advance in a sense, in that practically all production equipment needs to be power driven. The rapid increase in horsepower of prime motors means the expansion and increase of equipment such as machinery. In particular, it can be seen that the growth rate of modern industries was significantly faster than that of traditional industries, a sign that modern industries saw faster technological advances than traditional industries.

Table 3.2 Growth rate of technological innovation activities (%)

Period	Food	Textile	Wood	Printing	Chemicals	Kiln	Metal	Machinery	Others	Manufacturing
Total patents										
All periods	5.8	6.5	7.9	7.5	8.9	9.0	9.7	7.9	2.1	7.0
1889–1900	8.7	13.9	8.1	9.0	5.1	6.7	15.1	12.1	6.6	9.8
1901–1910	8.5	12.5	21.1	21.1	18.4	22.9	15.2	14.8	5.4	12.9
1911–1920	0.8	-4.2	2.9	2.9	7.0	6.0	5.9	2.2	-4.5	1.6
1921–1930	9.1	10.3	3.8	12.0	11.5	9.0	5.8	7.5	3.6	8.4
1931–1942	2.1	-0.2	4.4	-5.2	4.3	2.4	6.0	2.8	-1.1	2.7
Japanese patents										
All periods	5.7	6.3	5.3	7.3	8.6	8.7	9.4	7.2	1.9	6.6
1889–1900	6.7	13.1	7.1	3.9	2.1	3.9	8.8	8.5	6.2	7.6
1901–1910	9.7	12.5	10.8	22.7	17.9	22.0	15.6	12.7	4.3	11.4
1911–1920	0.6	-5.1	-1.8	4.8	7.8	6.7	8.0	0.6	-5.8	0.4
1921–1930	8.9	10.4	4.1	13.2	11.5	8.6	6.3	8.8	3.8	9.2
1931–1942	3.0	0.5	5.6	-4.9	5.5	4.2	8.5	5.5	0.5	4.5
Foreign patents										
All periods	0.6	4.8	0.9	3.4	8.9	8.4	4.6	6.2	3.2	6.2
1901–1910	1.5	12.2	10.6	19.2	20.0	26.1	15.0	18.8	19.7	17.7
1911–1920	2.9	3.8	7.2	-1.0	5.8	5.2	3.1	4.3	1.9	4.2
1921–1930	10.9	10.1	2.3	5.4	11.7	10.1	5.0	6.1	3.1	7.1
1931–1942	-10.8	-4.9	-13.6	-8.0	0.0	-4.9	-3.2	-2.6	-9.4	-2.5
Individual patents										
All periods	5.2	5.6	4.9	6.8	7.1	7.7	8.1	5.7	1.7	5.4
1889–1900	6.6	13.1	7.1	3.4	2.0	3.9	8.2	8.5	6.2	7.6
1901–1910	9.6	11.8	10.7	22.8	17.2	20.7	15.6	12.3	4.1	10.9

1911–1920	0.1	−5.6	−2.1	3.9	6.8	6.5	6.6	−0.6	−6.0	−0.5
1921–1930	8.1	9.5	4.1	13.0	8.9	7.4	2.9	5.6	3.6	7.0
1931–1942	2.2	−0.9	4.2	−5.9	2.7	2.0	7.3	2.8	0.0	2.0

Corporate inventions

All periods

1903–1910	14.6	24.6	14.1	16.1	20.8	20.9	14.9	16.5	9.4	16.5
1911–1920	22.5	94.6	12.5	37.5	42.8	58.2	9.6	28.0	23.1	32.1
1921–1930	15.0	0.9	16.1	18.1	17.1	10.1	23.8	14.2	3.7	11.8
1931–1942	16.7	16.0	8.2	15.3	20.7	15.5	15.8	19.0	7.8	18.4
	7.2	5.0	18.4	0.8	9.4	9.4	10.2	8.8	6.4	8.6

Utility models

All periods

1910–1920	5.0	3.0	4.1	8.4	7.3	6.6	13.9	7.2	3.8	5.4
1921–1930	3.1	−3.8	1.4	8.1	3.4	4.8	15.5	3.8	0.9	1.6
1931–1937	9.6	10.8	9.2	13.5	13.4	11.1	16.5	13.5	8.7	11.5
	1.4	2.5	1.1	1.5	4.6	3.3	7.6	3.6	1.6	2.9

Source: Data from the Japanese Patent Office.

Note: The figures are moving averages over seven years.

Table 3.3 Growth rate of economic activity indicators (%)

Period	Food	Textile	Wood	Printing	Chemicals	Kiln	Metal	Machinery	Others	Manufacturing
Number of factories										
All periods	8.7	5.2	12.3	8.3	7.0	6.9	9.3	10.6	9.1	7.3
1900–1910	8.5	6.7	15.6	11.1	4.8	7.7	4.9	8.1	10.8	7.4
1911–1920	18.2	6.3	15.7	9.4	11.3	9.2	15.3	14.4	11.2	10.3
1921–1930	2.5	2.8	7.1	7.7	3.4	4.2	6.0	6.0	5.3	3.9
1931–1938	5.1	5.0	10.1	4.0	9.3	6.5	11.8	14.9	9.1	7.7
Number of employees										
All periods	4.5	3.8	8.5	6.1	8.6	5.8	9.2	10.4	3.4	5.7
1900–1910	4.3	5.9	12.4	8.7	6.9	6.2	8.1	7.5	1.3	5.7
1911–1920	6.7	7.5	10.4	8.1	14.0	10.0	13.1	14.1	6.4	8.7
1921–1930	5.6	1.4	3.7	6.0	3.8	0.9	2.8	1.3	0.4	2.3
1931–1939	1.1	-0.1	7.0	0.7	10.0	6.1	13.3	20.0	6.0	6.2
Horsepower of prime motors										
All periods	12.0	10.8	17.3	16.6	14.5	16.4	21.4	16.5	12.3	13.5
1890–1900	10.8	11.7	17.0	33.0	10.3	11.8	38.7	17.0	12.6	12.9
1901–1910	16.7	14.3	35.7	13.8	21.4	29.9	8.6	25.0	15.0	17.3
1911–1920	15.5	12.6	15.8	9.9	16.3	14.7	29.5	21.8	16.8	16.7
1921–1930	13.0	9.8	9.7	17.3	8.0	14.5	6.9	8.5	9.0	9.3
1931–1937	0.9	3.0	4.4	3.3	17.8	9.7	21.8	7.3	6.4	10.6

Production volume										
All periods	2.9	7.0	3.8	9.6	6.0	5.7	9.6	10.7	3.5	5.3
1878–1890	3.0	11.1	-0.1	11.8	2.5	1.5	6.4	6.1	5.0	4.3
1891–1900	3.8	5.7	5.1	12.8	4.4	5.1	2.1	12.9	1.6	4.4
1901–1910	1.8	4.3	1.4	10.5	4.3	8.0	12.6	13.3	2.7	3.7
1911–1920	4.4	7.4	3.6	9.9	6.5	6.5	17.1	14.8	2.3	7.1
1921–1930	2.1	5.9	6.8	5.8	8.3	6.6	7.7	1.8	2.9	4.7
1930–1937	2.1	5.9	8.2	4.7	13.0	8.9	13.8	19.4	7.5	9.1

Source: For the number of factories and the horsepower of prime motors, see Ryoushin Minami (1976); for the number of employees, see Mataji Umemura et al. (1988); for production volume, see Miyohe Shinohara (1972).

Note: The figures are moving averages over seven years.

The structure of technological innovation activities in each industry is examined below. Table 3.4 shows the composition of patents and utility models by industry. It can be clearly seen that the machinery industry has an overwhelming majority. One reason is that technology classification is linked with mechanical technology. Secondly, there are many patents in the textile and chemical industries, while other industries have more utility models. The other industries are chiefly traditional industries, therefore technological innovations in these areas are generally improvements and minor inventions. As in Tables 3.2 and 3.4 also enumerates the industry-specific proportions of Japanese patents, foreign patents, individual patents, corporate inventions and utility models, in addition to the total number of patents. It is noteworthy that utility models are minor inventions, and generally supplement the development of major inventions.[9] In terms of proportion, machinery and other industries account for the vast majority of inventions, which can be explained as follows: The machinery industry is characterized by decentralization, whereas it is difficult to separate some other industries. It is called indivisibility in the economics field. The machinery sector not only requires large pieces machinery such as machine tools but also small devices such as jacks. From the perspective of the structure of inventions, machinery occupies first place. Foreign patents account for 60% to 70% of these inventions, indicating that industrialization in developed countries is, in large part, due to progress in mechanization.[10] Moreover, it can be seen that, apart from utility models, the chemical sector had a high proportion of patents, which was a growing trend. This shows that Japan had gradually shifted to heavy industrialization.

Below is the industry structure of production activities. Table 3.5 shows the landscape different from the forms of technological innovation. For example, the machinery sector does not show intense technological innovation activities. As traditional industries, the textile and the food industries occupy a large share, indicating that modern economic growth in Japan was mainly driven by these two industries. However, this landscape changed over time, as their share decreased and was replaced by modern industries such as machinery, chemicals, and metals, especially for production volume and horsepower of prime motors. This illustrates industrial upgrading. In 1938, this landscape became obvious. Modern and traditional industries had the same share, especially in the number of employees and horsepower of prime motors. The proportion of heavy industries such as metal, machinery, and chemicals were higher than those of light industries such as food, textiles, and wood.

From this simple observation of quantities, conclusions can be drawn in two respects: First, the production activities of traditional industries such as food and textiles are more active than technological innovation activities, while the opposite is true for modern industries such as machinery, metals, and chemicals. In other words, the technological innovation activities of traditional industries depend more on their production activities, namely so-called "demand-pull" technological innovation. Technological innovation in modern

Table 3.4 Industry structure of technological innovation activities (%)

Year	Food	Textile	Wood	Printing	Chemicals	Kiln	Metal	Machinery	Other	Manufacturing
Total patents										
1885–1899	7.0	15.9	2.4	1.2	9.6	1.3	2.1	35.4	25.2	100.0
1900–1909	5.4	15.6	2.1	1.4	7.6	1.5	3.7	47.7	15.0	100.0
1910–1919	4.8	13.7	1.8	1.8	14.4	2.3	4.5	49.5	7.3	100.0
1920–1929	4.2	9.5	1.2	2.5	18.0	3.9	4.4	51.3	5.0	100.0
1930–1939	6.0	11.1	0.7	2.0	23.7	3.0	5.1	45.5	3.0	100.0
Japanese patents										
1885–1899	7.1	14.9	2.5	1.1	9.8	1.3	2.0	35.1	26.2	100.0
1900–1909	6.4	19.8	2.7	1.1	7.0	1.4	2.6	40.0	18.8	100.0
1910–1919	6.2	17.5	2.3	2.1	15.4	2.5	4.0	41.3	8.7	100.0
1920–1929	5.7	12.5	1.5	3.3	20.4	4.5	4.5	41.5	6.0	100.0
1930–1939	7.6	13.0	0.9	2.5	24.1	3.1	5.3	40.3	3.2	100.0
Foreign patents										
1895–1899	8.4	7.5	0.9	1.9	8.4	0.9	6.5	65.4	0.0	100.0
1900–1909	2.7	4.8	0.7	2.1	9.2	1.7	6.4	67.2	5.2	100.0
1910–1919	1.4	4.1	0.4	1.0	11.9	1.8	5.7	69.9	3.7	100.0
1920–1929	1.3	4.1	0.5	1.1	13.9	2.8	4.3	68.9	3.1	100.0
1930–1939	1.4	5.5	0.3	0.6	22.6	2.7	4.4	60.1	2.4	100.0
Individual patents										
1885–1899	7.1	15.0	2.5	1.2	9.8	1.3	2.0	35.2	26.1	100.0
1900–1909	6.5	19.9	2.8	1.1	7.0	1.3	2.5	39.8	19.1	100.0
1910–1919	6.4	17.6	2.4	2.1	14.8	2.6	3.8	41.0	9.2	100.0
1920–1929	6.6	13.5	1.9	3.6	19.6	4.7	4.2	38.5	7.3	100.0
1930–1939	9.7	15.6	1.3	3.2	22.2	3.4	4.5	35.7	4.4	100.0

(*continued*)

Table 3.4 Cont.

Year	Food	Textile	Wood	Printing	Chemicals	Kiln	Metal	Machinery	Other	Manufacturing
Corporate inventions										
1900–1909	3.6	18.4	0.5	1.0	7.7	6.6	8.2	49.5	4.6	100.0
1910–1919	3.8	17.2	0.8	1.7	22.0	2.4	5.1	43.9	3.1	100.0
1920–1929	2.4	8.8	0.2	2.2	23.4	3.5	5.7	52.6	1.2	100.0
1930–1939	3.7	8.4	0.3	1.3	27.5	2.6	6.8	48.8	0.8	100.0
Utility models										
1910–1919	3.4	13.5	4.1	0.8	2.4	0.9	0.3	39.2	35.4	100.0
1922–1929	2.9	8.5	3.8	1.2	2.4	0.7	1.0	48.3	31.2	100.0
1930–1939	2.8	9.6	3.3	1.2	2.5	0.6	1.2	53.9	25.0	100.0

Source: Data from the Japanese Patent Office.

Note: The data on inventions is the total number in this period.

Table 3.5 Composition of various economic activity indicators (%)

Year	Food	Textile	Wood	Printing	Chemicals	Kiln	Metal	Machinery	Other	Manufacturing
(A) Number of factories										
1899	13.7	55.8	1.9	2.3	6.2	5.5	4.5	4.9	5.3	100.0
1909	14.4	53.0	3.6	3.2	4.9	5.7	3.7	4.9	6.7	100.0
1919	23.4	38.4	5.4	3.0	5.4	5.0	5.2	6.9	7.4	100.0
1929	19.8	34.2	7.6	4.4	5.1	5.2	6.5	8.7	8.4	100.0
1938	16.1	27.4	9.3	3.4	5.8	4.8	8.9	15.0	9.4	100.0
(B) Number of employees										
1899	14.2	52.2	2.5	2.2	3.3	4.0	2.7	5.3	13.5	100.0
1909	13.1	52.8	4.7	3.0	3.7	4.2	3.4	6.3	9.0	100.0
1919	9.6	48.1	5.6	2.8	6.0	4.8	5.4	10.4	7.3	100.0
1929	13.7	45.4	6.5	4.1	6.7	4.1	5.1	8.8	5.6	100.0
1939	8.9	25.5	7.0	2.5	9.6	4.1	9.6	27.3	5.5	100.0
(C) Horsepower of prime motors										
1899	7.1	54.3	1.0	1.0	15.0	2.7	10.7	6.2	1.9	100.0
1909	7.1	41.7	4.7	0.9	19.8	7.0	5.5	11.8	1.5	100.0
1919	5.9	30.0	4.3	0.5	20.6	6.2	13.9	17.0	1.7	100.0
1929	7.8	29.0	4.4	0.9	16.9	9.2	12.2	18.0	1.5	100.0
1937	4.0	17.7	3.0	0.6	27.9	9.1	23.3	13.2	1.2	100.0
(D) Production volume										
1899	47.3	26.2	4.0	1.0	8.6	1.5	1.4	2.7	7.3	100.0
1909	40.3	26.1	3.4	2.0	9.4	2.3	3.0	6.5	7.0	100.0
1919	30.2	27.5	2.3	2.7	8.9	2.1	7.9	14.1	4.4	100.0
1929	25.3	30.8	2.8	3.0	11.7	2.6	10.0	10.2	3.6	100.0
1937	15.0	25.2	2.7	2.2	16.0	2.6	13.9	19.1	3.2	100.0

Source: For the number of factories and the horsepower of prime motors, see Ryoushin Minami (1976); for the number of employees, see Mataji Umemura et al. (1988); for production volume, see Miyohe Shinohara (1972).

Note: The figures are moving averages over seven years.

industries must tap new markets, so it can be regarded as "technology-push" technological innovation. Secondly, technological innovation in traditional industries has a big advantage and occupies an important position in the early stage of economic development, and it is gradually replaced by modern industries as economic development progresses. This is brought about by the law of economic development, because modern economic growth (or economic development) is accompanied by an upgrading of the industrial structure, such as the transition from agriculture to industry or from light to heavy industries and from traditional to modern industries.

III. Innovation characteristics

The characteristics of technological innovation in various industries are studied by observing several indicators that reflect the intensity of technological innovation. Specifically, this book uses the three indicators: (1) the proportion of utility models (proportion of utility models in all inventions); (2) the proportion of Japanese patents (proportion of Japanese patents in all patents); and (3) the proportion of individual patents (proportion of individuals patents in all Japanese patents). According to the reality in Japan at the time, the author holds that the high level of the three indicators indicates a low level of technological innovation, whereas the large proportion of patents, foreign patents, and corporate inventions indicates a high level of technological innovation. In other words, if the indicators above are high, it shows the characteristics of traditional industries. If it is low, it shows the characteristics of modern industries.

Table 3.6 shows the distribution of these three indicators across the different industries. The proportion of utility models proves what we have estimated. The indicators of traditional industries (food, textile, wood, others) are higher than those of modern industries (chemicals, metal, machinery). At the same time, this proportion is rising in modern industries, which shows that Japan began to develop auxiliary technologies through its adoption of imported technologies. Like utility models, the proportion of Japanese patents is higher in traditional rather than modern industries. Similarly, the proportion of Japanese patents in many modern industries was low in the early stages, but gradually showed an upward trend. It almost had the same trend as the proportion of utility models, indicating that the Japanese made immense improvements to the technology they had imported. In terms of the proportion of individual patents, this change was wholly different from the other two proportions. Whether in traditional or modern industries, this accounted for upwards of 90% in the early twentieth century. This gradually fell, but the degree of decline was not exactly the same. The proportion in other industries such as food declined slightly, while the in industries such as chemicals, metal and machinery it plunges almost linearly. This shows that technological innovation in traditional industries was always dominated by

Table 3.6 Characteristics of industrial technological innovation (%)

Year	Proportion of Japanese patents	Proportion of individual patents	Proportion of utility models	Year	Proportion of Japanese patents	Proportion of individual patents	Proportion of utility models
Food				**Textile**			
1900	81.8	98.8	—	1900	91.6	99.8	—
1910	91.5	97.8	57.2	1910	92.2	93.8	67.5
1920	90.3	92.6	58.5	1920	83.8	88.8	67.5
1930	88.5	86.3	62.2	1930	84.2	81.7	69.6
1940	97.1	81.2	—	1940	90.2	69.5	—
Wood				**Printing**			
1900	90.1	100.0	—	1900	59.5	95.5	—
1910	90.6	99.1	88.6	1910	67.0	96.1	40.3
1920	85.0	96.0	91.6	1920	80.0	88.6	48.1
1930	87.5	94.8	91.1	1930	90.1	87.5	53.2
1940	95.1	82.1	—	1940	94.2	74.4	—
Chemical				**Kiln**			
1900	69.9	98.9	—	1900	73.0	100.0	—
1910	67.1	93.1	26.7	1910	69.8	90.1	32.5
1920	72.5	84.7	19.7	1920	74.7	88.1	26.1
1930	72.2	66.4	22.2	1930	72.0	77.8	32.4
1940	79.5	53.2	—	1940	83.7	64.6	—
Metal				**Machinery**			
1900	51.6	93.8	—	1900	69.1	99.4	—
1910	53.0	94.6	17.2	1910	58.0	95.6	55.4

(continued)

Table 3.6 Cont.

Year	Proportion of Japanese patents	Proportion of individual patents	Proportion of utility models
1920	64.4	82.9	24.0
1930	67.2	59.8	37.4
1940	84.8	54.9	—
Other			
1900	95.8	99.8	—
1910	85.9	98.2	86.9
1920	75.7	95.7	91.1
1930	76.5	94.0	95.2
1940	88.0	89.4	—

Year	Proportion of Japanese patents	Proportion of individual patents	Proportion of utility models
1920	50.2	84.6	59.7
1930	56.6	62.7	73.0
1940	73.4	48.9	—
Manufacturing			
1900	79.1	99.4	—
1910	69.6	95.4	65.2
1920	62.6	86.7	64.9
1930	67.2	70.3	71.7
1940	79.4	56.7	—

Source: Data from the Japanese Patent Office.

Notes:
1 See the text for the definition of indicators.
2 Figures are moving averages over seven years.

individual innovation, while modern industries gradually shifted from individual to organized innovation.

As observed above, the gap between the two industries in the proportion of utility models and Japanese patents gradually narrowed, while the gap in the proportion of individual patents widened. However, according to our definition and scope, the proportion of utility models and Japanese patents is larger than that of individual patents. Therefore, we can draw a basic conclusion: The technological gap between the two industries narrowed as a whole. In other words, although the proportion of individual patents expanded, it changed within a larger range. Therefore, the overall impact is not so great.

Section 3 Demand driver and technology impetus

I. Existing research

Through observation and analysis, we can see the differences between traditional and modern industries in production and technological innovation activities. In point of fact, this is closely related to the origin of technological innovation as well as the so-called "demand-pull" and "technology-push" hypotheses of the relationship between industrial development and technological innovation. These two hypotheses were controversial and much debated in Europe and the U.S., but the facts in Japan were not taken into account. We discuss this issue to see if it can explain the reality in Japan. The basic propositions of these two hypotheses are as follows: On the one hand, entrepreneurs introduce certain new inventions or discoveries to bring about new industries, enterprises, and products. This is usually referred to as technological innovation. The proposition that values this innovative activity is called the "technology-push" hypothesis, which originates from Schumpeter's "creative destruction"; on the other hand, the so-called "demand-pull" hypothesis was advanced by Schmookler, who, after comparing the investment and employment in such industries as railways, petroleum refining, papermaking, and agriculture, as well as changes in stocks and invention activities in the U.S., reached the following conclusion: Investment in capital goods spurred inventions and innovations, namely the relationship between demand→ investment → invention.[11]

There is much debate on these two different propositions. The basic understanding is that, generally, technological innovation played a big role in the early days of industrialization, and as industrialization intensified, demand gradually increased. However, no research on this was carried out in Japan, so no results are available. One reason for this may be a lack of data available for statistical analysis. It is difficult to analyze several industries and aspects like Schmookler. For example, Japan's financial market is dominated by indirect finance. In particular, the securities market was not developed before World War II and it was hard to obtain relevant data. However, other indicators can be used instead. Production volume is used as the indicator of demand, the horsepower of prime motors (which belongs to capital equipment investment) for investment, and patents and utility models for technological innovation.[12]

II. Hypothesis

Through the introduction above, we can see that there is a circular causal relationship between investment in equipment and technological innovation. In other words, the more progress that is made in technological innovation driven by technological inventions and discoveries, the more likely the expected profit will increase. Therefore, enterprises will increase equipment investment. If technological innovation is product innovation, it is necessary to develop and increase equipment that produces new products. If it is engineering and process innovation, enterprises will invest in equipment because it can increase average productivity and cut costs, and anticipate the expansion of scale of production. If new products are recognized by the market, new demand will be created. Likewise, if old products are good quality, at a low price, and are recognized by the market, demand will be created. New investment usually comes with new technological innovation. The relationship between demand and investment as the medium and technological innovation (such as invention activities) can be expressed by the relationship below:

(1) Technological innovation (invention activities) → investment → demand.
(2) Demand → investment → technological innovation (invention activities).

Which of these two forms can better explain the case in Japan before World War II? Given the existence of dual structure in Japan at the time, we give the following hypothesis: On the one hand, modern industries were completely new to Japan at the time. Therefore, investment activities based on technological innovation (including the import of technology) were required to develop the market (demand). Because of this, modern industries should be more inclined towards Model 1; on the other hand, traditional industries were inherent in Japan, hence the existence of the market (demand). The demand in this market may grow due to the increase in income and exports, and the growing demand will inevitably require the increase in the amount of equipment required. Moreover, in order to scale up the market and participate in domestic and international competition, it is necessary to improve and update the existing technology. Thus, it is more likely that traditional industries will belong to Model 2. In which industries the two models are more suitable will be tested in the next section.

III. Verification of the hypotheses

In order to verify the above hypothesis, data on patents is used to represent technological innovation, and horsepower of prime motors is used to represent equipment investment for quantitative analysis. As technological innovation and equipment investment may affect each other, the two are used as explained variables, and the Koyck (geometric) lag model is established. Only one lag period is used here.

$$GH_t = a + bGP_t + cGH_{t-1} + u_t \qquad (1)$$

$$GP_t = a + bGH_t + cGP_{t-1} + u_t \qquad (2)$$

In the formula, H represents the horsepower of prime motors; P represents the number of Japanese patents + number of utility models; G represents the growth rate; u represents the margin of error; t represents the year. In other words, the growth of investment in equipment in this period is affected by the increase in technological innovation in this period and the previous period (Model 1). Conversely, technological innovation in this period may also be affected by the increase in equipment investment in this period and the previous period (Model 2).

The situation from 1891 to 1937 is described, and the results are shown in Table 4.7. Judging from Model 1, it has a good effect, except for the food industry. No serial correlation was detected for DW h value, and the t and F values were also significant. The coefficients of the lag terms of these industries are chiefly between 0.6 and 0.8, indicating that technological innovation in the previous period has had a strong impact on investment in equipment in this period. In Model 2, other industries do not have good results except for the textile industry. Compared to Model 1, the judgment coefficient and the t and F values are relatively low, indicating that the impact of equipment investment on technological innovation is negligible.

By summarizing the calculation results of the two models, it can be determined that there is no relationship between technological innovation and equipment investment in the food sector. In the textile industry, Model 2 offers a better explanation than Model 1, therefore its equipment investment has a bigger impact on technological innovation. In other words, this industry belongs to "demand-pull" growth. In other industries, Model 1 had a greater effect than Model 2, indicating that technological innovation had a bigger impact on investment in equipment. In other words, technological innovations tap markets in these industries, creating technology-push growth for the demand.

Section 4 Concluding remarks

After analysis in this chapter, the following conclusions can be drawn: First, technological innovation activities in Japan were more active than other developed countries before World War II. This also indicates that Japan had an "advantage of backwardness" in economic development at that time. In other words, more technology can be imported from advanced countries in

Table 3.7 Relationship between patent and horsepower of prime motors

Industry	a (t value)	b (t value)	c (t value)	R²	F value	DW	DW h value
Model (1)							
Food	7.335 (2.679)	-0.062 (-0.323)	0.380 (2.811)	0.166	4.392	2.169	-1.549
Textile	3.059 (2.204)	0.056 (0.654)	0.632 (6.532)	0.496	21.672	2.053	0.239
Wood	1.722 (1.059)	0.171 (1.949)	0.823 (11.417)	0.757	68.399	1.736	1.035
Printing	3.240 (1.454)	-0.007 (-0.087)	0.796 (8.393)	0.626	36.857	1.805	0.880
Chemicals	2.401 (1.767)	0.153 (2.065)	0.720 (9.027)	0.687	48.372	2.302	-1.222
Kiln	2.400 (1.574)	0.259 (3.535)	0.687 (8.494)	0.729	59.166	2.399	-1.670
Metal	10.003 (2.403)	-0.303 (-1.342)	0.666 (6.021)	0.543	26.150	1.840	0.831
Machinery	2.768 (1.511)	0.047 (0.406)	0.811 (9.233)	0.661	42.905	2.150	-0.651
Other	3.525 (2.653)	-0.078 (-1.215)	0.684 (7.386)	0.640	39.071	1.884	0.524
Manufacturing	3.016 (2.179)	0.018 (0.233)	0.741 (9.289)	0.676	45.969	1.715	1.157
Model (2)							
Food	4.797 (2.528)	-0.077 (-0.760)	0.409 (2.954)	0.179	4.811	2.013	-0.136
Textile	1.823 (1.268)	-0.078 (-0.687)	0.804 (8.903)	0.646	40.108	2.318	-1.380

Wood	1.645 (0.723)	−0.014 (−0.124)	0.571 (4.200)	0.312	9.962	2.144	−1.509
Printing	6.689 (1.704)	−0.106 (−0.639)	0.342 (2.475)	0.147	3.778	2.068	−0.713
Chemicals	2.623 (1.236)	0.009 (0.062)	0.650 (5.001)	0.432	16.703	1.993	0.054
Kiln	0.278 (0.106)	0.287 (1.618)	0.426 (2.734)	0.388	13.973	1.933	−0.642
Metal	9.107 (3.853)	−0.153 (−2.371)	0.360 (2.704)	0.288	8.901	2.011	−0.096
Machinery	2.515 (1.405)	0.006 (0.063)	0.633 (5.462)	0.407	15.075	2.305	−1.682
Other	6.160 (2.289)	−0.448 (−2.277)	0.450 (3.544)	0.372	13.047	2.114	−0.785
Manufacturing	5.128 (2.501)	−0.217 (−1.641)	0.642 (5.735)	0.452	18.111	2.347	−1.913

Source: Data on the horsepower of prime motors is from Ryoushin Minami (1976), and data on patent and utility models is from the Japanese Patent Office.

Note: The calculation period is from 1891 to 1937.

the early days of economic development, as evidenced by patents obtained by foreigners who had filed application and obtained grants in Japan at the time. Of course, if imported technology is to serve its purpose in Japan, it must be absorbed and even improved to gain "intermediate technology" or "suitable technology." Japan indeed carried this out, because the Japanese filed more and more applications for patents and utility models.

Second, technological innovation activities in modern industries are more active than production activities, while the opposite is true in traditional industries. However, it mainly refers to the measurement relationship between technical innovation and production activity indicators. In point of fact, in terms of the number of small-scale technological innovations, traditional industries are not less than modern industries (a great many utility models). Besides, technological innovation activities in traditional industries depend more on market demand (demand-pull), while innovation activities in modern industries are prone to be determined by supply factors (technology-push). As there was a market for traditional industries, innovation was determined by market demand. There was not much of a market for modern industries, and innovation was required to tap into the market.

Third, technological innovation in traditional industries was chiefly small-scale with technological improvement at the center, while modern industries had large-scale innovations (higher complexity) and imitated imported technologies. The gap between the two was relatively large in the early stages, but later narrowed because many modern elements (modernization) were introduced in the traditional industries, while modern industries also incorporated some technologies suited to the importer country (localization). Moreover, as the economy developed, traditional industries had a dwindling share of the market while that of the modern industries increased. Therefore, technological innovation in traditional industries decreased accordingly, while modern industries gradually assumed a dominant position.[13]

Notes

1 There are legions of English publications on technological innovation. For example, Freeman (1982), Stoneman (1983), Coombs et al. (1987), Dosi et al. (1988), and Liu Xielin (1993).
2 Guan Quan (2001, 2003) sorted out the research on technological innovation in modern Japan.
3 Industry classification here is based on Japanese customs at the time, where the manufacturing sector is divided into nine major segments, including food, textiles, chemicals, machinery and appliances, metals, kiln, wood and wood products, printing, and others.
4 On Gerschenkron's hypothesis, see Gerschenkron (1962); on its adaptability in Japan, see Ryoushin Minami (1981).
5 (Japan's) Patent Office (1955).
6 Japan launched its statistics on industrial activities shortly after the Meiji Restoration period. The *Statistics Table of Agriculture and Commerce* was the

earliest record of these activities, which included agricultural and commercial data in addition to industry. This directly affected the *Statistics Table of Agriculture and Business* compiled by the Beiyang government in the early days of the Republic of China. There was subtle difference between the two. In other words, Chinese statistics were surveyed and compiled under the guidance of Japanese experts. The *Statistics Table of Factories* started in 1909, and was surveyed every five years to begin with. It was carried out every year after 1919 and continued until after World War II. It was renamed the *Statistics Table of Industry* after the war. This survey is more detailed and accurate than its predecessor, and it was directly used in the *Manchuria Statistics of Factories* (1933–1941) compiled for the statistical survey in Manchukuo, as well as *North China Statistics of Factories* (1939) and *North China Statistics of Factories* (1943) compiled after Japan occupied North China. For details, see the relevant chapters by Guan Quan (2018).

7 Japan's patent system was set up in the form of law in 1885. To begin with it included only three types of invention patents, pattern designs and trademarks. Utility models were added in 1905. In 1921, the number of patent types increased from 136 to 207; see (Japan's) Patent Office (1955).

8 The corporate invention refers to an invention by a company. Its invention activities are carried out within a company (including scientific research institutions). As it uses a company's experimental equipment, the ownership belongs to the company. On the issues of individual inventors, see Chapter 5 of this book or Guan Quan (2000).

9 On the definition and analysis of major inventions and minor inventions, see Chapter 7 of this book, as well as Guan (2001) and Guan Quan (2011b).

10 During this period, foreign patents applied for and approved in Japan came from developed countries. They had a higher development level than Japan at the time.

11 On the "demand-pull" hypothesis, see Schmookler (1957, 1966). On the "technology-push" hypothesis, see Schumpeter (1990, 1999).

12 On this relationship in Japan after World War II, see Hitotsubashi University Institute of Innovation Research (2001).

13 This point can also be seen from the analysis of other chapters, in particular Chapter 2.

4   Regional nature of the power revolution

Section 1 Introduction

Before World War II, industrialization in Japan took place in different areas. On the one hand, modern industries had made a dramatic appearance; on the other hand, traditional industries had improved and upgraded. The support of technological advances is required, irrespective of particular industries. For example, the textile sector has new textile machines, the machine sector has various machine tools, and the chemical sector has chemical reaction devices. In addition to these specialized technologies, for each independent sector, there is general technology applied to all industries, namely power technology, because mechanized production necessitates the use of power devices, whether it be a steam engine, motor, or internal combustion engine.

Ryoushin Minami conducted a classic study of the process and characteristics of the power technology progress in Japan before the war. Minami advanced the view that two power revolutions took place in the Japanese manufacturing sector during the nearly half century from the end of the nineteenth century to the early twentieth centuries. The first occurred from 1890 to 1905 – the transition from waterwheel to steam engine; the second occurred from 1905 to 1930 – the transition from steam engine to electricity.[1] The study conducted by Minami is mainly geared to the various sectors in the manufacturing industry, especially classification, such as textiles, food, chemicals, and machinery, and also the analysis of specific industries, such as silk reeling, matches, and printing, but there was no research on regional differences. Other studies were also conducted on the use and popularization of prime motors at factories, such as Tejiro Kanbayashi (1943), Kazoo Yamaguti (1956), Toshio Hurushima (1966), Yoshiro Matsuda et al. (1984), Takeshi Abe and Takeo Kikkawa (1987), Fumio Makino (1987), Yoshio Sugiura (1988), and Yosuke Murashita (1989, 1990). There is also an analysis of regional changes, either for the earlier Meiji period or the cases of individual regions, but there is no comprehensive, long-term analysis of dynamic changes among the regions.

In order to fill this gap, this chapter adopts the same data and analysis methods as those adopted by Minami, and applies it to the analysis of all regions in modern Japan. Specifically, it is geared to the period from the late nineteenth century to the early twentieth century, namely some 50 years before the end of World War II. As industrialization in Japan gradually caught on, it also performed differently in terms of power. For example, weaving, silk reeling, textiles, and food are dominant industries in industrial development in Japan during this period. An important feature of these industries is a heavy reliance on raw materials and traditional production technologies. In other words, due to different products in different regions, development in these industries varied, and not all regions developed simultaneously.[2] The silk reeling sector in sericulture regions such as Nagano, Yamanashi, and Gunma had sound development. Major urban regions such as Tokyo, Kanagawa, and Hyogo did not necessarily develop a certain industry, but introduced and developed industries in an all-round manner. Due to developments in different industries, the types of power used also varied. Waterwheels or steam engines were required for sericulture and silk reeling, while internal combustion engines and electric motors were more suited to machinery and metals.

Section 2 Motorization of plants

I. Distribution of factories

According to the definition by Minami, for the analysis of the motorization process at factories, it is necessary to calculate the proportion of factories that use a certain type of motive motors. This proportion is the motorization rate. In order to calculate this proportion, it requires the data on the number of all factories and the number of factories using power. When studying changes in the power in regions, data can be obtained from the *Statistics Table of Agriculture and Commerce* of the Ministry of Agriculture and Commerce and the *Statistics Table of Factories* of the Ministry of Commerce and Industry. The former includes the number of factories and the number of factories using power in each region in 1884–1919, and the latter includes the data for 1909, 1914, 1919, and every year thereafter, but there are some problems with using these two types of data. First, the scope of respective survey is different. The former covers factories with more than 10 people and the latter covers factories with more than five people. Second, the credibility of the former is in doubt. Data for some years are incomprehensible. Third, the latter lack regional data in 1929 and data are missing for some regions in 1922.

We calculated the number of factories and the number of factories using power for 1892–1919 based on the *Statistics Table of Agriculture and Commerce*, and those for 1909, 1914, 1919 and thereafter based on the *Statistics Table of Factories*. Factories had only two kinds of power: waterwheels and the steam engine before 1895. Thereafter, internal combustion engines and electric motors emerged. In the 51 years from 1892 to 1942, the number of factories nationwide and the number of factories using power soared by 20 and

50 times, respectively. The greater increase in the number of factories using power demonstrates the progress and effect of the power revolution.

Table 4.1 shows the distribution of factories in the regions. Regardless of the year, the number is largest in the Kinki area, followed by South Kanto and the Tōkai regions. The proportion is relatively small in economically

Table 4.1 Regional distribution and motorization rate of factories

Region	1899	1909	1920	1930	1940
Factory share (%)					
Hokkaido	1.6	0.8	2.4	2.8	3.2
Tohoku	6.3	4.1	4.4	4.1	4.1
North Kanto	3.6	5.0	4.0	4.4	3.6
South Kanto	9.1	16.9	16.4	17.8	20.7
Hokuriku	11.2	10.6	8.6	7.9	6.8
Tōsandō	15.9	6.7	4.5	5.2	4.5
Tōkai	11.7	12.2	14.4	13.6	14.1
Kinki	20.9	27.0	27.8	26.1	24.8
San'in	3.0	1.3	1.1	1.3	0.9
Sanyodo	5.9	4.1	4.2	5.9	5.3
Shikoku	4.3	4.8	4.3	4.0	3.3
Kitakyushu	5.4	5.7	5.8	5.2	4.6
Minamikyushu	0.8	0.7	2.1	1.7	1.5
Okinawa	0.0	0.1	0.1	0.1	2.5
Nationwide	100.0	100.0	100.0	100.0	100.0
Motorization rate (%)					
Hokkaido	40.9	63.6	80.5	75.6	74.8
Tohoku	31.6	41.2	69.3	83.7	77.0
North Kanto	26.6	39.2	74.1	81.8	85.5
South Kanto	56.5	26.5	71.9	89.5	90.4
Hokuriku	13.9	18.5	68.1	83.5	91.3
Tōsandō	47.3	50.9	83.1	89.4	87.6
Tōkai	39.0	37.8	63.7	86.4	86.3
Kinki	28.2	22.4	63.5	82.5	87.1
San'in	29.9	28.3	53.3	75.9	86.5
Sanyodo	30.5	26.7	66.8	77.6	85.9
Shikoku	20.6	19.8	52.1	76.1	82.3
Kitakyushu	38.8	20.0	48.9	67.6	74.9
Minamikyushu	43.4	29.7	24.8	53.7	71.4
Okinawa	100.0	0.0	67.7	32.4	7.1
Nationwide	34.5	28.4	65.2	82.6	84.1
East Japan	36.6	38.3	70.9	83.7	84.4
West Japan	35.3	27.3	55.6	73.7	80.3

Source: *Statistics Table of Agriculture and Commerce* by (Japan) Ministry of Agriculture and Commerce over the years, *Statistics Table of Factories* over the years by the Ministry of Commerce and Industry.

Note: Factories with more than 10 people in 1899, and those with more than five people after 1909.

backward Okinawa, Minamikyushu, San'in, and Hokkaido. It basically shows the degree of industrialization in various regions of Japan in the late nineteenth to early twentieth centuries. From the perspective of changes over the years, there was large increase in South Kanto, jumping from 9.1% to 20.9%. In 1899, the figure was only about half that in Kinki area. By 1940, the two were almost the same. Other regions that saw a rapid increase include Hokkaido, Okinawa, and Minamikyushu. By contrast, Tōsandō (15.9% → 4.5%), Hokuriku (11.2% → 6.8%), and San'in (3% → 0.9%) saw varying degrees of decrease.[3]

We wanted to obtain data on the size and distribution of factories, but the data on factory size and horsepower of prime motor in the regions is available for only four years: 1909, 1914, 1919 and 1920. In 1909 and 1920, the situation was as follows: Nationwide, the proportion of factories with 5–29 employees is in excess of 80% in the two years, and the distribution is ordered by factories with 30 to 49 employees, 50 to 99 employees, 100 to 499 employees, 500 to 999 employees and more than 1,000 employees. The distribution in each region is essentially close to that of Japan. Tōsandō, Hokkaido, Kitakyushu, and Okinawa generally have large-scale factories, which can be said to be a feature of Japan before the war. Similar to the size distribution, data for the industry distribution is only available for 1909, 1914, and 1919–1929. The situation in Japan is omitted because it is the same as that described by Minami.

The most noteworthy is the textile sector. While the share of the textile sector declined from 1909 to 1929, but it was still comparatively large. Its proportion varied greatly in different regions. For example, Tōsandō, North Kanto, Hokuriku, and Tokai, where traditional silk reeling, textiles, and weaving are developed sectors occupy 50% to 70%, while Hokkaido, Okinawa, Kitakyushu and others account for less than 20%. The food sector also had a large share, at 17–19% over the three years. The share of other industries remained at 7–9%. These light industries were the mainstay of Japanese manufacturing at least until the 1930s. Of course, as the economy developed further, the advantages of this position were gradually replaced by heavy industries such as machinery and metal. During this period, the proportion of these two industries increased from 3% to 7%. In the southern Kanto region, these two industries saw more significant expansion.

II. The motorization of factories

The issue of motorization is examined below. Figure 4.1 shows the motorization rates in East Japan (excluding Hokkaido) and West Japan (excluding Okinawa).[4] There are two discrete curves in the figure, with a factory with more than 10 people in the early stages and a factory with more than five people in the later stages. Therefore, the position shown in the early stage is higher than that of the later stage. It cannot be completely connected throughout.[5] In other words, while the motorization rate in the early stages is lower than

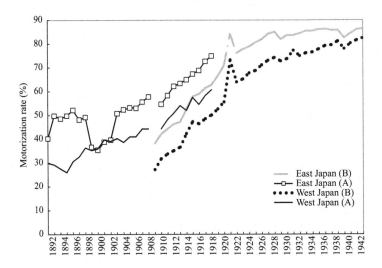

Figure 4.1 Changes in the motorization rate of factories: East Japan and West Japan.

Source: *Statistics Table of Agriculture and Commerce* by (Japan) Ministry of Agriculture and Commerce over the years, Statistics Table of Factories over the years by the Ministry of Commerce and Industry.

Note: The scope of the two types of data is different, so A and B are added for differentiation.

that in the later stages, the rate in the early stages is relatively high due to the impact of the size of factory (more than 10 people). However, given the actual industrial development in Japan at that time, factories with 5 to 10 employees accounted for a large proportion. If the motorization rate is judged based on factories with more than 10 employees, it is easy to overestimate the actual situation. The best observation is the tendency of factories with more than five people. In this way, it can be judged that the motorization rate in Japan was between 10 and 20% at the end of the nineteenth century.

The motorization rate is slightly higher in East Japan than in West Japan (5%–10%). If the curve for the whole nation is drawn, it should be between East Japan and West Japan. Moreover, in both East Japan and West Japan, a more rapid upward trend began in 1909. In 1909, the two stood at 25–40% (the national average was 28.4%). By 1920, it had reached 55–70% (national average of 65.2%) and had soared to 70–85% in 1930. Thereafter, motorization continued but the speed of development gradually slacked off. According to Minami, the power revolution was completed in Japan at this time.[6]

The lower part of Table 4.1 shows the trend of motorization in various regions. Except in Okinawa, the regions witnessed rapid motorization from the end of the nineteenth century to 1940. By 1909, there was still a large gap, but this gradually narrowed. For example, Hokkaido saw the highest motorization rate in 1909, but it saw an average rate by 1930. Another example is Tōsandō, which had developed sericulture and reeling industries, and had begun to see a high motorization rate by the end of the nineteenth century. However, the motorization rate in Hokuriku, Shikoku, and Kitakyushu in 1909 was not even half of that in Tōsandō, but this gap gradually narrowed after 1920. Further, the motorization rate has always been higher in East Japan than that in West Japan, which may be attributable to the concentration of modern industries there.[7]

III. Reasons why motorization became popular in factories

According to the observation above, there was a certain regional disparity in motorization in factories from the end of the nineteenth century to the 1920s, but it achieved a rapid rise in popularization, especially in the late 1920s and early 1930s. There is a reason for this popularization. It is discussed here in terms of quantity.

Below, a popularization function is designed. The explanatory variables are as follows: The first is the proportion (X_1) of factories with more than 30 people, which represents the size of factory. Excluding some industries such as textiles, factories with more than 30 people would have been large factories at the time. The larger the factory, the easier it was to use power earlier. The second is the nature of an industry. According to the Minami's research, the motorization rates in the textile, machinery, metal, printing, and wood sectors are higher than those in the manufacturing sector as a whole. The greater the proportion of these industries, the higher the motorization rate in these regions. Due to the limitations of data, the proportion (X_2) of textile factories, proportion (X_3) of mechanical factories, and proportion (X_4) of wood factories are selected here. What is also important for this chapter is whether the differences between East Japan and West Japan are reflected statistically. Therefore, the dummy variable (X_5) for East Japan and West Japan has been added. The calculation formula is as follows:

$$\alpha = a + b_1 X_1 + b_2 X_2 + b_3 X_3 + b_4 X_4 + b_5 X_5$$

Where, α is the motorization rate (%); X_1 is the proportion of factories with more than 30 employees to all factories (%); X_2 is the proportion of textile factories (%); X_3 is the proportion of machinery factories (%); X_4 is the proportion of wood factories (%); X_5 is a dummy variable for East Japan and West Japan (excluding Hokkaido and Okinawa). The results of the calculations for 1909 and 1920 using this formula are as follows.

1909:

$$\alpha = -9.280 + 0.914 X_1 + 0.218 X_2 + 1.567 X_3 + 1.134 X_4 + 3.797 X_5$$

$$(-1.999) \quad (7.565)^* \quad (2.974)^* \quad (3.424)^* \quad (6.004)^* \quad (1.369)$$

$$\bar{R}^2 = 0.765$$

1920:

$$\alpha = 30.859 + 0.851X_1 + 0.078X_2 + 1.056X_3 + 0.642X_4 + 10.070X_5$$

$$(-5.590) \quad (5.525)^* \quad (0.942)^* \quad (2.031)^* \quad (3.012)^* \quad (3.183)$$

$$\bar{R}^2 = 0.607$$

The figures in brackets are t values; those with asterisk "*" are significant at a statistical level of 5%; $\bar{R}^2$ is the coefficient of determination after correction for degrees of freedom. The calculation results are "fairly good." It is "fairly good" because the cross-sectional analysis of such regions does not have regular changes such as time series data have, and has greater uncertainty. In this sense, these can be said to be good results. The coefficients of determination for the two years are high, indicating that this equation is valid. In terms of t value, the dummy variable in 1909 and the proportion of textile factories in 1920 did not pass the test of significance at the 5% statistical level, while the others showed statistical significance. In both years, the high value showed in the t value is the proportion of factories with more than 30 people among all factories, indicating that the scale of factory in this period is critical for the technological advance and popularization of motorization.

The proportion of wood factories has a high t value, indicating that this industry has higher demand for power than other industries. The results of the proportion of machinery factories are not prominent, indicating that this industry, whilst modern, can have both small or large factories due to its flexibility or divisibility. It is highly divisible, and small factories could operate without power. In the early days of industrialization, there were generally no large factories and most of these adopted semi-manual and semi-mechanical operations. A similar problem exists in the proportion of textile factories. The textile industry adopted both traditional production and modern production methods. The earlier the period, the more likely it was that traditional production methods were used. They did not necessarily use much power. The dummy variables for East Japan and West Japan in 1909 did not pass the statistical test but did pass it in 1920. That is to say, the differences between the two regions did not pose a problem in 1909, but these had widened by 1920. In fact, the gap was not that big (see Table 5.1).

Section 3 Popularization of prime motors

I. Estimation of horsepower of prime motors

As motorization intensified at factories, the number and horsepower of prime motors increased, and the average horsepower of prime motors and horsepower intensified. The ratio of prime motor's horsepower to employees in factories also increased. In order to calculate these indicators, accurate data on the horsepower of prime motors is required. Minami conducted research on industry calculations. The discussion here concerns the regions. As regards the estimation of the horsepower of prime motors in the manufacturing sector, the data available for use are the same. It can be obtained from the *Statistics Table of Factories* of 1909, 1914, 1919 and ensuing years and the *Statistics Table of Agriculture and Commerce* from 1884 to 1919. However, the difference between the two is described above, and new problems occurred during the calculation of the horsepower.

First, although the number of prime motors is recorded in these data, the data on horsepower is not always available. Therefore, these have been estimated using Minami's method (1965). For example, there were 43 Japanese waterwheels in Tokyo in 1909, with a horsepower of 143. There were seven waterwheels of unknown horsepower. Thus, it can be estimated according to the following calculation method. 143/43 = 3.3, and then 3.3 is multiplied by 7 waterwheels of unknown horsepower, leading to the horsepower of 7 × 3.3 = 23.1. In this way, the horsepower of Japanese waterwheels in Tokyo is 143 + 23.1 = 166.1, which is rounded to 166. Another problem is that there is only data on the number of prime motors without reference to the horsepower. For example, in 1909, there was only one turbine waterwheel in Kumamoto Prefecture but the horsepower is unknown. This is common in the *Statistics Table of Agriculture and Commerce,* especially for Japanese waterwheels. The same is also true of steam turbines, turbine waterwheels, and impact turbines in the *Statistics Table of Factories* from 1938 to 1942. There is no choice but to abandon this. The second is the classification of prime motors. This varies according to records over the years. Specifically, these include electric motors, steam engines, turbosteamers, gas engines, kerosene engines, water turbines, impact turbines, and Japanese waterwheels. We integrate these into five types: Motors, steam engines, gas engines, kerosene engines, and waterwheels. Third, there are problems with the data for certain years in some regions, these are either extremely high or extremely low. For example, the horsepower of steam engines in Kanagawa was 442 and 1,441 in 1895 and 1897, respectively, but was 321,024 in 1896. In this case, this number was revised as the average of horsepower in the two years before and after. Of course, it is highly necessary to make such adjustment. Fourth, from 1909 to 1914, generators are expressed using watts instead of horsepower. In this case, it was converted with one horsepower for 746 watts (in turn, 1 kilowatt = 1.34 horsepower).

II. Changes in the horsepower of prime motors

The regional changes in prime motors' horsepower are examined from several perspectives. First of all, a change in the horsepower of prime motors is observed. Table 4.2 shows the growth rate of the horsepower of prime motors.

Table 4.2 Growth rate of horsepower of prime motors by region (%)

Region	1895–1900	1901–1910	1911–1920	1921–1930	1931–1940
Hokkaido	8.4	42.8	13.2	0.9	6.5
Tohoku	2.8	18.7	6.8	10.5	13.5
North Kanto	13.9	17.4	5.5	7.3	11.3
South Kanto	15.3	14.7	15.4	8.5	12.1
Hokuriku	21.6	15.7	12.1	13.0	14.1
Tōsandō	−14.4	18.4	10.3	9.7	9.2
Tokai	15.9	16.3	12.3	8.5	11.3
Kinki	9.7	17.1	15.1	9.8	8.6
San'in	4.3	14.0	9.7	11.3	20.1
Sanyodo	11.4	16.3	14.7	9.2	14.8
Shikoku	21.7	16.8	14.1	7.7	14.1
Kitakyushu	19.2	18.2	5.0	7.7	15.4
Minamikyushu	13.1	14.5	11.3	13.7	17.1
Nationwide	11.1	17.7	12.0	8.4	11.4
East Japan	9.2	16.1	12.4	8.9	12.2
West Japan	13.0	17.0	11.5	9.4	11.1

Source: *Statistics Table of Agriculture and Commerce* published by (Japan's) Ministry of Agriculture and Commerce over the years and *Statistics Table of Factories* published over the years by the Ministry of Commerce and Industry.

Note:
1 Factory with more than 10 people before 1910, and those with five people after 1911.
2 Figures are five-year moving averages.

Overall, except for the negative growth in the initial period in the Tōsandō area, all regions saw positive growth in all periods. In other words, the horsepower of prime motors was increasing during the 46 years (a five-year moving average) from 1895 to 1940. In terms of growth rate, it was the highest from 1901 to 1910, and the variance of regions was the smallest, although it was much higher in Hokkaido than in other regions. Although the growth rates in the three periods of 1911–1920, 1931–1940, and 1895–1900 were not as high in these periods, thy reached double digits. There were some – but not very large – differences between regions from 1911 to 1920 and from 1931 to 1940. The regional difference was the largest from 1895 to 1900. After 1901, there was not much difference between East Japan and West Japan.

Below is the examination of regional distribution of horsepower of prime motors, as shown in Table 4.3. On the whole, the regional distribution of horsepower of prime motors is highly similar to that of factories, but there are some differences. For example, the proportion of horsepower of prime motors in South Kanto, Kitakyushu and other regions is far higher than that of factories, while that in Tohoku, Hokuriku, Tōsandō, San'in, Shikoku and other regions is lower than the proportion of factories (see Table 4.1). Although the structure of the factory size by region is not shown here, it differs from the distribution of factories, as discussed earlier. For the distribution of

Table 4.3 Regional distribution and electrification rate of horsepower of prime motors (%)

Region	1899	1909	1920	1930	1940
Proportion of horsepower of prime motor (%)					
Hokkaido	1.5	4.9	10.5	5.0	3.2
Tohoku	3.9	3.0	1.9	3.0	3.8
North Kanto	4.7	4.0	2.2	1.9	2.2
South Kanto	17.8	21.4	21.0	20.0	20.4
Hokuriku	2.4	1.4	2.8	4.2	4.8
Tōsandō	2.1	2.7	2.1	2.5	1.9
Tokai	10.3	10.9	9.3	9.6	9.8
Kinki	24.4	26.7	30.6	37.0	28.1
San'in	0.4	0.4	0.3	0.3	0.7
Sanyodo	5.2	4.5	4.9	5.4	7.2
Shikoku	2.8	1.5	2.4	1.9	2.9
Kitakyushu	24.0	18.2	11.2	8.4	13.5
Minamikyushu	0.6	0.4	0.5	0.6	1.3
Okinawa	0.0	0.0	0.2	0.1	0.1
Nationwide	100.0	100.0	100.0	100.0	100.0
Electrification rate (%)					
Hokkaido		26.4	45.9	81.1	87.1
Tohoku		26.4	48.8	80.4	86.5
North Kanto		48.1	68.2	92.8	97.1
South Kanto		36.9	85.2	92.9	98.2
Hokuriku		21.4	72.3	96.4	98.4
Tōsandō		5.2	48.0	86.1	96.9
Tokai		10.5	54.5	91.8	97.4
Kinki		23.8	55.9	89.1	97.8
San'in		22.5	45.8	91.1	95.6
Sanyodo		14.3	44.3	88.9	97.8
Shikoku		13.9	38.5	70.6	94.9
Kitakyushu		17.7	73.9	89.5	95.8
Minamikyushu		7.2	45.7	88.9	95.0
Okinawa		0.0	11.8	7.1	22.0
Nationwide		24.0	62.2	89.4	96.6
East Japan		28.9	73.9	91.8	96.9
West Japan		20.0	57.0	88.5	97.0

Source: *Statistics Table of Agriculture and Commerce* published by the (Japan's) Ministry of Agriculture and Commerce over the years. *Statistics Table of Factories* published by the Ministry of Commerce and Industry.

factories, those with between five to 29 employees have a large proportion, but the horsepower of prime motors is more evenly distributed in large-scale factories. The motorization rate of large enterprises is relatively high, and the horsepower of prime motors should be higher as this is not concentrated in large enterprises due to the large numbers of SMEs.

III. Measurement of demand function of prime motors

As observed above, the horsepower of prime motors also rapidly increased along with the motorization of factories. The author attempts to find the reason for the increase in the horsepower of prime motors. The following relationship is designed with reference to the research Minami (1976). A prime motor is a part of a producer's durable equipment, and its increase is part of real fixed investment. Therefore, the principle of investment function can be used for the demand analysis of the horsepower of prime motors. The theory of the investment function mainly includes the profit principle and the acceleration principle. The former is used here. Specifically, the profit (P) or its proxy variable output (Y) is used as the explanatory variable of investment (I), and the following results:

$$I = aP \text{ or } I = aY$$

Here, I is replaced by the increment (ΔH) of the horsepower of prime motors in the previous year, plus the error term (u_t), and the following calculation formula results:

$$\Delta H_t = a + b Y_t + u_t$$

In the formula, the subscript t is the year.

Due to the limited data, calculation here only covers 1909–1940, with the results shown in Table 4.4. It can be seen that there is a certain difference in different regions, and it is fairly good throughout the country. The t value for each region is significant, but the coefficients of determination vary greatly. In general, this result is tenable: if the profit (output) is higher, the result of investment, namely productive durable equipment and its horsepower, will increase.

Section 4 Progress of the power revolution

I. Trend of the power revolution

There are four types of changes in the ratio of the horsepower of various prime motors to the horsepower of total power in 14 regions, as shown in Figures 4.2 to Figure 4.4. First of all, the so-called first power revolution – the transition from waterwheel to steam engine – can be observed from the ratio of waterwheels and steam engines to the total horsepower. Although not described in the figure, the national average should be equivalent to the level between those in Figure 4.2 and Figure 4.4. The proportion of steam engines kept rising before 1900, reaching 90% by the turn of the century. It continued its decline throughout the early 20th century until 1940. In contrast to the changes in steam engines, the proportion of waterwheels gradually declined around 1900 and then increased, to a degree, in 1920. Judging from

Table 4.4 Measurement results of demand function of prime motors

Region	a	t value	b	t value	$\bar{R}^2$	DW
Nationwide	−100 153.914	−3.525	0.060	16.087	0.896	0.647
Hokkaido	3 046.955	1.151	0.039	2.778	0.183	0.529
Tohoku	−9 980.034	−5.463	0.126	13.151	0.851	0.622
North Kanto	−3 551.519	−2.670	0.044	7.592	0.654	0.775
South Kanto	−14 912.917	−2.511	0.052	16.272	0.898	0.788
Hokuriku	−10 946.265	−5.969	0.088	16.723	0.903	0.748
Tōsandō	−1 635.542	−0.671	0.027	3.121	0.226	0.932
Tokai	−10 783.255	−3.180	0.052	13.683	0.861	0.526
Kinki	−19 231.178	−1.814	0.047	10.359	0.780	0.836
San'in	−1 771.940	−4.000	0.112	10.853	0.796	0.548
Sanyodo	−10 069.311	−3.216	0.106	12.237	0.832	0.575
Shikoku	−4 125.058	−2.572	0.071	8.777	0.717	0.493
Kitakyushu	−3 534.754	−0.553	0.075	8.316	0.694	0.639
Minamikyushu	−402.790	−0.455	0.083	5.443	0.488	0.467
Okinawa	1 978.676	3.130	0.524	5.327	0.477	0.718

Source: See Guan Quan (1997) for the horsepower of prime motors; data on the production volume from the Ministry of Commerce and Industry (1961) (data 1).

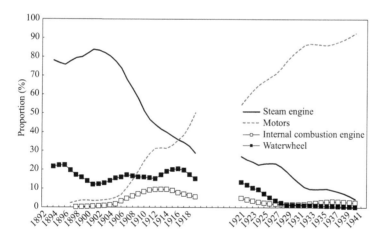

Figure 4.2 Change in the proportion of horsepower of prime motors by type: Hokkaido, Tohoku, Hokuriku, Tokai, San'in.

Source: *Statistics Table of Agriculture and Commerce* by (Japan) Ministry of Agriculture and Commerce over the years, *Statistics Table of Factories* over the years by the Ministry of Commerce and Industry.

the changes in steam engines and waterwheels, Minami's statement on the first power revolution was tenable.

We take a look at the ratio of the horsepower of motors (electrification rate). It was almost zero at the end of the nineteenth century, but then it began to shoot up. It surpassed the steam engine by the middle of the second decade of the twentieth century and continued to rise, reaching nearly 90%

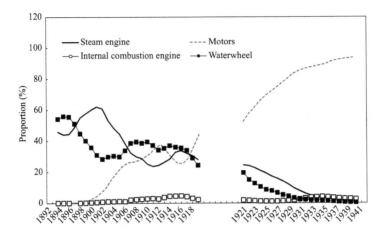

Figure 4.3 Proportion of horsepower of prime motors by type: North Kanto, Tokai, Minamikyushu.

Source: *Statistics Table of Agriculture and Commerce* by (Japan) Ministry of Agriculture and Commerce over the years, *Statistics Table of Factories* over the years by the Ministry of Commerce and Industry.

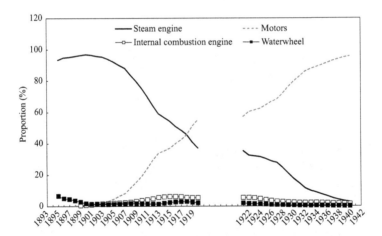

Figure 4.4 Proportion of horsepower of prime motors by type: South Kanto, Kinki, Sanyodo, Shikoku, Kitakyushu.

Source: *Statistics Table of Agriculture and Commerce* by (Japan) Ministry of Agriculture and Commerce over the years, *Statistics Table of Factories* over the years by the Ministry of Commerce and Industry.

after 1930 (see Figure 4.3). This is the so-called second power revolution. Figure 4.3 shows differences among the regions. First, through the comparison of Figure 4.3 and Figure 4.4, the types of regions have a big difference in terms of waterwheels. In the regions shown in Figure 4.4, the waterwheel was replaced at the turn of the century, and remained at a low level. Thus, in West Japan, the second stage of the power revolution (from steam to motor engines) passed off smoothly. In Figure 4.3, waterwheels account for a high proportion, and the process of their being replaced by steam engines is not clear. At the turn of the century, steam engines had an advantage to some degree, but waterwheels saw a later increase. In other words, this region saw the coexistence of waterwheels and steam engines from the Russo-Japanese War until the late second decade of the twentieth century. Especially after the Russo-Japanese War, they coexisted. After the 1920s, electric motors began to show their obvious advantages, and the reeling industry was also on the wane. The second power revolution had successfully launched. The region in the middle is shown in Figure 4.2. The characteristics show that during the first power revolution and thereafter, there were fluctuations due to the influence of waterwheels, but generally speaking, the two power revolutions got off to a smooth start.

The electrification rate divided by size is not shown in the figure. Nationwide, it differs somewhat from the electrification rate as observed above. The motorization rate is higher in large-scale factories, while the electrification rate is evenly distributed in factories of varying scales, mainly due to the characteristics of motor engines. In other words, motor engines can approach infinite miniaturization, whereas it is impossible for steam engines. Thanks to miniaturization, it can be installed in any place and on any equipment with different requirements. This is a key advantage of electric motors.[8] The industrial distribution of the electrification rate is also not described in the figure. The national average is 24.0%. In 1909, metal (83.3%), machinery (49.0%), printing (42.5%), and kiln (27.6%) were relatively high. Other sectors also joined in 1920. In the later period, the gap between industries gradually narrowed.[9]

II. Conclusion of the power revolution

The regional changes in the motorization of factories and the power revolution of electrification are discussed above. It can be seen that the power revolution gradually occurred alongside certain regional differences, and the gap between regions gradually disappeared. In other words, the gap between regions gradually narrowed along with the power revolution. Is this true? Figure 5.5 shows the number of factories, horsepower of prime motors, horsepower intensity, and coefficient of variation of actual production volume per capita (where horsepower of prime motors and horsepower intensity are five-year moving average) among the regions. Only the number of factories continued to increase. By contrast, the horsepower of prime motors continued to fall. However, the horsepower intensity showed another variation: It began to rise rapidly at the end of the nineteenth century, peaked around 1910, then began to plunge, and decreased slowly. The period for observing the actual production volume per capita is short, basically a period of relatively stable decline and then increase. The number of factories saw relatively stable changes as a

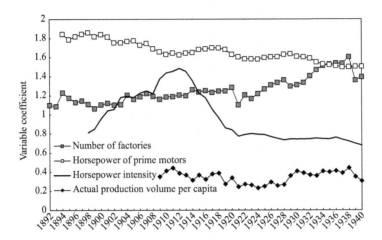

Figure 4.5 Changes in regional disparities: Coefficient of variation.

Source: *Statistics Table of Agriculture and Commerce* by (Japan) Ministry of Agriculture and Commerce over the years, *Statistics Table of Factories* over the years by the Ministry of Commerce and Industry.

whole. It rose slightly before 1920, but neither clearly nor rapidly. After 1920, it saw a sharp upward trend. By contrast, the change in the horsepower of prime motors was basically downhill all the way.

Based on these changes, the following judgment can be made: The changes in the number of factories and the horsepower of prime motors saw no significant progress due to industrialization and urbanization before 1920, and the regional disparity between factories was small. Factories for food, reeling, weaving and others saw development in various regions. After 1920, however, great progress was made in industrialization and urbanization, and factories began to spring up in cities. Due to the concentrated advantage in transportation, information, and labor, cities were more efficient. Prime motors were initially used in large factories and there was a large regional gap during this period. As the effects of electrification intensified, electric motors could be installed in smaller factories, and the gap between regions gradually narrowed.

This section concerns horsepower intensity (as the proxy variable for capital intensity here). As prime motors became more popular, the gap between the regions widened rapidly. At this time, only large-scale factories could install prime motors. There is a large regional gap in terms of horsepower intensity. Later, as electrification intensified, the gap between the regions began to narrow. Production volume per capita (proxy variable for real labor productivity) was also basically similar. Owing to the effect of electrification, the gap between the regions gradually narrowed before 1920. In other words, thanks to the use of prime motors and electricity, factories saw an improvement in production methods (technical progress) and increased labor productivity. However, the gap widened again in the 1920s due to the impact of other urban factors, such as advantages in traffic, logistics, and information.

In general, motorization, especially electrification, helped to narrow regional disparity, but this disparity may not necessarily be narrowed due to the role of other factors. The role of motorization has become more important during the middle of the second decade of the twentieth century, principally because of the application of new technology of electricity. It is worth mentioning that in the early stage of economic development (referred to as the industrialization period), the regional gap will likely widen, which can be observed in many countries. This can be attributed to gaps between regions in terms of geographical location, natural resources, talent, the amount of funds and these gaps could not be easily filled during this period. As the economy developed further, traffic and communication technology has become more popular; there is more equal access to education and human resources; and big cities have a more pronounced role in driving the surrounding areas. The gap between regions gradually narrows. This is what Kuznets calls the inverted-U hypothesis for the income gap.[10]

Finally, after several decades of technological development, the production functions in various regions of Japan saw significant changes. The direction of this change shifts from labor-intensive to capital-intensive change.

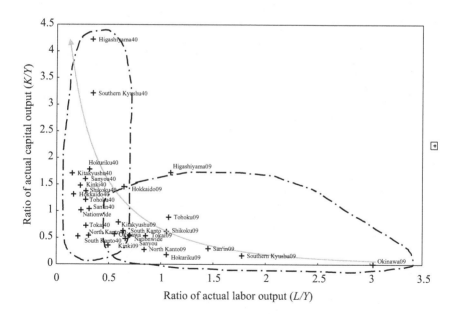

Figure 4.6 Technological changes in regions (1909, 1940).

Source: *Statistics Table of Factories* by the Ministry of Commerce and Industry (1909, 1940).

This is shown in Figure 4.6. Overall, since 1909, the regions have moved from the lower right corner of the horizontal axis to the upper left corner of the vertical axis. This figure is plotted according to the approximate production function. The horizontal axis refers to the actual labor-output ratio (the labor coefficient), and the vertical axis refers to the actual capital-output ratio (the capital coefficient). The curve in the graph represents the isoquant curve in theory. On the one hand, the isoquant curve indicates that, given the same amount of factor input, the closer it is to the origin, the more cost (or input) it saves, indicating technological advances. On the other hand, its position in the lower-right corner of the figure indicates that it is labor-intensive, and its position in the upper-left corner indicates that it is capital-intensive. The vast majority of the regions in the picture are in the lower-right corner in 1909 and these moved to the upper-left corner in 1940, showing changes in the type of technology.

Section 5 Concluding remarks

This chapter has studied the issue of the power revolution in Japan before World War II. The power revolution was the application and popularization of general industrial technology. Therefore, if this technology was improved and popularized, it could spur the development of industry as a whole. Ryoushin Minami conducted pioneering research into the industrial aspect of the power revolution in Japan. This chapter examines regional changes according to Minami's methods and ideas. First of all, the relevant data were estimated. As the early-stage data was incomplete, appropriate improvements and adjustments were required. In particular, there were a slew of problems in analysis. By revising the data, analysis and examination can be carried out concerning changes in power and the corresponding industrial changes in the regions, and the following conclusions were drawn. First, as regards the changes in the power revolution, it is generally consistent with Minami's view, although there is a slight gap among the regions. Second, power is the general technology, and the regional disparity narrowed because of the power revolution in the regions. In particular, electric motors were popularized on a greater scale, because smaller factories could also adopt electric motors. Third, as power technology became more popular, industrial focus gradually shifted from West Japan to East Japan, which determined the regionality of industrial concentration after World War II.

Notes

1 Ryoushin Minami (1976), Minami (1987).
2 On the development of industry in modern Japan, see Kazoo Yamaguchi et al. (1966), Mataji Umemura et al. (1983).
3 For the analysis in this chapter, the custom of dividing regions in Japan at the time was followed. These regions are equivalent to China's regions, though

obviously they not as large (Japan's territory area is only equivalent to China's Yunnan Province). Below is the relationship between the regions (14) and current administrative divisions. There are currently 47 administrative divisions (43 rural prefectures, 2 urban prefectures, 1 metropolitan district, 1 "district") in Japan. (1) Hokkaido: Hokkaido; (2) Tohoku: Aomori, Iwate, Miyagi, Akita, Yamagata, Fukushima; (3) North Kanto: Ibaraki, Tochigi, Gunma; (4) South Kanto: Saitama, Chiba, Tokyo, Kanagawa; (5) Hokuriku: Niigata, Toyama, Ishikawa, Fukui; (6) Higashiyama: Nagano, Yamanashi, Gifu; (7) Tokai: Shizuoka, Aichi, Mie; (8) Kinki: Shiga, Kyoto, Nara, Osaka, Hyogo, Wakayama; (9) Sanin: Tottori, Shimane; (10) Sanyodo: Okayama, Hiroshima, Yamaguchi; (11) Shikoku: Tokushima, Kagawa, Ehime, Kochi (12) Kitakyushu: Fukuoka, Saga, Nagasaki, Kumamoto, Oita; (13) Minamikyushu: Miyazaki, Kagoshima; (14) Okinawa.

4 Customarily, the entire Japanese archipelago is divided into two parts: East Japan and West Japan. These two regions vary somewhat in terms of geography, climate, and culture. Of course, the differences are not great. The division of East and West Japan is based on the aforesaid 14 regions; (7) Tokai and (8) Kinki are the dividing line; from north to south or from east to west, regions (1)–(7) belong to East Japan, regions (8)–(14) belong to West Japan.

5 These come from different sources, from the *Statistics Table of Agriculture and Commerce* in the early period and from the *Statistics Table of Factories* in the later period.

6 Ryoushin Minami (1976).

7 Customarily, West Japan is more developed than East Japan, because Kyoto and Nara are the ancient capitals of Japan, and industrial and commercial cities around them became a focus for the handicrafts sector. This region is characterized by a wealth of SMEs. Although Tokyo was in the heartland of the Tokugawa Shogunate in pre-modern times, it was not as developed as Osaka due to constraints on the development of industry and commerce at that time. After the Meiji Restoration, this landscape changed. Tokyo became the capital. Free from the constraints of the feudal era, Tokyo's industry and commerce saw rapid development, especially in emerging industries.

8 See Minami (1976).

9 Researches on industry were carried out by Ryoushin Minami (1976) and Minami (1987).

10 Kuznets advanced this issue, see Kuznets (1955). It was followed by a great many studies, which fueled a lot of controversy. Research on modern Japan was conducted by Ryoushin Minami (1996).

Part III

Conditions for innovation and development

5 Industrial development and human resources

Analysis of inventors

Section 1 Introduction

The three chapters in this part study the necessary conditions for industrial development and technological advance or technological innovation, including human resources, market conditions, and government policy.[1] This chapter discusses a special part of human resources—inventors. Human resources have multiple aspects. From a micro perspective, these include entrepreneurs, technicians, managers, and workers. These people contribute to the enterprise at different levels and from different perspectives. No enterprise can develop without visionary entrepreneurs; corporate development goals cannot be achieved without well-trained managers and technicians; it is hard to solve a host of specific problems without disciplined and skilled workers.

This group of inventors is studied here because of our understanding that the driving force for industrialization and even economic development is technological innovation, which directly involves the managers, technicians and research and development (R&D) personnel of an enterprise. Managers are responsible for determining whether to develop and apply certain technology; technicians are responsible for the management and maintenance of routine technology; and the R&D personnel are engaged in technological innovation. If we shift our gaze beyond the enterprise, technological innovation involves other people in society in addition to the corporate employees. We collectively refer to these people engaged in technological innovation as "inventors."

Studies on the relationship between inventors and technological innovation from the perspective of economics are few and far between, but see Schmookler (1957), Jewkes et al. (1969), and Japanese Tadashi Ishii (1979) and Yukihiko Kiyokawa (1995). However, the research on modern Japan is restricted to the fiber sector.[2] It should be said to be a case study of the industry. The analysis in this chapter is geared to the manufacturing industry as a whole rather than individual industries.

Section 2 Statistical analysis

I. Preliminary discussion

It is well-known that economic development in Japan before World War II was achieved through the mutual competition and promotion of traditional industries and modern industries. As mentioned in the preceding chapter, one of the reasons for dividing the industry into traditional and modern industries in this period is that the two industries have different technical systems.[3] In other words, traditional industries mainly relied on existing technology, while modern industries imported Western technology. Different technical systems mean that the hardware used in capital equipment is different, and the knowledge structure of the personnel and other aspects also vary. Therefore, the technical innovation activities they are engaged in also differ.

Does the above deduction hold water? Verification is carried out through statistical analysis. We noticed the educational background and the position (identity) of inventors. Educational level can be roughly divided into three levels: elementary, intermediate, and advanced. Various classification methods are available for positions and identities. It is assumed that people engaged in invention activities are the insiders in related industries. They are divided into four types: craftsmen, workers, technicians, and managers.

Figure 5.1 shows the relationship between these identities and inventors, with traditional industries on the left and modern industries on the right. In fact, two aspects are assumed: First, there are craftsmen in traditional industries but workers and technicians are not included. There are workers and technicians in modern industries but craftsmen are not included.[4] While this assumption is not entirely reasonable, it can be easily explained and analyzed. Second, the managers in traditional industries are also engaged in R&D, but this is not the case in modern industries. Thus, in Figure 5.1, traditional industries do not have workers and technicians, while modern industries do not have managers.

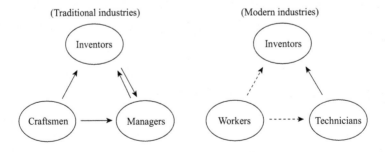

Figure 5.1 Types of inventors in traditional and modern industries (concept map).

Note: The solid line represents the usual type, and the dotted line represents the special case.

As regards traditional industries, consideration can be given to two aspects: First, craftsmen are engaged in R&D, then the results are applied to production at enterprises, and craftsmen directly become managers, such as Hejiro Hukami in the third section. Enterprises in traditional industries are chiefly SMEs. These enterprises did not have more detailed division of labor, and the routine production activities and technological innovation were not clearly separated. Moreover, the technical system of traditional industries is not so abstruse and complicated, and a great many craftsmen can be competent for carrying out innovation by means of experience and dedication. Second, it is rare that workers are promoted to be technicians or become inventors in modern industries. Usually, professional technicians are engaged in R&D activities and become inventors, such as Yuiti Torihaku, Yasujiro Niwa, and Masatugu Kobayashi in the third section. Enterprises in modern industries are mostly medium- and large-sized enterprises. The division of labor and production systems are relatively developed, and R&D activities are generally conducted by professional technicians. Moreover, the technical system of modern industries is relatively complicated and has certain difficulty. Therefore, corresponding scientific knowledge is required to carry out R&D, and they have high educational level.

According to the above discussion, a view can be put forward: Inventors in traditional industries are chiefly managers with low educational level, while inventors in modern industries are highly-educated technicians. It is verified through statistical analysis.

II. Explanation of information

There were few researches on inventors in the past, mainly due to problems in two aspects: First, there was no sufficient preparation in economics theory. The other is a lack of data suited to statistical analysis. Since the purpose of this chapter is empirical analysis, more efforts are made in data mining. While there is not much statistical data on inventors, there are data for statistical analysis. Information on inventors is available mostly in the form of biographies, which generally record the birthplace and achievements of relevant people. A brief description in the order of publication date is given below.

(1) Shigetaro Nara (1930): Mainly the winners commended by the country, recording in detail the lives of 199 people, motivations for inventions, contents, and others.
(2) Osaka Invention Association (1936): About 9,946 people in such fields as machinery, chemicals, and electrical engineering, including resumes, inventions, among others. It contains a detailed description of nearly 400 people.
(3) Japanese Invention Dictionary (1939): A detailed record of 1,038 representative inventors in 43 fields including machinery, chemicals, electrical engineering, fiber, and others, including resumés, and inventions.

(4) Kentaro Matsuhara (1952): Recording the detailed life and inventions and their influence on 61 people including 50 inventors awarded the "Medals with Blue Ribbon"[5] as at 1951.
(5) Shigetaro Nara (1961): Recording the lives, inventions and related influences regarding 260 inventors commended by the country.

The above materials have respective strengths and weaknesses. (1), (4), and (5) contain detailed records of inventors, but these are not classified for convenient reference. (2) It includes many inventors, but the description is not detailed enough. Eventually, we chose (3) as the main data for statistical analysis, supported by other data.

III. Statistical analysis

From the above (3), 864 people were selected (268 in machinery, 168 in chemicals, 195 in electrical engineering, 100 in fiber, and 133 in others) as objects of analysis. One of our goals is to examine the differences between traditional industries and modern industries. In view of this, we select three variables:[6] Ratio of patentees (X_1), ratio of highly educated people (X_2) and ratio of technicians (X_3). The higher the variable, the better it can represent modern industries. Otherwise, it is a traditional industry.

Table 5.1 shows the statistical characteristics of inventors in each field. For the ratio of patentees (X_1), it is the lowest in the field of others (59%), highest in chemicals (98%) and electrical engineering (92%), followed by fiber (78%) and machinery (68%). For the ratio of highly educated people (X_2), it is the lowest in fiber (33%), the highest in electrical engineering (96%), relatively high in chemicals (79%), and average in others (53%) and machinery (49%). For the ratio of technicians (X_3), it is also the highest in electrical engineering (94%), followed by chemicals (69%), and it is relatively low in other fields. On the whole, the three variables for inventors in traditional industries are low, while the three indicators are high in modern industries. Therefore, it can be roughly judged that the above indicators are suitable for judging inventors in two industries. However, this judgment is the intuitive feeling based on the above figures, without rigorous statistical analysis.

In order to better analyze the above inference, the principal component analysis,[7] one of the methods of multivariate statistical analysis, is used. The results of the statistical analysis are shown in Figure 5.2, which can describe the different characteristics of inventors in various industries overall (cumulative contribution rate: 92.6%). It should be comprehensively judged based on two principal components in Figure 5.2. However, the characteristics of inventors (contribution rate: 76.0%) can be roughly determined based on the first principal component. For example, modern technology fields such as communications, electrical machinery, power transmission and transformation, metals, electrochemical engineering, grease, chemicals, and dyes are mostly concentrated on the right side in the figure, while traditional sectors

Table 5.1 Characteristics of inventors by industry

Industry and technology classification	Number of patents	Ratio of patentees (X_1)	Ratio of highly education people (X_2)	Ratio of technicians (X_3)
Machinery industry (average)	268	68	49	47
(1) Mechanical device	23	87	87	57
(2) Prime motor	22	73	68	82
(3) Fluid operation	13	69	54	39
(4) Weapons and gunpowder	4	100	50	100
(5) Institutions and organizations	5	80	20	0
(6) Transportation	26	62	54	39
(7) Cleaning and hygiene	12	83	42	42
(8) Construction and civil engineering	24	79	71	50
(9) Mining	5	100	80	80
(10) Working machinery	5	80	40	40
(11) Manufacturing machinery	25	72	8	28
(12) Press machinery	3	33	33	33
(13) Printing and photography	22	91	73	86
(14) Stationery and calculator	10	80	50	40
(15) Household appliances	23	48	22	26
(16) Sports and entertainment	12	58	42	25
(17) Wearing gear	11	18	27	46
(18) Kitchen utensils	12	8	33	17
(19) Mechanical miscellaneous	11	73	82	64
Chemical industry (average)	168	98	79	69
(20) Chemicals	16	100	100	69
(21) Fuel and combustion equipment	16	100	75	88
(22) Metal	34	97	97	84
(23) Kiln	9	100	67	67
(24) Manufacturing methods	23	96	65	62
(25) Dyes, dyeing, coatings	16	94	56	50
(26) Food and favorites	25	92	76	67
(27) Grease	15	100	87	87
(28) Hygiene materials and cosmetics	14	100	86	50

(*continued*)

Table 5.1 Cont.

Industry and technology classification	Number of patents	Ratio of patentees (X_1)	Ratio of highly education people (X_2)	Ratio of technicians (X_3)
Electrical industry (average)	195	92	96	94
(29) Electrical machinery	54	85	98	98
(30) Electric lamp and electric heater	27	85	100	81
(31) Power transmission and control	41	90	88	100
(32) Electrical communication	61	97	100	100
(33) Electrical chemistry	12	100	92	92
Fiber industry (average)	100	78	33	41
(34) Loom	19	79	41	50
(35) Reeling machine	35	77	47	59
(36) Fabric	19	68	37	18
(37) Knitting	10	70	40	40
(38) Mat	8	88	0	38
(39) Net-making machine	9	89	33	44
Other (average)	133	59	53	37
(40) Agriculture	89	38	16	25
(41) Sericulture	15	80	47	25
(42) Aquatic products	17	59	65	53
(43) Drying and freezing equipment	12	58	83	46
Statistics (average)	864	79	62	58
Ratio of patentees (X_1)		1.000		
Ratio of highly educated people (X_2)		0.538	1.000	
Ratio of technicians (X_2)		0.601	0.771	1.000

Source: *Japanese Invention Dictionary* (1939).

Note:
1 The figure in the variable column (X_1, X_2, X_3) is the ratio (%).
2 Ratio of patentees = number of patentees ÷ (number of patentees + number of utility model holders) × 100. Patentees include those who have both patents and utility models.
3 Ratio of highly educated persons = number of senior high school graduates and above ÷ all × 100. Senior high school graduates include graduates from specialized schools.
4 Ratio of technicians = number of technicians ÷ (number of technicians + number of managers) × 100. Managers include self-employed people; technicians include teachers.
5 The figure in the bottom statistics column is the correlation coefficient.
6 The industries here are actually technology classification.

such as kitchen utensils, press machinery, wearing gear, agriculture, and household appliances are chiefly on the left side in the figure.[8] According to the advance design, if the numbers of the three variables are high, the modernity of this field (industry) is strong. Conversely, if the numbers of the

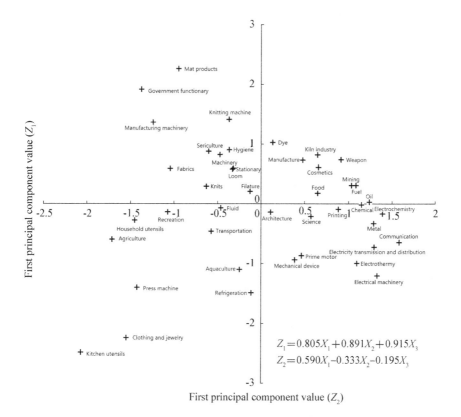

Figure 5.2 Results of principal component analysis: Analysis of characteristics of inventors.

three variables are low, it is a traditional field (industry). The coefficients of each variable of the first principal component are positive and in excess of 0.8, indicating that the three variables are have a high value for judging and distinguishing the characteristics of various sectors. Accordingly, judgment can be basically made according to the first principal component.

Section 3 Case study

I. Traditional industries: The invention and application of the plow

In modern times, the improvement in plows has been intimately related to the popularity of plowing with cattle and horses. Prior to that, plowing with cattle and horses was popularized in West Japan but not in East Japan. Long-bed plows are mainly used in West Japan, while bedless plows are used in only a few regions in Kitakyushu. In fact, people expect the emergence of short-bed plows with the advantages of both long-bed plows and bedless plows.[9] A plow, known as the "Higo plow"[10] that is close to this type of plow was invented in Kumamoto. To meet this expectation, there were some inventions in the late nineteenth century. For example, Suejiro Otyu invented the Kumamoto pointed plow by improving the local plow, and obtained a patent in 1909 (No. 5317); Isono Seisakujo in Fukuoka City also invented the "Oma plow" and the "Xinza plow"; Hejiro Hukami, also in Fukuoka, spread the excellent Fukuoka plowing method with cattle and horses; Genzou Matsuyama from Nagano invented the dual-purpose plow, which was popular in East Japan, where plowing with cattle and horses was not popular. After that, Shintiro Takakita improved the short-bed plow, and Hejiro Hukami invented the secondary plow, contributing to the popularity of short-bed plows.[11]

As regards the technical innovation activities of plows, there were a total of 196 patents and 1,524 utility models before World War II. These inventions are shown in Figure 5.3. It can be seen that there are far more utility models than patents (the former is about eight times more than the latter), indicating that this technology is simple traditional technology. As the traditional technical system is relatively simple, it is not easy to achieve an epoch-making technological innovation. Utility models showed an S-shaped change in the middle of the 1930s, which means that the growth accelerated along with the popularization of technology. In other words, only individual inventors carried out original R&D in the early days. As this technology gradually caught on, more people were involved in it. There are several highlights in the change of patents, which basically correspond to high-caliber inventions by Genzou Matsuyama, Shintiro Takakita, Hejiro Hukami, among others.

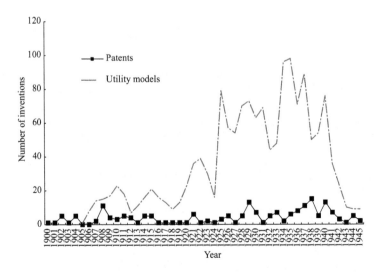

Figure 5.3 Invention of the plow.
Source: (Japan) Patent Office (1958).

II. Cases of modern industries: The invention of communication machinery

Prior to World War II, Japan had experienced a great deal of technological innovation in electrical communication technology. Here are some representative outcomes. As regards wireless communication, the filter was the first problem to be solved. Sosuke Asano of the Teishinshō Electric Laboratory, invented the mercury filter in 1903, followed by a magnetic iron powder filter invented by Mitsuru Saiki and tantalum and mineral filters invented by Yuiti Torihaku. The next problem to be solved was radio wave generators. In 1911, Yuiti Torihaku, Etaro Yokohama, and Masajiro Kitamura successfully developed TYK wireless phones (Patent No. 22347). In 1914, this achieved great results in the 14-kilometer experiment, and was the first practical use of wireless telephones in the world.

Early wireless technologies, similar to telecommunications and telephone technologies, could be easily imitated. However, this changed in the era of vacuum tubes. Due to the high specifications required for vacuum technology, material technology, and micro-processing technology, Japan relied on foreign technology for a period of time. Professor Hidetugu Yagi of Tohoku University made new discoveries while guiding his students' graduation thesis. Shintaro Uda of the Yagi Institute conducted more in-depth research. In 1926, they invented the Yagi antenna (Patent No. 69115), which is the prototype of the TV antenna used today. However, it did not attract much attention in Japan at that time. It was not until the Pacific War that the Japanese discovered that this technology was being used by the British when they saw the words "YAGI ARRAY" on the radio wave weapons used by its army.

In electrical communication technology, words are changed into symbols (telecommunications), then the language is changed into sound (phone), and then wireless communication. Finally, there is the transmission of images. From the middle of the nineteenth century to the 1920s, Europe and the U.S. achieved their respective success with photo transfer technology. These technologies were introduced to Japan in 1926. In order to send photos of Emperor Showa's ceremony of ascension to the throne (1928) rapidly, news agencies purchased related technologies from Germany and France, but the performance left a lot to be desired. At length, the NE-style photo transfer system developed by Yasujiro Niwa and Masatugu Kobayashi of the Nippon Electric Company was adopted. When Yasujiro Niwa went on a business trip to Europe (1924–1926), this technology was in a stage of practical application for photo transmission in Europe. Aware of the prospects of this technology, Yasujiro Niwa immediately launched R&D with success in Japan.

Figure 5.4 shows the inventions in the field of communication technology. The figure shows the following aspects: First, it showed a clear upward trend before World War II, and especially, the growth picked up after the 1920s. It indicates that this technology matured and entered the stage of practical use. Second, the number of patents obtained by foreigners stands out. During this period, foreigners obtained 3,571 patents, 3,479 more than that by the

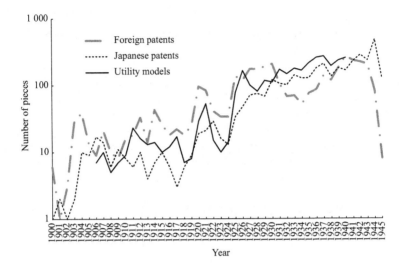

Figure 5.4 Invention of communication technology.
Source: (Japan) Patent Office.

Japanese. It surpassed the Japanese before the 1930s. This shows that this technology was basically copied from foreign technology. Third, there were few utility models (such as comparison with plows). This tendency is shown by the fact that the number of patents is more than double utility models. It goes to prove that this technology is based on modern science and technology, rather than simple extension of existing traditional technology.

III. Comparative analysis

Following the above statistical analysis and case study, the types of inventors in traditional industries and modern industries are summarized in Table 5.2, which shows many differences between the two. In terms of educational level and positions, it is the same as the results of statistical analysis. The majority of the inventors in traditional industries did not graduate from elementary schools, while all the inventors in modern industries had graduated from universities. In another example, inventors in traditional industries are chiefly individual managers, while those in modern industries are mostly technical personnel of large enterprises or university teachers.

From the perspective of the motivation for inventions, there are certain inevitable factors for the accumulation of experience and thoughts in routine work in traditional industries, while modern industries rely on scientific experiments and internal connections to a greater extent, which can produce certain accidental factors. This is because the technical system in traditional industries depends on traditional experience, whereas modern industries adopt experimental science. From the perspective of the originality, both

Table 5.2 Invention activities and inventors in traditional and modern industries

Inventors	Inventions	(1) Education	(2) Title	(3) Motivation	(4) Originality	(5) Organizational form	(6) Application	(7) Competitive invention
(Plow)								
Genzou Matsuyama	Dual-purpose plow	Elementary school	Manager	Experience	Originality	Individual	Fast	Yes
Shintaro Takakita	Dual-purpose plow	Elementary school	Manager	Experience	Improvement	Individual	Fast	Yes
Hejiro Hukami	Secondary plowing	None	Self-employed	Experience	Improvement	Individual	Fast	Yes
(Electrical communication)								
Yuiti Torihaku	Radio telephone	University	Technician	Change of ideas	Improvement	Organization	Slow	No
Hidetugu Yagi	Yagi antenna	University	Professor	Scientific experiment	Originality	Organization	Slow	No
Yasujiro Niwa	NE-Fax	University	Technician	Foreign business trip	Improvement	Organization	Slow	No

Source: *Japanese Invention Dictionary* (1939).

industries have seen original results and have also made some improvements. As Japan's level of technicality was generally low before World War II, it was difficult to obtain original outcomes. From the perspective of the organizational forms of technological innovation, traditional industries mostly feature individual behavior, while modern industries are characterized by organized innovation activities. Traditional industries have a relatively simple technology system which can be handled by individuals with proficient skills and a pioneering spirit. In comparison, technology in modern industries is complex and interconnected, and is achieved through concerted efforts. Moreover, in terms of funding, traditional technology can usually be improved without a great deal of tests or equipment, and this can be done by individuals with limited funding. Modern industries feature complex technology systems and require state-of-the-art testing equipment, which requires major investment.

In terms of the use after invention, it is relatively fast in traditional industries, because they have a market of a certain scale. Once an invention achieves success, it can be easily rolled out. However, as this advantage is not available for modern industries, heavy marketing must be undertaken. Therefore, we hold that traditional industries are demand-pull, while modern industries are technology-push. Finally, because of differences in the respective markets, technological innovation in traditional industries are chiefly conducted by SMEs in an atmosphere of fierce competition, whereas those in modern industries are generally carried out by large monopoly enterprises.[12]

It should be noted that this discussion is based on typical cases. In reality, many industries fall into the grey area between traditional and modern industries. Technological innovation developments in these industries should also have dual characteristics. Generally speaking, there are two possibilities: one is the introduction of foreign technology to improve traditional industries, such as the textile industry; the other uses technology copied from Europe and the U.S., similar to that which exists in traditional industries in terms of technology and production organization, such as matches and soap.

Section 4 The socioeconomic background

I. Educational development and talent supply

In modern Japan, all kinds of talents are cultivated to meet the needs of industrial development. In the early days of economic development, both primary and higher education saw great development thanks to the support of the government. In modern society, the people achieved literacy, laying a social foundation for the government to implement policies; it has also trained a wealth of professionals to import advanced Western technology. Although the development of secondary education got off to a late start, it developed faster than primary and higher education, which was closely related to the fact that economic development at the time required a wealth of skilled workers

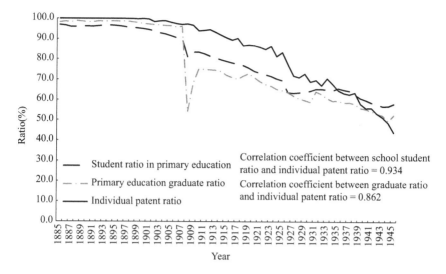

Figure 5.5 Primary education and individual patents.

Source: Patents: (Japan) Patent Office (1955), Students: (Japan) Investigation Bureau of Ministry of Education, Culture, Sports, Science and Technology (1962).

Notes:
1 Ratio of primary education students = number of primary education students ÷ total number of students × 100%.
2 Ratio of individual patents = number of individual patents ÷ total number of Japanese patents × 100%.

with a certain educational level. It can be said that before World War II, the development of education in Japan corresponded to that of industry.[13]

Through the analysis above, we draw the following conclusions: Technological innovation in traditional industries is chiefly realized by those with a low educational level, while in modern industries it is the result of the collective creation by highly educated technicians. This view is confirmed from a different perspective (education). Figure 5.5 shows the changes in the ratio of primary education graduates (or current students) (the ratio of the number of primary education graduates (or number of current students) to the total number of graduates) and the ratio of individual patents (the ratio of the number of individual patents to the total number of Japanese patents). According to these figures, before the Russo-Japanese War, the proportion of the two reached more than 90%, and then gradually declined. After 1920, the former fell to about 70%, while the latter was still more than 85%. Although there was great progress in secondary education in this period, there was still no obvious effect on technological innovation. By around 1940, the two dropped to some 50%, which indirectly indicates that secondary education gradually showed its effect. It can also be verified from this figure that there is a highly positive correlation between the number of primary education graduates and current students and the number of individual patents. In other words, the correlation coefficient between the ratio of graduates and the ratio of individual patents = 0.862, and the correlation coefficient between the ratio of current students and the ratio of individual patents = 0.934.

The above discussion chiefly concerns the importance of primary education (related to traditional industries) and higher education (related to modern industries), but it does not mean that secondary education is insignificant. In fact, as the economy develops, secondary education becomes increasingly important. From the perspective of the growth rate, the number of students of secondary education institutions during the period before World War II (1885–1945) accounted for 17.7%, far higher than that of primary education (5.4%) and higher education (9.6%). In particular, when the modern education system was basically established (1885–1910), the growth rate of primary education was up to 34.3%, while the growth rates of primary education and higher education were 9.5% and 12.8% during the same period.[14]

II. Industrial development and demand for talent

Industrial development does not merely indicate an increase in the number of enterprises or the expansion of scale. It is also accompanied by technological advancements featuring the improvement of employee skills and the performance of capital equipment. As the industry develops and expands, more skilled labor and management personnel as well as professional technicians are required, in addition to unskilled labor. From the perspective of technological advance and technological innovation, the growing number of professional technicians is of great importance. In fact, Japan saw a significant increase in the number of professional and technical personnel before World War II.

According to the research by Hoshimi Uchida, there were a total of 86 technicians in 1880, but this figure had risen to 1,565 by 1900, and 14,162 in 1920. According to the *Statistics Table of Factories*, there were 53,000 technicians in 1920, which is 2.7 times more than that by calculated by Hoshimi Uchida. The number did not increase greatly after that. Growth picked up again from the late 1930s, and, by the 1940s there were 158,000 technicians.[15] Of course, not all technicians are engaged in technical innovation activities, but they can gain technical know-how in the daily maintenance of machinery and by "learning by using," and also sometimes by carrying out R&D. Technological innovation activities are not purely theoretical thinking and lab experiments. These require various repeated applied experiments and inspiration from actual operations.

The relationship between technical staff and technological innovation is analyzed using specific data below. In order to examine the differences in the contribution of technical personnel to technological innovation activities in various industries, two variables—the intensity of technical personnel and the number of corporate patents—are used for analysis. Figure 5.6 and Figure 5.7 show the correlation between the two. Thirty-eight industries at two time points from 1919 to 1920 and from 1939 to 1940 are selected here. In view

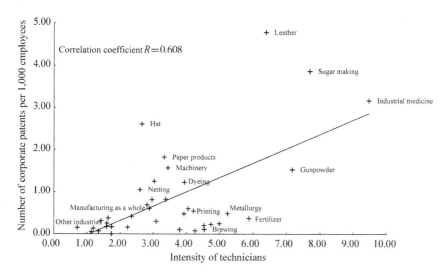

Figure 5.6 The relationship between the intensity of technical personnel and number of corporate patents (1919–1920).

Source: The number of employees from the *Statistics Table of Factories*, and the patents from (Japan) Patent Office.

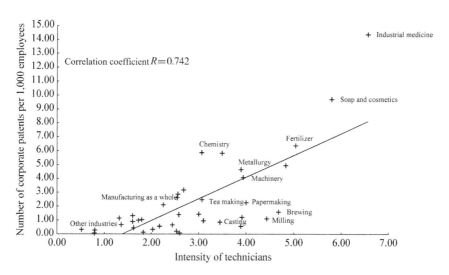

Figure 5.7 The relationship between the number of technical personnel and the number of corporate patents (1939–1940).

Source: The number of employees from the *Statistics Table of Factories*, and the patents from (Japan) Patent Office.

of the correlation coefficient, it is relatively high (0.6–0.7) at the two time points, indicating a strong positive correlation between the two. This means that organized technological innovation activities (shown by the number of corporate patents) were chiefly created by technical personnel with professional know-how. This also proves our previous views and proposition.

Organized R&D efforts were basically made after government and private research institutions were founded on a large scale after the 1920s. In other words, these government and private research institutions played a crucial role in technological innovation. In 1923, there were 162 private research institutes, 43 national research institutes, and 65 public industrial experimental institutes. By 1931, the corresponding figures were 193 (with 1,349 researchers), 73 (829 researchers), and 83 (551 researchers), respectively. By 1939, the corresponding figures were 383 (with 8,988 employees), 118 (5,306 employees) and 173 (3,950 employees). Of course, if the researchers of these institutions apply for patents for these inventions, they are corporate patents, and the members of these institutions have scientific research of a high caliber. For example, the ratio of patents (the ratio of patents to the sum of patents and utility models) by four top research institutions in Japan (the Institute of Physical and Chemical Research, the Tokyo Institute of Technology, the Osaka Institute of Technology, and the Electric Laboratory) was 80–90% from 1913 to 1945.[16]

The increasing importance of organized technological innovations signifies the declining status of individual inventors, but this does not mean that the latter has been fully replaced by the former. Unlike production activities, technological innovation activities feature originality and personality. In other words, in addition to teamwork, R&D also calls for genius. As regards this point, J. Schmookler, E. Mansfield, and JD Jewkes also hold the same view.[17] However, as industrial technology becomes more complex and integrated, individual inventors cannot hold a candle to enterprises or research institutions in terms of funding, human resources, or the coordination role of organizations.

Section 5 Concluding remarks

From the above analysis, we can draw the following conclusions: First, there are many differences between traditional industries and modern industries in terms of inventors. For starters, inventors in traditional industries are chiefly business managers with a low educational level, while modern industries have technical personnel with a high education level. Second, experience is usually gained in the routine "learning by doing" for technological innovation activities in traditional industries, while modern industries mostly achieve this through scientific experiments. Third, technological innovation activities in traditional industries are chiefly carried out by individuals, while these are more organized in modern industries. Moreover, it is usually easier to achieve inventions in traditional industries, while these are slower in modern industries. Finally, technological innovation activities in traditional industries are generated by fierce market competition, while these are often conducted under monopolistic conditions in modern industries.

Second, individual inventors played a great role in the early stages of economic development, but were replaced by organized collective R&D activities in the later stages. This is intimately related to the large proportion of traditional industries in the early days of economic development. As the economy developed, the proportion of modern industries increased greatly. At the same time, this is also related to the fact that enterprises in traditional industries are SMEs, whereas many large-scale enterprises belong to modern industries; this is also indirectly related to the so-called "Schumpeter hypothesis."[18]

Third, technological innovation in traditional industries is principally demand-pull, while technological innovation in modern industries is basically driven by technology and are generally carried out under existing market conditions. Therefore, in traditional industries, the phrase "necessity is the mother of invention" makes sense. This is not the case in modern industries, where it is likely that there is either no or only a small market, which requires technology promotion and market development.[19]

Fourth, the development of education, as a social and economic factor that produces inventors, is vital, as it produces sufficient human resources for innovative activities. Accordingly, the development of industry will then keep pace. Only when the industry development reaches a certain level is there a need for innovative talents. It is also found that primary education plays a critical role in the early stage of economic development while secondary education is more important in the latter stages. Higher education always plays an important role, especially in modern industry.[20] Moreover, as they develop, this creates a growing demand for technical personnel. The role of technical expert R&D teams made up of professional technicians is increasing. In particular, technicians at government and private scientific research institutes play a more important role.

Notes

1 Corresponding conditions must be met for both economic development and technological advance. In addition to the conditions discussed here, there should also be factors such as education, resources, and even culture, which can be collectively called "social competence." On economic development conditions and social competence, see Ryoushin Minami (2002) and Guan Quan (2014).
2 As regards Japan before World War II, the fiber industry was the largest industry. The research results regarding this industry far outnumbered those of other industries. This also applies to modern China.
3 See Chapter 2 and Guan Quan (1997).
4 On the definitions of and differences between craftsmen, workers, and technicians, see Kounosuke Odaka (1993).
5 A kind of medals awarded to those who contributed to modern Japan. It is divided into categories according to color, including industry, government, science, religion, culture, and others. Blue is a reward for industrial professionals and inventors.

6 The data, although incomplete, records the date of birth of inventors, name of inventions, content, time, and types of awards.

7 The basic principle of the multivariate statistical analysis method like principal component analysis is introduced in Chapter 2.

8 There are also some industries situated in the center of the chart, such as silk reeling and dyeing. These industries have dual characteristics, both as traditional industries and modern industries. For example, Takafusa Nakamura defines the silk reeling industry as a new traditional industry. See Takafusa Nakamura (1976) and Takafusa Nakamura (1997).

9 The so-called "bed" of a plow is the part touching the ground: some are short, while some do not have any—these are called "bedless" plows.

10 Higo, the present-day Kumamoto, is the name of an ancient place name in Japan.

11 On the technological development of modern plows, see Hiroshi Shimizu (1953, 1954) and Kaichi Arashi (1957). On the economic significance of the penetration of plowing with cattle and horses, see Fumio Makino (1996).

12 On this issue, corresponding discussions are given in Chapters 4 and 7 of this book.

13 On the development of education in modern Japan, see the Survey Bureau of (Japan) Ministry of Education (1962).

14 Survey Bureau of (Japan) Ministry of Education (1962).

15 Hoshimi Uchida (1988) said that the technical staff are limited to graduates of universities and industrial and technical institutes. Thus, his number is lower than that in the *Statistics Table of Factories*. For example, the distribution of technical staff by Hoshimi Uchida and *Statistics Table of Factories* in 1920 are as follows: 635:3,071 employees in metal; 1,324:7,731 in machinery; 302:2,663 in kiln; 570:4,272 in chemicals; 180:5,061 in food; 1,103:17,814 in textile; 1,071:4,254 in shipbuilding; 207:1,609 in papermaking. Each industry varies, and the difference between the two is 5 to 28 times.

16 (Japan's) Ministry of International Trade and Industry (1979).

17 Schmookler (1957), Mansfield (1968), Jewkes et al. (1969).

18 See Chapter 6 for details.

19 This is complementary to the discussions in Chapter 3.

20 On this, see Guan Quan (2014).

6 Industrial development and market structure

The Schumpeter hypothesis

Section 1 Introduction

This chapter studies market issues, which is one of the conditions for technological innovation. There are two market issues: the size of the market, and the market structure. The first means that the market will expand as the economy develops. An expanding market indicates the expansion of market capacity. From a market perspective, it means the development of an industry, at least the quantitative growth. When the market expands, the supply and demand of commodities within it also rise. The increase in supply and demand indicates a growing number of market participants, including producers, and sellers, as well as others in transportation and storage. In pre-modern times, people lived in rural areas in a relatively closed community. Due to the poor traffic network, and sometimes for political reasons, human mobility was very low, and there was a lack of circulation for goods closely related to the life of the people. Although, at the time, people shared highly similar production and living conditions, there was little exchange or communication, which hindered technological advances and the formation of economies of scale. Since the beginning of modern times, thanks to large-scale mechanized production and the development of the transportation system, all markets, such as commodities, and the labor, and capital markets, achieve development, thus greatly spurring economic development.

This chapter focuses on the second aspect, which is the market structure. Big and small markets, and the monopoly and competitive markets. According to the principles of economics, a competitive market is more conducive to economic activities, in that resources have a rational allocation under competitive conditions. In contrast, monopolies are prone to lead to market distortion. Monopolists are minority suppliers in the market, and can fix the prices of goods and services at will. It is easy to set prices higher than that on the competitive market, causing losses to consumers. Moreover, if there is only one or a few suppliers in the market, monopolists will also cause more serious problems, such as offering low-quality goods and services. This situation exists in quite a few countries to varying degrees. Before World War II, zaibatsu had a monopoly in some fields in Japan. After World War II, state-owned railway companies in Japan saw a decline in service quality for a long time; they were finally split. Antitrust is now the consensus in most modern countries, but methods and attitudes in different countries vary: in some countries it is more stringent, while in others it is more relaxed. Of course, some developing countries lack an anti-monopoly mechanism, due to their political, economic, and social constraints, but it is generally considered that these countries have poor economic systems.

Schumpeter pointed out the importance of technological innovation in the modern capitalist economy, with a particular emphasis on the role of entrepreneurs in technological innovations. He put forward the so-called "Schumpeter hypothesis," which contained two important propositions: (1) monopolistic enterprises have more possibilities for technological innovation than competitive enterprises; and (2) Large enterprises have more possibilities for technological innovation than SMEs. Together with the supplement by John Kenneth Galbraith, this became an important proposition. Centering on this proposition, many economists carried out empirical analysis on European and American enterprises, including Kamein and Schwartz (1982), Baldwin and Scott (1987), and Cohen and Levin (1989). The results vary, some are positive and some negative.[1] Some economists also conducted research on the situation in Japan, including Kenichi Imai (1970), Noriyuki Doi (1977, 1993), Masu Uekusa (1982), Naoki Murakami (1986, 1988), and Ryuhe Wakasugi (1996). These findings show negative results. The Japanese research was geared to the period after World War II, but the pre-war period rarely mentioned.

The lack of research for the period before World War II is chiefly due to a lack of necessary data – there is hardly any data on R&D activities at the enterprise level. Generally, R&D function used for the study of technological innovation requires data on the R&D input and output, such as the amount of investment in R&D, the number of researchers (inputs) as well as the number of new products or patents (output). These data are few and far between. However, analysis is still not out of the question, only that it is not as rigorous as post-war analysis. This chapter attempts to breakthrough on this issue by tapping relevant data and adopting close analysis methods.

Another purpose of this chapter is to discuss the role of Japanese zaibatsu before World War II, especially the role of technological innovations. It is well-known that zaibatsu had a status that cannot be ignored in the Japanese economy before World War II. Did zaibatsu contribute to the development of the Japanese economy and technological innovation? This issue is closely related to the "Schumpeter hypothesis" discussed in this chapter. It is therefore a focus of our research.

Section 2 Quantitative analysis

I. About the data

According to the Schumpeter hypothesis, two issues need to be discussed: One is the relationship between the size of enterprises and technological innovation, namely whether large enterprises are more conducive to technological innovation. The second is whether monopolistic enterprises are more conducive to technological innovation. To this end, it is necessary to acquire data on the size of enterprises and technological innovation. However, it is extremely difficult to acquire these data at the enterprise level in Japan before World War II, because Japan was still a developing country at that time. In particular, regarding technological innovation, Japan learned from European and American companies, and as a result, there are few data records at the enterprise level. As we know, the *Statistics Table of Factories* fully reflects industrial activity and records important information, such as the number of factories, number of employees, horsepower of prime motors, and the amount of raw materials and fuel used. However, the relevant data divided by the size of enterprises is limited indeed. Thus, it is hard to use the *Statistics Table of Factories* to study the issues such as technological innovation and differences among enterprises.[2]

However, the *Industrial Survey Report* on Tokyo, Osaka, Nagoya, Yokohama, Kobe and other large cities, which were published from 1933 to 1935, recorded some indicators divided by the amount of capital, such as the number of factories, capital, horsepower of prime motors, production volume, number of employees, amount of raw materials and fuel used, wages, interest, taxes and other data closely related to the operation of enterprises. Although these data cannot directly reflect the status of technological innovations, it is possible to gain information that can reflect the production efficiency and technological level of enterprises by calculating the appropriate indicators. Of course, this survey has its problems. The data only covers the years from 1932 to 1933. This imposes some limitations on our analysis, making it hard to study technological advance and changes in technological level, and to compare it to other data. In addition, as it was published by each city independently, the data on some cities is incomplete. Thus, this book mainly uses the data on Tokyo and Nagoya, supplemented by the data on Osaka, Yokohama, and Kobe.

II. Statistical analysis

According to the above discussion, two kinds of data are used here to study the relationship between the size of the enterprise and technological innovations. First, the production input coefficient is studied according to the *Industrial Survey Report* of the above cities, based on capital. Second, the records of practitioners and inventions (patents and utility models) in the *History of Enterprises* are used to study the relationship between the two.

First, we select two representative industries from the manufacturing sector: Industrial medicine (modern industry) and wood products (traditional industry). Figures 6.1 and 6.2 show the isoquant curve of the two industries. The horizontal axis is the labor coefficient (L/Y) and the vertical axis is the capital coefficient (K/Y).[3] These show that the average production points of the two industries are generally concentrated near the isoquant curve, and capital and labor generally have a substitution relationship. Small enterprises have relatively low labor productivity and low capital coefficient, while large enterprises

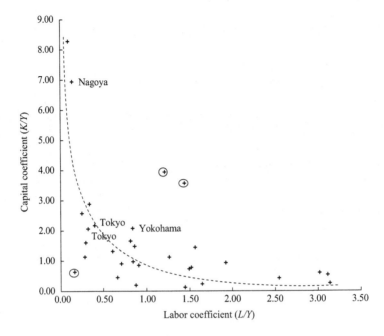

Figure 6.1 Production coefficient of industrial medicine by capital.

Notes:
1 There are 31 samples, but those less than 100 yen in Tokyo, less than 5,000 to 10,000 yen in Nagoya, and less than 10,000 to 50,000 yen in Yokohama are not included.
2 Regression formula: ln K = –0.086 – 0.805 ln L, adj. R2 = 0.544 (–1.488) (–5.766) The F value is 33.248, and the figure inside ( ) is t value.
3 Those marked with "○" are excluded from calculation.
4 The isoquant curve is drawn by hand.
5 Labor coefficient (L/Y) = number of employees ÷ value added (1,000 yen). Capital coefficient (L/Y) = fixed capital ÷ value added (yen). Value added = (production volume + commissioned production, repair revenue) – (costs of raw material + fuel and power fees).

possess a great deal of capital equipment that can replace labor in order to boost productivity. This shows that large enterprises and SMEs are within the same production technology system. When the size of the enterprise changes, the capital and labor coefficients change accordingly. This change belongs to the mutual substitution relationship between capital and labor in the same production technology system, rather than a wholly different production system.[4]

Next, data from the *History of Enterprises* is used to analyze the relationship between enterprise size and technological innovation. Specifically, out of more than 1,000 manufacturing companies in the *History of Enterprises*, we selected forty-one that record both the size of the enterprise size and the level of inventions.[5] Figure 6.3 shows the relationship between the employees of these enterprises and the number of inventions per 100 people. It can be seen that the relationship between the two does not indicate that large companies

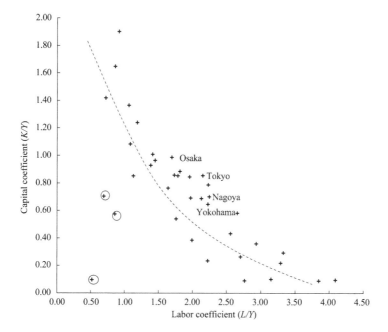

Figure 6.2 Production coefficient of wood products by capital.

Notes:
1 There are 40 samples. However, those more than 500,000 yen in Tokyo and Osaka and 100,000 to 500,000 yen in Yokohama were excluded.
2 Regression formula: $\ln K = 0.190 - 1.595 \ln L$, adj. $R2 = 0.712$ (3.480) (–9.495) The F value is 90.155, and the figure inside ( ) is t value.
3 Those marked with "○" are excluded from calculation.
4 The isoquant curve is drawn by hand.
5 Labor coefficient (L) = number of employees ÷ value added (1,000 yen). Capital factor (K) = fixed capital ÷ value added (yen). Value added = (production volume + commissioned production, repair revenue) – (costs of raw material + fuel and power fees).

have an advantage in technological innovation. In other words, the figure does not support the Schumpeter hypothesis. Although having more technological innovation results than SMEs, large enterprises do not have advantages of scale. Conversely, SMEs beat large enterprises in terms of the number of inventions per capita.

However, an explanation needs to be given before a conclusion is reached. In general, large enterprises have existed for a long time, thus accounting for their presence in the *History of Enterprises*. The smallest enterprise we found had more than 200 people. As a whole, the average size (of 38 enterprises) was 4,556 people.[6] In other words, although small enterprises show strong techno-logical innovation capabilities, enterprises with more than 200 people were also large companies in Japan before World War II, so they were not SMEs in the real sense of the word. In other words, we consider that medium-sized

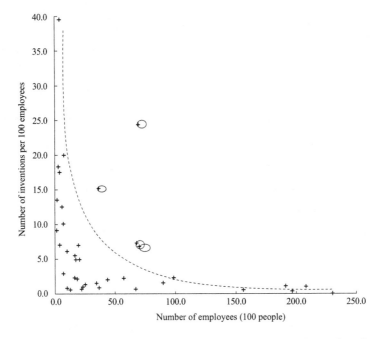

Figure 6.3 Correlation relationship between enterprise scale and technological innovation.

Notes:
1 There are 38 sample enterprises.
2 In addition to the aforesaid enterprises, there are data on Shibaura Engineering Works, Hitachi and Nippon Mining, but they are not calculated here.
3 Most of the figures cover the years from 1936 to 1945, and some around 1951.
4 The number of inventions is the sum of patents and utility models owned by various enterprises.
5 Regression formula: $\ln Y = 1.479-0.805 \ln X$ adj. R2 = 0.593 (9.076) (–7.107) The F value is 50.505, and the figure inside ( ) is t value.
6 Those marked with "○" are excluded from calculation.
7 The curve is drawn by hand.

enterprises have strong technological innovation capabilities, rather than large or small enterprises. There is another problem here: consideration only the number of inventions rather than their quality. The same patent may have great significance in one area, but may have less significance in other fields. This is one of the limitations of quantitative analysis, rather than a problem for this chapter. It will not have a big impact.

Section 3: Zaibatsu and technological innovation

As mentioned earlier, it is hard to deny that before World War II, Japanese zaibatsu occupied a not insignificant, perhaps even a decisive position in economic activity, however you evaluate it. How should we understand the role of zaibatsu? The purpose here is not to comprehensively evaluate the historical status and role of zaibatsu, but to conduct a discussion from the perspective of technological innovation and technological advances. In fact, research on the Japanese zaibatsu after World War II yielded fruitful results. It is usually divided into two schools: One is to study zaibatsu from the perspective of Marxist economic thought, which generally has a critical attitude toward its role and status. The other is to study zaibatsu from the perspective of management science and methods, and discuss the behavior of zaibatsu enterprises and their management reasons.[7]

In addition to these studies, Kazushi Okawa and Rosovsky spoke highly of zaibatsu from the perspective of economic development, holding that

> zaibatsu is the leaders of technologically advanced industries. They were the major importers and game-changers of Western European technology … Since the principal task at the time was development rather than economic democratization, zaibatsu, as the huge economic entities that are hardly accepted in other countries, are suitable and developed in Japan.[8]

This view is obviously diametrically opposed to the previous studies on zaibatsu, but their views are not confirmed, and did not receive much attention thereafter.

This is at least attributed to the following reasons. First, before World War II, zaibatsu was dissolved as one of the economic supports for war crimes when the U.S. army occupied Japan. The leaders of zaibatsu were disbanded, and some directly involved in crimes were even tried at courts. In other words, the nature of zaibatsu was fixed by the U.S. army in the post-war nationalization movement and it was hard to reverse the verdict.[9] Second, after World War II, Japan saw far better economic development than that before World War II, and these were achieved without the aid of zaibatsu. People no longer think that zaibatsu is a good thing and rarely speak in its defense. Third, many people who had some relationship with zaibatsu were still alive for a long time after World War II, including those in the political and economic community. They were reluctant to mention the past to avoid arousing trouble. Fourth, the negative impact of the monopoly power of zaibatsu on economic activity has been recognized by major countries and this has become a classic theory in economics. There is no moral and theoretical support, even if someone wished to defend the concept.

I. Zaibatsu and the import of technology

The import of technology into traditional and modern industries differs in the following respects: First, modern industries basically emerge based on imported technology, and a wealth of advanced technologies were imported from European and U.S. countries. In contrast, traditional industries mainly rely on existing technology, so that imported from abroad is highly limited. Second, modern industries are highly reliant on technology-exporting countries through direct investment or technology transfer, while traditional industries depend more on independent methods such as imitation or partly importing technology.[10] Third, as modern industries are generally dominated by a small number of large companies, technology is generally imported by large enterprises, while traditional industries are competitive, composed of numerous SMEs. Therefore, the mainstay for technology import is inevitably SMEs.

The technology import in the shipbuilding industry dominated by large enterprises was mainly made by companies related to zaibatsu. A total of 40 pieces of major technology were imported from 1904 to 1921: 21 by Mitsubishi Shipbuilding, 11 by Kawasaki Shipbuilding, 3 by Osaka Iron Works, 4 by IHI Shipbuilding, and 1 by Harima Shipbuilding. These five enterprises are big companies who had adopted the zaibatsu system.[11] The technology import in the aircraft manufacturing industry is very similar to that of the shipbuilding sector. From 1913 to 1939, 50 companies imported pieces of technology: Mitsubishi Heavy Industries (21), Kawasaki Aircraft (10), Nakajima Aircraft (10), Aichi Aircraft (3), IHI Aircraft (1), Tokyo Gas (1), Sumitomo Heavy Industries (2), Japanese Musical Instruments (1), Japan Airlines (1), and other major enterprises of the zaibatsu system.[12]

This is wholly different in traditional industries. For example, tools of agricultural production mainly relied on the improvement and R&D of domestic technology. In 1885, when the patent system was set up, 99 patents were granted, of which 18 were agricultural implements, accounting for 18.2%. For example, a tea-making machine (No. 2 to No. 4) by Kenzou Takabayashi and a mat-weaving machine (No. 23 to No. 24) by Minki Isozaki were influential inventions at the time.[13] In other words, technology import and innovation in traditional industries such as agricultural implements had practically no connection with zaibatsu.

The above may be too stark a comparison. On the one hand, two extreme technology categories were selected, but most industries are in between these two categories. In other words, although this industry is a modern industry, it is influenced by zaibatsu, but it does not necessarily import many advanced technologies. On the other hand, although zaibatsu had basically no influence on traditional industry, it also imported technology from developed countries. The reason is simple: Since zaibatsu pursues wealth, it definitely chose more lucrative industries; the so-called "profit-making industries" are mostly related to modern industries due to high productivity and high profit. Compared to old zaibatsu, emerging zaibatsu was more involved in the heavy industry sector, which was closely related to wars. Therefore, it was shaped by the occupying forces.[14]

II. Zaibatsu and technological innovation

The characteristics of the aforesaid technology import are still apparent in technological innovations. In other words, zaibatsu had a tremendous role in modern industries, but played a smaller part in traditional industries. For example, the ratio of individual patents has always remained high in traditional industries such as food and wood products. The number of individual patents in agronomy (technical classification) which is a traditional industry was up to 1,570, while there were only 22 (1.4%) corporate and government patents. In general, individual patents have no connection with large enterprises and zaibatsu.

Comparison is made based on the actual situation of several industries (technical fields). Table 6.1 shows the inventions by enterprises involved in photography, dry batteries and internal combustion engines. Regarding photographic technology, a total of 1,724 inventions were approved by 1937, including 304 (17.6%) inventions by legal persons and governments. The remaining were inventions by individuals and foreigners. In terms of dry batteries, there were a total of 657 inventions before the war, including 293 owned by legal persons and governments, accounting for 44.6% of the total. This proportion is far higher than that of photographic technology. Finally, we take a look at internal combustion engines. From 1927 to 1937, there were 300 inventions, including 237 (accounting for 79%) by the Japanese. It is well-known that internal combustion engine technology is modern technology invented in Europe in modern times. Therefore, the Japanese technology should have been imported from Europe. However, following a period of absorption, the Japanese had been able to conduct R&D in this field independently and had reached a high level. Of the 300 inventions, 39 were by foreigners, 100 by Japanese corporations and governments, and 161 by individuals (including 19 by foreigners). Legal persons and the governments account for up to one third, indicating that this industry had distinctive characteristics of modern industries, because it had the capability and characteristics of organized technology R&D. More importantly, some of these large enterprises, such as Kobe Steel, Niigata Iron Works, Tokyo Gas Electric, Mitsubishi Heavy Industries, Mitsubishi Shipbuilding, Ikegai Iron Works, Institute of Physical and Chemical Research, Nakajima Aircraft, Aichi Watch and Electric Manufacturing, Kawasaki Shipbuilding, Hitachi Shipbuilding, and Hitachi Manufacturing were big enterprises in the zaibatsu system, and occupied an important position in technology R&D.

Through the observation and analysis above, it is basically possible to make the following conjecture: As large enterprises in the zaibatsu system occupied an important position in modern industries, zaibatsu enterprises played an important role in technological innovation activities (e.g., internal combustion engines). By contrast, traditional industries were rarely affected by zaibatsu, and their technological innovation was achieved to a great extent through competition (such as agricultural machinery). Big enterprises of the zaibatsu system did not have a great influence on other industries (such as photography, cameras, and dry batteries) with an intermediate nature (grey area). As stated above, while zaibatsu was powerful and covered many sectors, other industries have an intermediate nature without the influence of zaibatsu and have achieved a certain level of modernity because economic development has led to the emergence of more industries and technologies who were influenced by other forces. This is also the result of economic development.

Table 6.1 Comparison of inventions by zaibatsu enterprises and non-zaibatsu enterprises in certain industries

Photography, camera	*Dry battery*	*Internal combustion engines*
Konishi Roppo Shop [106]	Panasonic [64]	Kobe Steel Works [13]
Institute of Physical and Chemical Research [37] (RIKEN)	Takasago Industry [57]	Japan Aerospace Exploration Agency [10]
Morita Joint Venture [21]	Yuasa Battery Manufacturing [21] (Mitsui)	Niigata Iron Works [10]
Tokyo Electric [21] (Mitsui)	Mitsubishi Electric [16] (Mitsubishi)	Tokyo Gas Electric [9] (Nissan)
Toyo Photography Industry [18]	Nihon Dengyo Kosaku [15]	Mitsubishi Heavy Industries [7] (Mitsubishi)
Nippon Kogaku [13] (Mitsubishi)	Sakizo YaiDry Battery [15]	Minister of the Navy [5]
ASK [11]	DENKA [15]	Mitsubishi Shipbuilding [5] (Mitsubishi)
Ichidacho Offset Printing [10]	Tokyo Shibaura Electric [15] (Mitsui)	Ushimadotyo Iron Works [4]
Fujifilm [8] (Mitsui)	Furukawa Electric [10] (Furukawa)	Institute of Physical and Chemical Research [4] (RIKEN)
Fine Printing [6]	Teishinshō Minister [10]	Ikegai Iron Works [4]
Shimadzu Corporation [4]	BAJ [10] (Mitsubishi)	Aichi Watch and Electric Manufacturing [3]
Photography Method [4]	Tokai Dry Battery [7]	Toda Foundry [3] (Nissan)
Photo Chemical Laboratory [4]	Japan Dry Battery [5]	Hanshin Iron Works [3]
Tokyo Neon Light [3]	Asahi Dry Battery [5]	Nakajima Aircraft [3] (Nakajima)
Sendagi Works [3]	Okada Dry Battery [4]	Hitachi Works [2] (Nissan)
Chemical Imaging [3]	Isomura Sangyo [3]	Kawasaki Shipbuilding [2]
Saito Chemical Research Institute [3]	Toho Chemical Research Institute [2]	Mitsubishi Electric (Mitsubishi)
Ogi Industry [2]	OKI [2] (Anda)	Japanese Engines
Daijiro Sakurai Shop [2]	Takehisa Dry Cell [2]	Uraga Senkyo Kabushiki Kaisha (Sumitomo)
Fuji Electric [2] (Furukawa)	Okada Electric Chamber of Commerce [2]	Engine Manufacturing
Tokyo Electric Co. Ltd. [2]	Tokyo Electric [2] (Sumitomo)	RIKEN Alumite Industry (RIKEN)
Mitsubishi Shipbuilding (Mitsubishi)	Toyo Dry Battery [2] (Mitsubishi)	Joint Venture Sakaeya Asbestos Textile
The China Time	Tokyo Institute of Technology	Shibaura Works (Mitsui)

Table 6.1 Cont.

Photography, camera	Dry battery	Internal combustion engines
Ataka Chamber of Commerce	Tokyo Electric Commerce	Yokohama Senkyo (Mitsubishi)
昭美染合资	Kawanishi Machinery	Daiichi Machinery Works
Osaka X-ray Joint Venture	Japan Dry Battery Manufacturing	Kurimoto
Omoto Kenkyushitsu	Kasei Chemicals (Kasei)	Joint Chamber of Commerce
Japan Dye Manufacturing (Sumitomo)	Minister of the Navy	Osaka Machinery Works
Chemical Research Institute	Shimadzu Works	Joint Venture Founded
Hitachi Works (Nissan)	Taiwan Invention Association	
Dainippon Bakelite (Mitsui)	Asahi Carbon Industry	
Sankyo		
Field Marshal		
Kasahara Business		
Takatiho Seisakujo		
Goto fuundou		
Mitsubishi Aviation Industry (Mitsubishi)		
Aviation Research Institute		
Gunze Limited (Mitsui)		
Relief Printing		
Shibaura Works (Mitsui)		
Toyo Western Electric		
Total: 304	Total: 293	Total: 100

Source: Photography and camera: Dai Tamura (1937); dry battery: Kendo Miyazaki (1960); internal combustion engine: Toshiyama Murayama (1939).

Note:
1 Inventions include patents and utility models.
2 As at the end of March 1937 for photographs and cameras, as at 1945 for dry batteries, and 1927–1937 for internal combustion engines.
3 Dry batteries only include patents.
4 The figure in [ ] [is the number of pieces (1 for the figure without brackets), and the name inside () is the name of zaibatsu.

III. The Institute of Physical and Chemical Research

The analysis below is of a special case of zaibatsu highly related to techno-logical innovation. As an emerging zaibatsu organization, the Institute of Physical and Chemical Research (RIKEN) showed its unique characteristics. Established in 1917, it is a semi-official and semi-private research institu-tion. Masatoshi Okouti, the third director, advocated a new interdisciplinary research method combining physics and chemistry, carrying out applied

R&D on the basis of pure academic research, with a view to changing the climate of imitating European and American technology. In order to fulfil the goal of combining academic research and industrial revitalization, RIKEN Industrial Co., Ltd. (a stock company founded in 1927) set about the R&D of vitamins and synthetic alcoholic products. In order to spur the industrialization of research outcomes, RIKEN Industrial gradually separated some research departments and acquired some SMEs who received RIKEN technology. In this way, RIKEN gradually became zaibatsu with a considerable number and scale of enterprises. By 1937, it had 23 direct companies and eight affiliates. This figure had reached fifty-eight by 1940.

Compared with other zaibatsu, RIKEN is small in scale, and the scale of its participants is not very large. However, RIKEN adopted a different corporate management policy. Rather than pursing corporate expansion, it was geared to the application of research results. In other words, its corporate profits were eventually applied to scientific research and application development. In a sense, its goal was to raise scientific research funding. In fact, RIKEN declined the government's scientific research funding from 1937 and raised its funding independently. After it developed economically, the scientific research activities of RIKEN were published in scientific papers and applying for patents. Some achievements received glowing plaudits. Some of its researchers held a doctorate degree, while others held Japan Academy awards and the Order of Culture. This shows that RIKEN cultivated a wealth of scientific researchers and was very different to other zaibatsu.[15]

The research status of RIKEN can be seen from another aspect. Japan had several important national-level research institutes prior to World War II: the Electrical Laboratory, the Tokyo Industrial Laboratory, the Osaka Industrial Laboratory, and RIKEN. From the second decade of the twentieth century to the end of World War II, Electrical Laboratory had 1,171 and 187 patents and utility models; RIKEN had 905 and 133; Tokyo Industrial Laboratory had 391 and 2; and Osaka Industrial Laboratory had 77 and 2.[16] RIKEN ranks second. If consideration is given to the fact that Electrical Laboratory and Tokyo Industrial Laboratory are older, RIKEN had indeed achieved resounding success from the perspective of technological innovation and application.[17]

Section 4 Concluding remarks

Based on the above theoretical and empirical analysis, several preliminary conclusions are drawn from this chapter. First, in terms of absolute number, large enterprises gained more technological innovation results and technological innovation capabilities than SMEs. In terms of the proportion per capita, however, there is no evidence to prove this. In other words, the "Schumpeter hypothesis" cannot be verified on the basis of the actual situation in Japan before World War II. Of course, it is not completely negated due to the limited data and materials, but technological R&D and innovation in the early days in Japan was basically carried out by SMEs in traditional industries. This tallies with the actual situation at that time, where Japan mainly copied Western technology. Modern industries were not fully capable of carrying out independent R&D, but in traditional industries, some improvement could be made to advanced technologies.

Second, before World War II, both monopolistic modern industries and competitive traditional industries saw active technological innovation, and some achievements were made which had epoch-making significance and impact. From the perspective of dual structure, technological innovation activities in traditional industries were competitive, while technological innovation in modern industries tended to be monopolistic. Of course, this is intimately related to their different market structures. Traditional industries faced fierce market competition, and were not dominated by individual large enterprises. Therefore, R&D was carried out in the face of fierce competition. In modern industries, some large enterprises had a monopoly on the market. At the same time, because the technology system in modern industries was complicated, technological innovation activities was generally carried out by large enterprises.

Third, zaibatsu played an important role in the import of technology and technological innovation in modern industries, because zaibatsu occupied a not insignificant, even a dominant position, in these industries. However, zaibatsu is not exactly the same, with traditional zaibatsu and so-called emerging zaibatsu. Because they operate in different sectors, there are certain differences. This is especially true of RIKEN in terms of technological innovation. As an emerging zaibatsu with a unique background, it made excellent achievements in technological innovation, and forged a path to success in commercial operations.

In general, before World War II, technological innovation activities in Japan were reflected in the improvement of traditional industries, while some important innovations in modern industries were copied from Western technologies. The two made key contributions to the rapidly growing Japanese economy. However, due to the restrictions of the economic development stage in Japan at that time, traditional industries made a greater contribution. This is not to say that modern industries do not have high-level technological innovation, or the wrong research direction. Given the specific circumstances at the time, traditional industries had more pragmatic economic benefits. In fact, technological innovation in modern industries is of greater significance for long-term future industrial development than traditional industries, because industrialization and modernization happened mainly thanks to modern industries.

Notes

1 See Schumpeter (1950) for the original text. There are many studies, such as Kamien and Schwartz (1982), Baldwin and Scott (1987), Cohen and Levin (1989).
2 Production volume by size is only recorded for certain years (e.g., 1929).
3 The labor coefficient is also the labor-output ratio, and the capital coefficient is also the capital-output ratio.

4 Kounosuke Odaka (1989) studied the fiber industry in the same way.

5 Japan's Hitotsubashi University has set up a database which contains a wealth of literature on the history of enterprises. We have only looked at the modern manufacturing sector.

6 Hitachi Mining and Hitachi Works, which were excluded from the analysis, had some 50,000 employees each.

7 Regarding the issue of zaibatsu, there was Management Committee of Holding Companies (1950, 1951) earlier, and the Society of Business History (1985) later.

8 Kazushi Okawa, Rosovsky (1973).

9 Regarding the issue of rectifying zaibatsu after World War II, see the *Management Committee of Holding Companies* (1951).

10 Hoshimi Uchida (1990) summarized different methods of technology transfer.

11 (Japan) Ministry of International Trade and Industry (1979).

12 The remaining six were imported by the Army and Navy; see (Japan) Ministry of International Trade and Industry (1979).

13 Japanese Society for the History of Science (1967).

14 Japanese zaibatsu is divided into new and old zaibatsu. The old zaibatsu had been involved in economic activities since the Meiji period, or even earlier. These zaibatsu had close political connections and occupied a dominant position. They chiefly operated in mining, commerce, shipping, finance and others. Companies such as Mitsui, Mitsubishi, Sumitomo, Yasuda, Furukawa, and Sosuke were also called comprehensive zaibatsu. New zaibatsu emerged in the 1920s, and chiefly operated in the chemical, military, and other industries. They were professional. Though not large, they had strong development momentum and included Nissan, Nisso, Fuji, Nakajima, and Ohkura.

15 Regarding "theoretical research" on emerging zaibatsu and its scientific achievements, see Masaru Udagawa (1984) and Ken Saito (1987).

16 (Japan) Ministry of International Trade and Industry (1979).

17 The Electrical Laboratory and the Geological Survey Institute were the earliest research institutes in modern Japan (1891), while the Tokyo Industrial Laboratory was set up later (1900).

7   Technology policy

Analysis of patent system

Section 1 Introduction

In addition to being an economic powerhouse, Japan is also a major power in terms of technology and patents today. In fact, Japan gradually became an economic and technological power after World War II, especially after the rapid economic growth in the 1960s.[1] Although Japan lagged behind European and American powers in terms of overall technology level before World War II, it reached or approached international levels in some areas of technology at that time. World-class inventions include, "Masatika gunpowder" by Masatika Shimose (1891), "dry battery" by Sakizo Yai (1892), "cultured pearls" by Kokiti Motoki (1894), "adrenaline" by Jokiti Takamine (1901), "automatic loom" by Sakiti Toyoda (1901), "monosodium glutamate" by Kikunae Ikeda (1908), "Type 38 rifle Arisaka" by Kijiro Nanbu (1909, the 38th year of Meiji period), "Vitamin B1" by Umetaro Suzuki (1911), "permanent magnet steel" by Koutaro Honda (1917), "mercury arrester" by Ryotaro Mitsuda (1917), "Vitamin A" by Katsumi Takahashi(1922), "Manufacturing method of thermometer" by Kousuke Kashiwagi (1922), "Receiving antenna" by Hidetugu Yagi(1925), "television" by Kenjiro Takayanagi (1928), "electric clock" by Kawarada Masatarō (1945), "small gasoline engine" by Souitiro Honda(1949).[2]

Japan had a considerable number of technologies, having granted 160,000 patents and 340,000 utility models before World War II. Although not as good as that of the European and American powers, the figures are not to be sneezed at, given the date of establishment of Japanese patent system and the gap in levels of economic development. On the eve of World War II, in terms of annual number of patent applications, Japan surpassed France and Italy, but lagged behind the US, Germany and Britain. The growth rate of patent applications is even more impressive. From 1889 to 1942, the average annual growth rate was 5.3% in Japan, 0.8% in the US, 0.5% in Britain, 3.5% in Italy, 3.2% in Germany and 0.7% in France.[3]

Granted that quantitative analysis of technological innovation is necessary, the research on technological policy is also important, because the level and capabilities of a country's technological innovation are often influenced by its policies. However, as it is hard to evaluate the effect of technology policies, research in this area is sparse, especially research on the patent system.[4] Moreover, technology policies are manifold and vary greatly from country to country, increasing the difficulty of research. Therefore, there has hardly been any research on Japan's technology policies, especially its patent system. In view of this, particular attention is paid to this issue here, in the hope of exploring the underlying causes of Japan's economic development by studying the relationship between the patent system and technological innovations.

In addition to studying the patent system in Japan, we attach greater importance to one of its characteristics, namely the utility model system. We hold that the establishment of this system is a major step forward for the Japanese patent system and also serves as a model for system innovation in developing countries. The utility model system provided a favorable institutional environment for Japan's technological innovation at least prior to World War II and played a crucial role in economic development. We would even argue that it had a bigger role than the patent law before World War II, because technological innovation capability and level in Japan were low at that time, so quite a few inventions were the results of imitation and improvement. According to the requirements and standards on patents, these inventions are not protected and it is hard to play a role in economic development. Utility models protect these minor inventions so that they play their part. At that time, the industrial structure was made up of traditional industries in Japan, with SMEs accounting for a large proportion of companies. As these inventions were simple and inexpensive, they could easily be adapted by SMEs in these traditional industries. These inventions injected vitality into these industries and greatly spurred the development of these industries. This is an important point of this chapter.

Section 2 The establishment of the patent system and its characteristics

I. Establishment of the patent system

The Japanese patent system emerged as a government notice on the *Monopoly Rules* in 1871 after the Meiji government came to power. Although the *Rules* were abolished after one year without granting one patent, it has its historical significance as the earliest law that stemmed from Western Europe. In a sense, Japan's modern legal system started from patent law. We are unclear about the details on the formation and abolition of the *Monopoly Rules*, but some of the following are the facts.[5] With regard to its formation, the introduction to the Western patent system by those with foresight including Fukuzawa Yukichi and Takahira Kanda provided good teaching material for the Meiji government which had no knowledge of the patent system.[6] As regards its abolition, Korekiyo Takahashi, the first director of the patent office, held that, firstly, the technological level at that time was too low and high-level inventions were unlikely; secondly, there were no qualified examiners.[7] In other words, the social and technical conditions were not sufficiently developed to allow the patent system.

After the *Monopoly Rules* were abolished, the private sector gradually showed increased willingness to invent. From the abolition of the *Monopoly Rules* in 1872 to the enactment of the *Monopoly Regulations* in 1885, a total of 326 inventions were submitted to officials in various regions.[8] The fifty-six inventions submitted to the Ministry of Industry and the Ministry of Agriculture and Commerce in the same period cover rice grinding, brewing, fiber, chemicals, stationery, measuring instruments, among others.[9] Over 100 inventions of all descriptions could be also seen in other newspapers at the time, including water conservancy machinery, silk reeling machinery, alloys, weapons, vehicles, telecommunications machinery, furniture, papermaking, brewing, agricultural tools, and so on.[10]

During this period, discussions on the formulation of the patent system were carried out in the private sector. In a reader's letter to the *News of the Post* on July 9, 1873, a proposal submitted by Jusuke Kobayashito Tokyo Commercial Law Society suggests granting monopoly rights to rick-shaw inventors. Katsuro Nishimura suggested twice in 1874 to the Right Chamber of Dajōkan that the patent system should be established as soon as possible.[11]

After the *Monopoly Rules* were abolished, the government took a passive attitude toward the establishment of a patent system. As social and techno-logical conditions increasingly matured, the government paid attention to this. Due to frequent changes in the government bodies responsible for this work,[12] legislation was constantly delayed. Finally, a bill was proposed by the Ministry of Agriculture and Commerce in 1884. After being examined by the Minister of Dajōkan, the Bureau of Institutional Investigations, Senate, Chamber of Elders, and others, the *Monopoly Regulations* were announced on April 18, 1885, marking the establishment of the patent system in Japan. The patent law was amended four times prior to World War II, as Japan's patent system gradually matured. Incidentally, several other laws which were related to the industrial ownership system, such as the *Trademark Act* (enacted in 1884), the *Design Act* (enacted in 1888), and the *Utility Model Act* (enacted in 1905) were updated accordingly.

II. The Utility Model Act

As mentioned above, the most salient feature of the Japanese patent system was the *Utility Model Act* enacted in 1905. Although based on a similar law in Germany (1891), it had better force of law than the German prototype. The main difference between the two is shown in the following three respects: First, with regard to the objects of protection, German law covered only "tools or supplies of labor," while Japanese law was extended to cover all industrial products. Second, censorship was not required in Germany but was required in Japan. Third, the force of law of utility models in German law was much weaker than that of patents, while it was almost the same as patents in Japan.

A direct reason for the enactment of the *Utility Model Act* is that Japan saw huge developments in technological innovation after the Russo-Japanese War, but there were some sources before that. The *Monopoly Rules* in 1871 stipulate that the level of inventions is distinguished through the period of protection. At that time, the validity periods of patents included fifteen years, ten years, and seven years. The *Monopoly Regulations* in 1885 also stipulated that the patent periods included five years, ten years, and fifteen years. Although the validity period of patents was extended to fifteen in 1899, the *Utility Model Act* was soon enacted to supersede the validity periods of patents. In general, the protection period for patents is a part relatively subject to policy performance in the patent law. Policy makers could make appropriate amendments based on social, economic, and technical conditions,[13] as evidenced by Japan's experience before the war.[14]

Section 3 Economic interpretation of patent system

Researches on the economic significance of the patent system were carried out long ago.[15] In general, the outcomes of R&D are manifested as information with economic value and have the nature of a certain public product, such as non-competitive consumption and non-exclusive income. In other words, the outcomes from R&D can easily be used by other organizations. It is therefore difficult to attribute all R&D benefits to researchers or developers. This inevitably dampens the enthusiasm of individuals and enterprises for R&D. From another perspective, however, it is beneficial for society as a whole that the outcomes of R&D can be used by more people. This leads to a conflict between the interests of individuals or enterprises and those of society as a whole. In order to solve this problem and reach an appropriate level of R&D activities, it is necessary to bring into play some kind of policy intervention. The patent system was the most effective policy means to address this problem and has now been adopted by countries the world over.[16]

I. Economic theory of big inventions and minor inventions

While giving monopoly power of a certain period to the inventor (or owner) of new technology, the patent system also requires that new technology should be disclosed to the public. In other words, the patent system enables inventors to recoup R&D investment funds on the one hand, while, on the other hand, allows other researchers to engage in competition on the other hand. This is a general function of the patent system. Due to different levels of invention, exclusive possibilities also vary. In 1962, K.J. Arrow pointed out that developers receive different income if the costs after development decrease to varying degrees. This is the discussion on big inventions and minor inventions. A brief introduction is given below.[17]

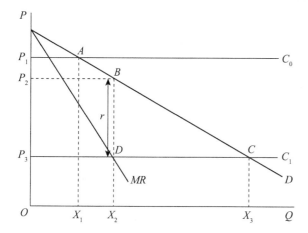

Figure 7.1 Economic significance of large inventions.

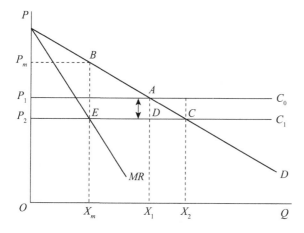

Figure 7.2 Economic significance of minor inventions.

Figures 7.1 and 7.2 show the marginal cost of goods produced by invention decreasing from C_0 to C_1, social benefits, individual benefits of inventors, and consumer surplus. There are two cases: the first case is large inventions, and the second is minor inventions. We first take a look at large inventions. Before invention, price and quantity are determined at point A. Assuming that the marginal cost following inventions falls from C_0 to C_1, the interests of the society as a whole in a competitive market is P_1ACP_3. However, as inventors apply for a patent right to protect their monopoly interests, it is possible to determine the price and quantity at point B. Inventors can obtain personal income of P_2BDP_3 by setting the patent royalties of r. As the market price falls from P_1 to P_2, consumer surplus will rise by P_1ABP_2.

The situation of minor inventions is the same as the former. The price and quantity are determined at point A before invention. It is assumed that the marginal cost after invention decreases from C_0 to C_1. The potential social benefit after invention is P_1ACP_2. When C_0-C_1 is small and the inventor requires monopoly, the expected price is P_m. However, this is higher than the market price. The price after the invention is the same as the price before invention, and is located at P_1. In this case, the benefits obtained by inventors requiring r as the patent royalty is P_1ADP_2, and the consumer surplus does not increase.

II. Our hypothesis

Judging by the theory introduced above, minor inventions yielded greater personal benefits from the protection of the patent system than large inventions. Therefore, we hold that in developing countries like Japan, where the level of R&D is far lower than that of developed countries before the war, the legal protection of minor inventions was often of greater significance. As mentioned earlier, an important feature of the patent system in Japan was the tendency to protect minor inventions. By distinguishing the validity periods of patents in the early stages and by enacting the *Utility Model Act* in the later stages, a great number of minor inventions emerged, especially in traditional industries. This also shows that the patent system in Japan was successful in protecting minor inventions.

Based on the above theory, we propose the following hypothesis: Japanese patents were more conducive to the development of traditional industries before the war. The earlier this favorable situation, the more important it is. In fact, the development of Japanese traditional industries relied on technological innovation to a great extent, which were promoted under the protection of its unique patent system.[18] This was the *Utility Model Act*, which clearly and strongly protected a wealth of minor inventions. Since utility models were chiefly applied to traditional industries, it can be said that the contribution of utility models to traditional industries was not to be sneezed at. If there was no *Utility Model Act*, a cornucopia of technological innovations in traditional industries would be impossible, because these could not be approved as patents and protected by law.

The *Utility Model Act* is identical to patent law in terms of protecting technical thoughts and creations. Therefore, many principles of the patent law can be applied to the *Utility Model Act*, such as the first-to-file system, the disclosure application system, censorship, and the trial system. However, there are many small differences between the two. Table 7.1 enumerates their main differences. As regards the objects of protection, the patent law refers to invention, while the *Utility Model Act* refers to each device. Inventions are defined as "high-caliber technical thought creation through the laws of

Table 7.1 Main differences between Patent Law and the *Utility Model Act*

Item	Patent Law	Utility Model Act
Object of protection	Invention	Device
Advanced	Not easy	Not easy
Application and examination procedures		
① Application and examination fee	Relatively expensive	Cheap
② Request for examination period	Long	Short
③ Methods of applying for disclosure	Complicated	Simple
④ Time for applying for change	Long	Short
⑤ Cooperative application system	Yes	No
⑥ Additional system	Yes	No
Period of right	15 years	10 years

Source: Japanese Patent Office (1955), Japanese Ministry of International Trade and Industry (1964), Kousaku Yoshifuji (1982).

Note: The standards here are based on the 1959 Patent Law and the Utility Model Act.

nature," while devices are defined as "technical thought creation through the laws of nature." The latter does not require a high level (and certainly not low level of protection). With regard to the conditions for the objects of protection, inventions should be novel, of an advanced nature and be applicable to industry. The same is true for devices. However, with regard to the level, invention requires "not easy," but devices require "not too easy." There are other differences in terms of application and examination procedures. The *Utility Model Act* is simpler than patent law.[19]

III. Verification of the hypothesis

In order to verify the above hypothesis, we select three indicators from the actual data that distinguish the level of inventions. The first indicator is the proportion of utility models (the ratio of the number of utility models to the sum of the number of patents and the number of utility models). The meaning of this indicator is twofold: First, because utility models are minor inventions, the higher the proportion, the lower the technological level in this industry. Conversely, the lower the proportion, the higher the technological level in this industry. Second, patents belong to the original core technological innovation, whereas utility models are the imitative auxiliary technological innovation. Core innovation was generally absent in traditional industries, which relied on utility models.

The second indicator is the ratio of Japanese patents (the ratio of the number of Japanese patents to the sum of the number of Japanese patents and the number of foreign patents). The meaning of this is twofold. First, Japanese people did not have the same technical knowledge as foreigners at that time. The higher this indicator, the lower the technical level in this industry, and vice versa. Second, Japanese inventions are in the majority in traditional industries, of course. In modern industries, this indicator means the degree of digestion of imported technology. In other words, the rise in the ratio of Japanese patents in modern industries does not indicate the declining technology level of this industry but, on the contrary, a kind of progress.

The third indicator is the ratio of individual patents (the ratio of the number of individual patents to the sum of the number of individual patents and the number of corporate patents). It can be said that except for some geniuses, individual inventions generally cannot hold a candle to those at a technical level, because modern technology requires a wealth of funds, information and talent. Most large technological innovations are the results of a collective effort.

Three indicators are now used to observe the actual situation in traditional and modern industries.[20] As can be seen from Figure 7.3 and Figure 7.4, each indicator and its change process varies greatly between the two industry groups. The ratio of utility models has been persistently high in traditional industries, but it is gradually rising from a very low level in modern industries. This tendency can be seen from the ratio of Japanese patents. As for the ratio of individual patents, it gradually decreased from its initial high level in both traditional and modern industries, but the degree of decrease varied. The decline was greater in modern industries than in traditional industries.

Through these observations, we can make the following three points: First, before World War II, there was a difference in technological levels between traditional and modern industries, and that modern industries had a higher technological level than traditional industries. Second, there was a wide technological gap between the two industries in the early stage of economic development, which gradually narrowed in the later stages. Third, the narrowing technological gap between the two industries was chiefly characterized by

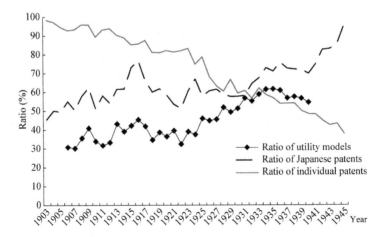

Figure 7.3 Characteristics of technological innovation in modern industries.
Source: (Japan) Patent Office.

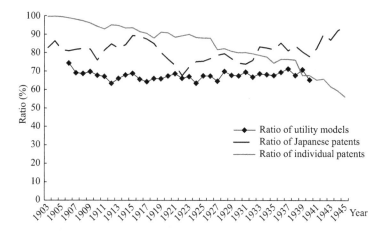

Figure 7.4 Characteristics of technological innovation in traditional industries.
Source: (Japan) Patent Office.

the practicability (increasing ratio of utility models) and independence (increasing ratio of Japanese patents) of technological innovations in the modern industries.

The above views can also be verified by relevant analysis. For example, the correlation coefficient between the ratio of utility models and the ratio of Japanese patents is high (0.745) initially (three-year average from 1906–1908), decreases (0.440) somewhat in the middle period (three-year average from 1922–1924), and nearly disappears (0.154) in the late stage (three-year average from 1938–1940).

IV. The significance and effect of the patent system: Expansion

Through the above investigation, we can sum up the significance and effect of the patent system in Japan. First, the establishment of the patent system in the early days of economic development played a positive role in the development of traditional industries. Even if the *Monopoly Rules* in the early Meiji period were not considered, the 1885 *Monopoly Regulations* were also formulated quite early. As we know, Britain was the first country to formulate the patent system (1624), followed by Germany (1877), the U.S. (1790), and France (1791). Except for Germany, other countries set up the patent system before the start of the modern economic growth. This also indicates in a sense that the industrial revolution occurred in Western Europe and then spread to North America.[21] It is well-known that in the early Meiji period, inventors of rickshaw (1870, three people including Yousuke Izumi), textile machines (1876, Tatchi Gaun) and others sustained huge losses due to a lack of protection from the patent system. These inventions belong to technological innovation in traditional industries instead of large inventions, but they still played a positive role in the economic development of Japan at that time. Second, the patent system in a developing country serves the function of obtaining technical information from advanced countries. Japan joined the *Paris Treaty* in 1899, after which foreign inventions can be examined in Japan and received the same protection. In this way, Japanese technicians were inspired by the foreign technology, which then allowed them to undertake imitative innovation.[22] Third, thanks to the *Utility Model Act*, minor inventions can be protected to the greatest extent possible in Japan. In the early stage of economic development when the technological level is low, this institutional innovation is a wise move and should deserve high praise and evaluation.

The author tries to expand the scope of application discussed here. Generally speaking, in the early stage of economic development when technological level and R&D capabilities are low, the technological knowledge and information held by the country are more focused on traditional industries. During this period, the protection and preferential treatment for the low-quality but numerous minor inventions have immense significance and effect. However, as technological level and R&D capabilities improve, technical knowledge is gradually transferred to modern industries. At this time, the policies should be adjusted in a timely manner. According to Figure 7.5,

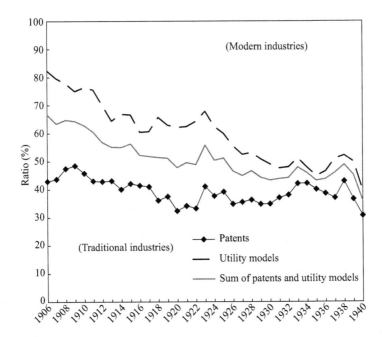

Figure 7.5 The importance of inventions in traditional and modern industries.

Source: (Japan) Patent Office.

Note: Ratio = (number of patents in traditional industries + number of granted utility models) ÷ (number of all patents + number of utility models) × 100%.

the total number of patents and utility models plunged from 66.6% in 1906 to 36.0% in 1940. Patents also fell from 42.9% to 30.7%. albeit to a small degree. The utility models nosedived from 82.4% to 39.6%. Seismic change occurred in traditional and modern industries in just thirty-five years. Judging by the changes in technology, Japan's modern industries replaced traditional industries as the mainstay of technological innovation in the first half of the twentieth century.

Section 4 The evaluation of related policies

With regard to the policy intervention of R&D, there are different types other than the patent system. First, the government directly engaged in R&D via national universities and research institutes. Second, support was given to various non-governmental research institutes, such as tax relief, provision of information and funding. Third, a number of private research institutes jointly carried out R&D on certain projects. However, this did not play a leading role in Japan before World War II. The methods below were more common.

I. Invention Expo

Since the early Meiji period, various expositions and Competitive Exhibitions were held frequently throughout Japan. As part of the government's shokusan kogyo, these expos played a positive role in the industry development at that time. Yukihiko Kiyokawa held that these expos served two functions, namely evaluation and public effect.[23] These two functions contributed to popularizing technology. On the one hand, the patent system offers legal protection to the outcomes of technological innovation; on the other hand, it requires that new technologies should be made available to the public. The two policies were originally contradictory. However, Japan gave full play to the two roles before the war. This policy was the Invention Expo.

Various expos and Competitive Exhibitions, chiefly industrial expos, reached a climax at the end of the Meiji period, which was at a low ebb and replaced by the patent system. During the replacement period (1909–1932), a total of four invention expos were held. While it is smaller than other representative expos in scale at the time, its exhibits were all new inventions such as patents and utility models. It is on a par with other fairs in terms of effect.[24] These four invention expos were hosted by the Japanese Invention Association. The government began to host such expos after the 1930s. From 1933–1943, Japan's Patent Office held 11 invention exhibitions, as well as many other professional (such as electrical and chemical) expos and exhibitions. Like other expos or exhibitions, these also carried out evaluation and review events, and held seminars, lectures, and so on, with a view to popularizing scientific knowledge and promoting technological innovation.

II. Reward policy for inventions

The award policy for inventions closely related to the patent system includes, inter alia, the commendation system, the subsidy system, and the patent right extension system. As a kind of commendation system, the medal system had been established according to the Medals Regulations of 1882; the government congratulated those who had made a contribution and awarded blue medals to inventors. Nevertheless, the Blue Medal had a wide scope of application. Before World War II, 2,000 people received this honor, including twenty-eight inventors. It can be seen that, at the time, people's interest in invention and the level of invention were relatively low. It also reflects the difficulty in evaluating inventions. Some well-known inventors who received this award included Tatchi Gaun (1882), Sakiti Toyoda (1911), Kishi Keijirou (1918), Naosaburo Minorikawa (1928), Tadaoki Mitsumoto (1944), Riiti Satake (1944), among others.

Another relevant policy is the patent right extension system, which was established in 1909 under British influence. However, Britain's purpose was to consider the interests of inventions and grant for losses resulting from the war, while Japan attached greater importance to the interests of the country. For example, "secret patents" related to military secrets could be extended unconditionally. Despite some drawbacks, this system had a certain role. Before World War II, a total of 112 inventions were approved for extension, including world-famous inventions such as the "automatic shuttle change device" by Sakiti Toyoda, the "calculating rule" by Jiro Henmi, the "steam generator" by Tsunekiti Takuma, and "special alloy steel" by Koutaro Honda.

III. Japanese Invention Association

Japan Invention Association was renamed in 1910 from the Industrial Ownership Protection Association founded in 1904, and it was inherited by the Corporation Invention Association after the war. At that time, it undertook rich and colorful activities, but one of its principal tasks was to issue commendations to inventors at both national and local level. Commendation is divided into the national commendation and local commendation. Some of the earliest to receive national commendation were Yuiti Torihaku, Etaro Yokohama and Masajiro Kitamura (inventors of the "TYK wireless telephone") (1911). Five national commendations were issued before the war. These were as follows: 106 inventions in the second commendation event (1926), 345 in the third (1933), 293 in the fourth (1938), and 162 in the fifth (1944), totaling over 900. A total of 1,278 people received local commendations during this time.[25]

Section 5 Concluding remarks

From the above analysis, the following conclusions can be drawn: First, the Japanese patent system had a salient feature, namely the *Utility Model Act* enacted in 1905. In addition to Japan, it had implications for many countries after World War II, including China.[26] Second, as the *Utility Model Act* helped protect minor inventions, it played an irreplaceable role in technological innovation in traditional industries and its industrial development. Third, the significance and effect of the patent system underwent a great many changes as the economy developed. Emphasis is given to two points here: One is the reversal of the roles of patents and utility models in traditional and modern industries. The earlier the role of the utility model in traditional industries, the more important it was. The later the role of patents in modern industries, the more prominent it was. As the level of technology improved, the significance of protecting minor inventions weakened. Fourth, technical policies played a positive role in the effective implementation of the patent system, which helped to guarantee it.

Notes

1 Since the 1980s, Japan has ranked first in the number of patent applications each year, which far outnumbered those in other developed countries. For example, in 2000, patent applications in Japan reached 437,000, which is twice as many as the U.S., and far more than those in other developed countries such as Germany. Recently, China has ranked first in the world in the number of patent applications. Economic development can be seen from the perspective of patents. Although the patent systems and technological levels vary in different countries, it cannot be measured by quantity alone.

2 (Japan's) Patent Office (1955).

3 (Japan's) Patent Office (1955).

4 Research on Japan's policy on technology includes: Tetsu Hiroshige (1973), Hoshimi Uchida (1986), Juro Hashimoto (1994). A comprehensive introduction to the Japanese patent system includes: the Japanese Patent Office (1955), the Ministry of International Trade and Industry (1964), Kazuo Ichikawa (1965), and the Japanese Patent Office (1984–1985).

5 Almost promulgated at the same time as the *Monopoly Rules; Law of Household Registration.*

6 Fukuzawa Yukichi introduced the Western patent system in *Conditions in the West* (Vol 3) (1867) based on what he saw and heard during his second trip (1861–1962). In 1867, Takahira Kanda wrote a thesis entitled "Privately speaking on protecting meridians" in the fourth volume of *Journal of Western Countries*, advocating the necessity of setting up a patent system. Other people, including Itirou Watanabe and Fumio Murata also discussed the significance of the Western patent system. For details, see the Ministry of International Trade and Industry (1964) and Kazuo Ichikawa (1965).

7 Korekiyo Takahashi (1936), pp. 218–219.

8 Toshiro Tamura (1988–1989).

9 Japanese Ministry of International Trade and Industry (1964), pp. 90–91.

10 Kohachi Nakamura (1944), p. 24; Kazuo Ichikawa (1965), p. 31–34.

11 For details, see the Ministry of International Trade and Industry (Japan) (1964), pp. 82–86; Kazuo Ichikawa (1965), pp. 35–47.

12 In 1878, it changed from the Ministry of Internal Affairs to the Ministry of Finance, and then to the Ministry of Agriculture and Commerce in 1881.

13 Kazuo Ichikawa (1965), p. 23.

14 Incidentally, the term of validity of patents varies from country to country, most commonly between 15 and 20 years. The shortest term among developed countries is Japan (15 years), followed by Britain (16 years), the U.S. (17 years), Germany (18 years), and France (20 years).

15 Much discussion is focused on the economic significance of the patent system. Machlup (1958), Arrow (1962), and Nordhaus (1969) et al. looked at the early stages while Kaufer (1989) later conducted comprehensive review.

16 Many problems exist in the patent system, including the following points. First, even if the patent system is brought into play, it is hard to solve all the problems of technological innovation. Second, the functions of the patent system cannot be fully used as the system per se has defects. Third, problems exist in the implementation. See Yuki Kamitaka (1984), pp. 105–116.

17 The introduction here is based on Arrow (1962), Nordhaus (1969), Kenichi Imai et al. (1972), and Takayuki Kami (1984).

18 The part about Japan in this book is by Guan Quan (2003). By comparing modern and traditional industries, it stresses the importance of the development of traditional industries from the perspective of technological innovation.

19 Kousaku Yoshifuji (1982), pp. 484–497.

20 The distinction between traditional and modern industries is based on Guan Quan (1997) and Chapter 2 of the book.

21 According to the research by Kuznets, the beginning of modern economic growth in countries was as follows: from 1765 to 1785 in Britain, from 1831 to 1840 in France, from 1834 to 1843 in the U.S., and from 1850 to 1859 in Germany. For details, see Kuznets (1999), Ryoushin Minami (1981).

22 As regards this point, different opinions hold that if a country did not join *The Treaty of Paris*, any imitation of advanced foreign technology will not be punished. However, the higher the technology level, the harder it was to imitate. Instead, it made developed countries more vigilant, and as a result, it became more difficult to introduce technology.

23 See Yukihiko Kiyokawa (1995).

24 The overview of the four invention expos is as follows: at the first expo, held in 1909, there were 1,175 exhibits and 502 exhibitors; at the second, held in 1914, there were 2,634 exhibits and 953 exhibitors; at the third, held in 1923, there were 4,128 exhibits and 1,012 exhibitors; at the fourth, held in 1932, there were 6,137 exhibits and 1,352 exhibitors. Incidentally, an introduction was given to the chief expos held during this period. At the Tokyo Industrial Expo, held in 1907, there were 93,854 exhibits and 14,876 exhibitors; at the Tokyo Taisho Expo, held in 1914, there were 160,293 exhibits and 65,102 exhibitors; at the Peace Memorial Expo, held in 1922, there were 141,016 exhibits and 75,074 exhibitors; at the Memorial Expo, held in 1928, there were 82,433 exhibits and 9,127 exhibitors. See Mitsuo Yamamoto (1973).

25 Japan Institute of Invention and Innovation (1974), pp. 190–192.

26 Before World War II, only Germany and Japan had passed a *Utility Model Act*. Many countries, including China, Italy, Australia, Brazil, Mexico, the Philippines, and South Korea, adopted this system after the war.

Part IV

Cases of innovation and development

8 Traditional industry

The rise and fall of the rickshaw industry

Section 1 Introduction

In this chapter, the author discusses the development of modern industries in Japan. Here, rickshaws transporting machinery, bicycles, and automobiles are selected. These three industries have seen a process development and change, representing an important part of the development of modern industries in Japan. Because the machinery sector is pivotal in industrialization, the development of the machinery sector represents in large measure the level of industrial development in a country. Although the machinery industry in modern Japan is not as developed as European and American countries and is smaller than the textile and food sectors, it is at the heart of industrial development.[1]

The three industries selected here have their own features. Invented by the Japanese during the Meiji period, the rickshaw could be said to be an innovative Japanese product. Popular in the Japanese market, it was also exported to China and many other Asian countries, becoming a crucial mode of transport. Moreover, it was the only export product in the machinery industry during the Meiji period. Of course, due to the growing popularity of bicycles, rickshaws were eventually replaced, and the industry gradually vanished.

Bicycles were invented by the Germans in the early nineteenth century. Later, following improvements by inventors in Britain and other countries, bicycles gradually became to an industry in the mid-nineteenth century and spread to Japan and other countries. Invented around the Meiji Restoration (1868), rickshaws were a tremendously popular mode of transportation throughout the Meiji period. In other words, while bicycles beat rickshaws in many ways, rickshaws also had their own unique advantages. They could carry passengers and serve as public transport, while bicycles did not have this function. Moreover, although bicycles caught on all over the world, they did not become popular in Japan before the end of the nineteenth century due to a lack of technology. However, the industry developed apace, and by 1937, it had become Japan's number one export in the machinery and appliances sector.[2]

Automobiles were invented in the mid-nineteenth century. Due to the complex structure and rigorous technical requirements, the industry was only developed in countries with great technical reserves, such as those in Western European. The U.S. did not mass-produce automobiles until the twentieth century. By comparison, this sector developed much later in Japan. Of course, due to its rapidly growing modern industries, Japan did produce automobiles as early as the early twentieth century, it just took longer for the automobile industry to be established. For this reason, Ford and General Motors, two major American automobile giants, began to set up plants in Japan in 1925 and 1926, respectively. However, the Japanese government expelled the two American companies from the Japanese market around 1936, using laws and policies they had formulated. In 1936, Toyota and Nissan, two Japanese car makers, were established, and Japan started to fast track its automobile sector. In fact, Japan was able to produce trucks, chiefly sedans, before that. However, the Japanese auto industry did not truly become globally competitive until after World War II, especially after the 1980s, due to domestic consumption levels and production technology problems. Japan is now a veritable auto powerhouse.

This chapter studies the relationship between the development and technological innovation in the rickshaw sector, one of the representatives of traditional industries. The reason for this has three aspects: First, this industry took shape based on the improvement in traditional Japanese technology. In this sense, it is a typical traditional industry, although it was born and took shape during the early Meiji period. Second, throughout the modern period (1868–1945), this industry underwent the entire process from its emergence to its demise. Therefore, the rickshaw sector is a very special "transitional industry." It played a transition role from traditional society to modern society. Third, this industry is not merely a simple traditional industry, as it played a pivotal role in the early days of industrialization. As the only mode of transport invented by the Japanese, rickshaws helped people get about more easily, promoted the emergence and development of an industry, and also became an important export commodity. However, few people have studied this industry to date. This chapter can be viewed as the only research outcome from the perspective of economics and industrial development. Previously, research was geared to the history of transportation. The author mainly examines the entire rickshaw sector from R&D to formation, growth, and decline. At the same time, the reasons for these changes are examined, especially the role of technological innovation and the market.

We take a look at the changing process of the rickshaw sector. Figure 8.1 shows the changes in the production, export, and domestic demand for rickshaws. On the whole, it shows an inverted U shape, first rising and then decreasing. This is true of production, export, and domestic demand. Domestic demand fell earlier while exports decreased much later, indicating that it increasingly met the needs of foreign markets. It is very different from changes in other industries in this regard and is more in line with the development model of traditional industries in Japan. The production volume started at 1,000 (1871) to begin with, hit a peak of 28,000 (1915), and finally fell to 300 (1945). The number of exports began to increase from 82 in 1880. After

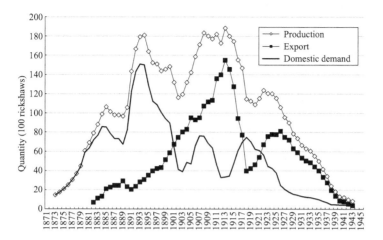

Figure 8.1 Production, export and domestic demand of rickshaws.
Source: Takao Shimano (1980).

Note: Domestic demand = production volume-export.

reaching 20,000 in 1915, growth remained sluggish, and by 1945 only 100 were exported. In terms of the difference between production and export in this industry, it peaked at 22,000 vehicles in 1893. Due to the time lag between domestic demand and export, the production volume saw two peaks. In the 1890s, production mainly met domestic demand. After the domestic demand saturated, exports gradually became the engine of production. Another characteristic of this industry is the lack of imports, and, as such, it can be judged as a traditional industry. As can be seen from Figure 9.1, this industry basically ran through the entire modern period, basically coming to an end at the end of World War II. This is a rare phenomenon. We call it a temporary or transitional supplement. It is a temporary product which appears when there is demand but no supply before the real modern industries were introduced. It lasted for over 80 years in Japan, and is still in use in some countries.[3]

Section 2 The development and decline of the rickshaw industry

I. Invention and popularization of rickshaws

After the Meiji Restoration, industrialization took place in various industries in Japan, including both traditional and modern industries. Traditional industries made a greater contribution in the earlier stages, in particular. Generally, traditional industries refer to industries that existed before modern times, such as silk reeling, food, and weaving. Individual industries took shape after modern times. A case in point is the rickshaw sector.[4] Before the Meiji Restoration, the Japanese basically got about by walking, supplemented by horse- and ox-drawn carriages, and sedan chairs. During the Tokugawa

Shogunate era, the Japanese government imposed harsh restrictions on traffic by setting up checkpoints everywhere, which greatly impeded the development of transportation.[5] After the Meiji Restoration, these restrictions were lifted, and some new modes of transportation, such as horse-drawn carriages and railways were imported. Especially, railways became the mainstream mode of transportation. However, due to its huge investment and large area, railways were not suitable for urban transportation. In this context, Yousuke Izumiet al. invented the rickshaw in 1869, obtained a manufacturing license the following year, and then launched their business. This simple, clean, and convenient mode of transportation soon caught on throughout the country, because rickshaws required simple production techniques, and could be made by a great many blacksmiths or carpenters. The development of the Japanese economy indicated a huge demand for transportation, which promoted the popularization of rickshaws and the industry development.[6] As the economy developed and urbanization intensified, people had more opportunities to use transportation. In the era when convenient transportation was not available, rickshaws became the favorite mode of transport at the time, and even spread to China and other Asian countries.

It is generally believed that rickshaws were invented by Yousuke Izumi, Tokujiro Suzuki, and Takayama Kosukei. In 1870, they applied to the relevant authorities of Tokyo Prefecture for the license to manufacture and operate rickshaws. It is generally recognized that the invention of rickshaws was inspired by wheelbarrow and carriages. Few people used rickshaws when Yousuke Izumi obtained the permit to manufacture and operate rickshaws, but they emerged all over the country within a few years. According to statistics, there were 114,000 rickshaws nationwide in 1875. Assuming that scrapped cars are not included, the average annual increase should be 23,000 vehicles in five years. In 1883, the number reached 170,000. At this time, there were 1,680 rickshaw makers nationwide, each one of whom made eight rickshaws per year.[7] According to the earliest statistics on rickshaws in the *Provincial and County Tables of Products in the 7th Year of the Meiji Period*, in 1874, two-thirds (31) of forty-six prefectures proper, urban prefectures and circuit (excluding Okinawa) nationwide produced rickshaws, with an output of 20,000.[8]

In this way, rickshaws and their production technology caught on across the country. There were two reasons for this. First, rickshaw technology was relatively simple in the early stages, it amounted to no more than a modification to the existing design for wheelbarrows. A great many carpenters who made wheelbarrows could make rickshaws. Second, at a time when the patent system had not been established, technical imitation was not considered an illegal act.

Two months after Yousuke Izumi obtained a manufacturing permit, the operation of rickshaws carrying four persons from Kyobashi to Mura Namamugi was approved. Rickshaw operation was launched for the route from Yokohama to Fujisawa in October of the same year, the route from Kanagawa to Kawasaki in November, and the route from Kawasaki to

Fujisawa the following January. Yousuke Izumiet al. also launched operations in Yokohama and there were two rickshaw operators in Nagoya in March 1871. They operated 34 rickshaw business places in prominent areas in the city. From 1872 to 1873, Yoshibe Hotta and Jinnsuke Iwatsu, who were blacksmiths, began to produce rickshaws.

The rickshaw spread to Osaka six months after the Tokyo rickshaw manufacturing permit was granted. In December 1870, Osaka Prefecture enacted the rules for operating rickshaws. The movement of rickshaws from Tokyo to Osaka can be regarded as the beginning of the popularity of rickshaws nationwide, as, shortly afterwards, Osaka became the second largest supply area of rickshaws after Tokyo, supplying them to such areas as Kinki, Shikoku, and Kyushu. In fact, by 1874, Osaka had become a production base on a par with Tokyo. In Kyoto, Sadajiro Inoue, who was a carpenter, obtained a business license in January 1871 and began to produce rickshaws. By1872, there were 1,581 rickshaws operating under the jurisdiction of Kyoto Prefecture. Nara and Okayama also purchased rickshaws from Osaka. Fukuoka formulated rules for the operations of rickshaws and trucks in April 1872. Operation of rickshaws began in Niigata Prefecture and Ishikawa Prefecture in 1871, and in Shimane Prefecture, Kagoshima Prefecture, Aomori Prefecture, and Akita Prefecture in 1873.[9]

As rickshaws became more popular, they replaced traditional sedan chairs. The first issue of *News Magazine*, issued in May 1871, stated that "there are about 25,000 rickshaws in Tokyo, and 25,000 people are required if one person pulls each rickshaw. Previously, there were 10,000 sedan chairs and 20,000 people were required if a sedan chair is carried by two persons. By this calculation, a number of 5,000 passengers can be added. While one third of sedan chairs still remains, the growth rate of rickshaws is staggering. This shows that rickshaws have a lower fee and faster speed than sedan chairs. This is after all the great power of machinery." Two-thirds of sedan chairs, namely 7,000, were replaced by rickshaws in just one year.[10]

The fact that sedan chairs were replaced by rickshaws can also be seen from other sources. The *Japanese Statistical Yearbook* records the number of rickshaws by region from 1886–1888. The vehicles used to carry passengers include sedan chairs, rickshaws, and horse-drawn carriages. In 1887, the rickshaw accounted for 95.7% on average (approximately 74,388) nationwide. The number of sedan chairs (1,946) barely outnumbered those for carriages (1,372). Rickshaws had completely replaced sedan chairs in less than fifteen years.[11] The reasons for this are probably the progress of the times, in addition to high cost[12] and slow speed of sedan chairs. As sedan chairs were carried by people, the bearers served passengers with their physical strength. Although they are being pulled, rickshaws are supported by wheels, which brings together the relationship between the passenger and the puller. Nevertheless, we argue that the decline of the rickshaw lies in the inequality in a sociological sense, because it is an unequal means of transport when compared to bicycles or cars.

II. Growth of the rickshaw industry

As mentioned in the preceding section, imitation occurred in various places as rickshaws spread throughout the country, indicating that rickshaws resulted in a new popular industry. This came into being naturally, and this characteristic also determined the subsequent development of this industry. This is a balance between the potential demand for rickshaws and production technology (supply).

It can be observed from Figure 8.1 that the rickshaw sector saw rapid development in the 1890s, and maintained this momentum until the outbreak of World War I (1914). Moreover, its growth in the early stages was chiefly driven by domestic demand and gradually driven by exports. The growth of domestic demand in was supported by demand and supply. On the demand side, Figures 8.2 and 8.3 show the correlation between urbanization and the number of rickshaws. Rickshaws were the chief mode of transportation in cities. The higher the urban population ratio, the greater the demand for rickshaws. Generally, urban income is higher than rural income, and this relationship can be reflected in regional disparities. The domestic demand for rickshaws began to fall in 1889, but external demand continued to rise in 1898, showing a high positive correlation relationship.[13] Even in 1909, when demand for rickshaws began to fall, it showed a high positive correlation relationship. In other words, the regions with intensified urbanization had a stronger demand for rickshaws, because urbanization meant a high population density and good road conditions. Of course, it should not be forgotten that the higher income in cities compared to rural areas is also one reason.[14] This shows that rickshaws were suited to the social environment at that time as a mode of transportation in cities. This also created demand factor for the rapid development of the rickshaw sector in this period.

What about the supply perspective? The earliest data shows a total number of 20,154 rickshaws, as stated in the *Provincial and County Tables of Products in the 7th Year of the Meiji Period* above. At this time (1874), just four years since the rickshaw was approved for operation, two-thirds of prefectures and counties were producing them. Tokyo (5,858 rickshaws) and Osaka (4,248 rickshaws) account for about half of the total number nationwide, which is also a major feature of this sector. Compared to other regions, consumption level and production capacity was high in these two regions.[15]

As rickshaw technology was relatively simple in the early stage, ordinary carpenters could produce them. However, as rickshaws caught on, people made improvements, and their design and structure became more complicated. The aforesaid *Provincial and County Tables of Products in the 7th Year of the Meiji Period* shows the manufacturers of various parts of rickshaws, such as metal appliances, wheels, iron tools, cages, and pulling bars. Moreover, the names of some parts and components were recorded in the exhibit catalogue of the Third Domestic Industrial Expo in 1890, indicating that the contract system had been adopted for the production forms of rickshaws in the early stages.

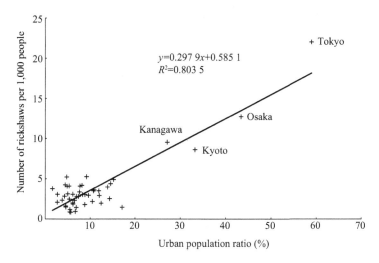

Figure 8.2 Relationship between urban population ratio and the number of rickshaws (1889).

Source: Mataji Umemura, Nobukiyo Takamatsu, and Shigeru Ito (1983).

Note: The figure is the 5-year moving average.

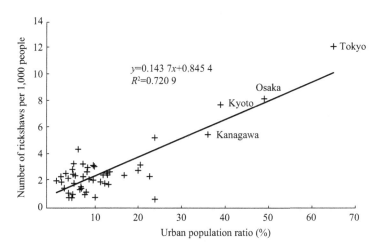

Figure 8.3 Relationship between urban population ratio and the number of rickshaws (1909).

Source: Mataji Umemura, Nobukiyo Takamatsu, and Shigeru Ito (1983).

Note: The figure is the 5-year moving average.

At the Fifth Domestic Industrial Expo in 1903, labor within the industry was further subdivided, and diversified parts and components were produced. Of the 41 producers, 27 were manufacturers of parts and components. In the mature period, a rickshaw was composed of 573 parts, including carriage, wheels, frame, and hood.[16] It was produced by division of labor and then assembled. At this time, the production was basically achieved through the contracting system. For example, Ito Store, which specialized in exporting rickshaws, made its own cages and spray paints, as well as assembly. Each division produced products using the piece-rate system in which masters guided their apprentices. The Inoue shop was four kilometers away from most of its contractors.[17] The *Factory Overview* 1909 included twenty-one rickshaw manufacturers, with a ratio of 12:9 for complete rickshaw manufacturers to parts manufacturers. At this time, the only factory with power equipment was the parts producer. The average number of employees was 5–6, which also included large plants such as Osuke Akiha (55). By region, there were 13 enterprises in Tokyo, and many parts factories were dotted throughout Sakai (city) in the Osaka region. As Sakai had previously been a region which produced cannons, this demonstrated the advances in metal processing.

III. Decline of the rickshaw industry

In fact, the decline of the rickshaw sector can be seen in Figure 8.1. Domestic demand began to grow in 1893, and exports began to decline in 1915. These two points in time illustrate the decline of the sector from different aspects. That the rickshaw industry went downhill gradually is due in large measure to the development of other modes of transportation such as bicycles. Figure 8.4 shows the process of bikes replacing rickshaws. The rickshaw ownership ratio (1) had gradually been decreasing since the 1890s, and had plunged rapidly in the first decade of the twentieth century. This coincides with the growth period of bicycles, so it can be concluded that the changes are caused by their development. The change in rickshaw ownership ratio (2) is about 20 years later than ratio (1), starting to decline gradually in the 1920s. This is due to the popularity of automobiles. In other words, in the absence of the development of bicycles, the decline of rickshaws might have been delayed for twenty years.[18] Incidentally, carriage use began late in the second decade of the twentieth century, and then gradually withdrew from the market during the subsequent decade. According to Figure 8.4, were it not for bicycles, horse-drawn carriage would have been replaced by automobiles earlier than rickshaws.

The export of rickshaws continued to grow until the outbreak of World War I, and then began to decline. One reason is that countries such as China also began to produce rickshaws. The overwhelming majority of exports went to China in the early days, but this did not last, accounting for only 10% after 1890. Exports to India (then ruled by Britain), Hong Kong, and other regions grew rapidly. Exports to Hong Kong also declined at an earlier stage, but exports to India lasted until around 1900. It was during this period that exports to Malaysia and Singapore (then a British colony) began to rise, and

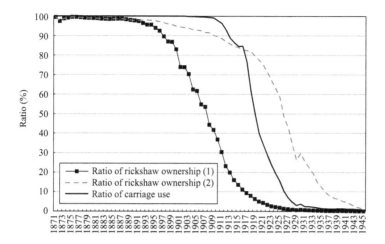

Figure 8.4 The decline process of rickshaws and carriages.

Source: Takao Shimano (1980).

Notes:
1 The denominator of rickshaw ownership ratio (1) includes rickshaw, bicycle, carriage, coach, tricycle, automobile;
2 The denominator of the rickshaw ownership ratio (2) removes the bicycle from the items of ratio (1);
3 The denominator of the carriage use ratio is carriage, coach, and automobiles.

occupied a high proportion thereafter. This change in the import, export, and production of rickshaws resembles the flying geese paradigm for an industry to develop in a country. From the perspective of Japan, an advanced country in East Asia at the time, this change is consistent with the view on product life cycle. In other words, rickshaws were originally developed by Japan as a mode of transport. When domestic demand reached saturation, rickshaws were exported to China. When China could produce rickshaws independently, rickshaws were exported to India and Southeast Asian countries with lower-level technology. Gradually, Japan lost its comparative advantage, with its rickshaws being replaced by products from countries such as China.

As rickshaws can be produced using simple technology, its production started early in China. Rickshaws were produced in as early as 1871, and exports to Southeast Asia began in around 1880. According to the inspection records in China by second-generation Osuke Akiha, many producers in Tianjin, Beijing, and Hong Kong, especially Shanghai, had over 100 producers.[19] There are few records on China's rickshaw industry, but the ownership in China is estimated at 293,000 in 1933, with an output of 59,000 rickshaws and 560,000 rickshaw pullers.[20] This is a not an insignificant industry. There are also few data records on the export of Chinese rickshaws. It can be confirmed that annual exports reached 2,000 and 7,000 Haiguan tael from 1914 to 1925.[21]

Section 3 Content and significance of technical innovation

I. Content of technological innovation

(1) Content of technological innovation

As mentioned earlier, the invention of rickshaws was inspired by wheelbarrows and carriages. Like other inventions, rickshaws left a lot to be desired at first. The early rickshaws were very amateurish, like a chair with a pulling bar on a wheelbarrow. Later, thanks to the efforts of people like Osuke Akiha, rickshaws gradually became a safe and comfortable mode of transport. Their main structure and related technologies are introduced below.[22]

Chassis body: In 1870, a rickshaw had four pillars on the body, covered with a hood like a dustpan. In 1871, a tumbler shape appeared, alongside rickshaws with cloth screens and springs. At this time, rickshaws with dustpan and a hood were in the majority. Later, Osuke Akiha, inspired by horse-drawn carriages, invented boat-shaped rickshaws. In addition, a rickshaw originally carried one person, however two-seater rickshaws appeared a few years later. By 1888, such rickshaws were in the majority.

Wheels: The center of the wheel of a rickshaw is called the hub, which is made of round wood and encircled by spokes. Spokes connect the wheels and the hub. The outside of the wheel is made of curved planks called a wheel plate. These wooden wheels were replaced by iron wheels in around 1907 and later replaced by rubber wheels. According to some statistics, 90 percent of the 154,000 rickshaws in 1912 had changed from iron to rubber wheels.[23] In the same year, solid tires were replaced by pneumatic tires, and this replacement was basically complete by 1914.

Pulling bar: There were two types of pulling bars to begin with. One was straight, while the other was slightly curved. The part held by the hand curved upwards slightly. To support the handles upon touching the ground, Osuke Akiha installed a curved appliance like a trunk on its front end in around 1880.

Fenders: Early rickshaws hardly had fenders. After 1871, improvements were made to a few existing fenders, which changed from the original flat type to slightly rounded fenders.

Springs: Springs were installed on rickshaws in about 1871. It is said that this was also Osuke Akiha's idea. Wood shavings were used to soften the shock before springs were installed. To begin with, springs resembled a rhombus with two pine leaves facing each other, but gradually round springs were used. A special spring was used using the Taisho period (1912–1925).

Hoods: Fukuzawa Yukichi brought a pram with a hood from the U.S. in 1867. Inspired by this, Kanzaemon Utida invented a hood for rickshaws. To begin with, the hood did not have spring that opened and closed. Instead, the canvas was tied to several pillars with ropes. It is said that the hood with springs was invented by Osuke Akiha around 1875 by using oilpaper. The exhibit in the Second Domestic Industrial Expo, in 1881 adopted this hood. Hoods made of rubber also appeared around 1880.

As mentioned above, technological innovations and improvements were made from various perspectives in various ways to meet the explosive demand, so that rickshaws, as a new mode of transportation, reached maturity in a short period of time. While these technological innovations were not epoch-making, it can be imagined that without them, the rickshaw sector would have been greatly weakened.

(2) Technological innovators

We cannot talk about the production and technological innovation of rickshaws without mentioning Osuke Akiha. First-generation Osuke Akiha was born in Edo (later Tokyo) in 1843. His family made and sold military and horse equipment, and he later became the foster son of carpenter Simousa Yasukei Saburou. In the early years of the Meiji period, he saw Western horse-drawn carriages, so he bought several carriages for operation on the route between Tokyo and Kawasaki. Business was booming and he employed eighty people. He cooperated with Mitsubishi Steamship, and for a long time operated thirty vessels in the area of Go Rokuro. While Yousuke Izumi and others invented the rickshaw, and applied for a permit for mass produc-tion, Osuke Akiha set up Akiha Shoten. Soon afterwards, he began making rickshaws, focusing on their improvement. At that time, the body of a rick-shaw was relatively crude and ugly. He bought devices, painted the rickshaw body, and installed springs on the axles. The shape of rickshaws was improved with reference to Western carriages. Cloth or leather screens were used to dec-orate inside the body. Various parts of the body were equipped with metal decoration. The hood was supported by springs, and trunk-type devices were installed in front of the pulling bar. He also invented fenders and wheels for two-seater rickshaws. His rickshaw was called "Osuke Akiha" in Osaka, and it won the Phoenix Design Award at the First Domestic Industrial Expo in 1877. He won the third prize at the Second Industrial Expo in 1881 and the Third Industrial Expo in 1890. He was active in the industry as the general representative of rickshaw manufacturing in Tokyo.

Second-generation Osuke Akiha was born in 1877 to a family of soy sauce makers in Chiba Prefecture. As the second boy in the family, he was named Shinji. When the first-generation Osuke Akiha passed away in 1895, he was fresh from Yokohama Eiwaku Gakko and was admitted to Tokyo Business School. In 1897 he became the foster son of the Osuke Akiha family, and adopted the name of Osuke. As he had received a modern education, he adopted a proactive business strategy and was proficient at using news and advertising. He won first prize at the Fifth Domestic Industrial Expo in 1903 and the Tokyo Industrial Expo in 1907. He also made several unsuccessful forays into rubber, automobiles, coal and other fields. His company had 115 employees in 1909 and 250 in 1910. These additional employees were basically hired to tap new fields. In 1920, he changed his personally-run business into a corporation (stock company) to improve business. However, he was dealt a hammer blow in the Tokyo earthquake in 1923, and never recovered.

There are also some strong performers in the rickshaw field, such as Kunitaro Unoue, Takesaburo Ito, Yasuyoshi Miyagi, Tozaburo Seiga, and Kiyoyoshi Wasa. In addition to production and export, they also made technical improvements to rickshaws. For example, Kiyoyoshi Wasa obtained No. 18444 utility model in 1910, Kunitaro Unoue obtained No. 28720 in 1913, Takesaburo Ito obtained No. 33497 in 1914, and Osuke Akiha obtained No. 34418 in 1915. Moreover, Eisuke Miyata (No. 15921 in 1910) and Rikiti Sumi (No. 14765 in 1909), who were highly active in the bicycle field, also obtained utility models for rickshaws.

II. The significance of technological innovation

(1) Contribution to industrial development

New means of transport emerged in the early Meiji period, including the railways, horse-drawn carriages, and rickshaws. These were all imports, except for rickshaws. These means of transportation saw rapid development for a considerable period of time, but carriages and rickshaws gradually declined after World War I. At the same time, bicycles began to develop rapidly in about the last decade of the nineteenth century, while buses, sedans, and motorcycles began to develop apace in 1920. The thirty years from 1870–1900 is an era of steam engine-powered railways, horse-drawn carriages, and hand-pulled rickshaws. These three modes of land transportation performed their respective tasks for the transportation of passengers: the railway for long-distance transport, carriages for medium distances, and rickshaws for short distances. However, this pattern was broken by the emergence and development of popular bicycles and automobiles. After the Russo-Japanese War, bicycles began to overtake rickshaws. In the 1920s, automobiles began to overtake carriages. In other words, bicycles replaced rickshaws, and automobiles replaced carriages.[24] Since then, the three modes of transportation—railway, automobile and bicycle—have been the main forms of passenger transport.[25]

In this way, the means of passenger transportation changed from rickshaws, carriages, and railways to bicycles, automobiles, and railways in the Taisho period (1912–1925). The contribution of rickshaws to industrial development tallies with the consumption structure and capital accumulation of the Japanese people during the Meiji period (1868–1911) and the Taisho era. During the early Meiji period, the government had to borrow money from foreign countries to build the railways. In this sense, the invention and popularization of rickshaws are of great significance. Conversely, in the absence of the invention and use of rickshaws and ensuing improvements, the balance of passenger transport would have been broken, or their efficiency would have been compromised, because rickshaws were more efficient than sedan chairs. Moreover, given the inadequate railway capacity and people's limited consumption capacity at that time, it was not possible for people to use railways and carriages. In other words, rickshaws provided more opportunities for ordinary people to get about, and also spurred the development of an industry.

(2) Contribution to the patent system

The invention of rickshaws and their ensuing technological improvements was significant for the development of the transportation machinery sector, and also for the formulation of the government's technical policies on the patent system. As the invention and improvements of rickshaws only represented a slight technological advance, there was no protection system in place at that time. As a result, rickshaws caught on in a short space of time. This might have been a good thing for the development of an industry, but it was a bad thing for inventors and reformers, as they did not receive due returns for their painstaking efforts.

Japan formally established a patent system in 1885. In fact, the *Monopoly Rules* were announced by Dajōkan in 1871, but were abolished one year later without approving one patent. Rickshaws were not granted patent rights as they had become popular when this announcement was made. There was no formal patent law in Japan until the government promulgated the *Monopoly Regulations* in 1885. At that time, many people advocated introducing a patent system in Western Europe, and there was heated debate over the patent rights of rickshaws. As rickshaws were popular at that time, inventors were not granted patent protection, which sparked great concern.

When the *Monopoly Regulations* were promulgated in 1885, inventors such as Yousuke Izumi filed an application apply, but because the rickshaw was a well-known mode of transportation by that time, no patent was granted. The rickshaw heralded the golden age in around 1897. There were 200,000 rickshaws in Japan, and they had become an important export product. Due to the limitations of this system, the inventors had long been forgotten, and were in desperate financial straits, so, in 1899 the "Proposal for granting annuity to rickshaw inventors" was submitted to the Imperial Diet, but was vetoed. In 1900, the Reward Bureau allocated 200 yen to the families of Yousuke Izumi and others.

(3) Limitations of technological innovation

Notwithstanding the positive significance of technological innovation, rickshaws also faced insurmountable limitations, mainly the rickshaw technical system. Later means of transport, such as bicycles and automobiles, were obviously superior to rickshaws, and also promoted their improvement. A rickshaw, as the name indicates, is a vehicle "that carries people, and that is pulled by people." A person's physical strength is limited, and a rickshaw does not conform to the idea of equality in modern society.

As mentioned in the preceding section, rickshaws had undergone many improvements since their invention. Except for some parts such as springs and pneumatic tires, improvements were chiefly minor and external decoration. For example, there were 43 invention patents for rickshaws and 78 utility models. More than half of these involved improvements in auxiliary technologies such as hoods, windproof lamps, and pedals. Japan's *Utility*

Model Act was enacted in 1905, and there was only the patent law before that. Before 1893, only one or two invention patents were granted per year, and this is the same for utility models. It was in a steady decline until it completely disappeared in 1927.[26] This shows a wholly opposite trend to the invention of bicycles and is one of the reasons why bicycles replaced rickshaws.

There are two reasons that rickshaw's technological innovation activities are few and far between. First, rickshaws had mature technology and had almost reached the completion state before the patent system was enacted (1885), and there was little room for any further improvement. Therefore, there were few achievements in the way of invention patents and utility models. Second, due to the limitations of technical system, there was not much room for further improvement of rickshaws.[27] In other words, a rickshaw is a simple mode of transportation, without power equipment. With a simple structure, there is not much room for improvement. The limitations of rickshaw technology can be seen from the review reports at the various expos held at the time. Some reviews are as follows:[28]

"Rickshaws are made in Japan, and its technology is improving day by day, but exhibits here tend to have novelty value without practicality. It pursues a beautiful appearance and sells for a high price."

(The 3rd Domestic Industrial Expo in 1890)

"Rickshaws have been rapid development in recent years, and many products debut at this expo. However, many products focus on external appearance, but little improvements are made in important components such as wheels, axles, and springs for a comfy ride."

(The 4th Domestic Industrial Expo in 1895)

"Compared to products in the previous expo, products at this expo see little improvement, and there are practically no products free from limitations."

(The 5th Domestic Industrial Expo in 1903)

"Compared to other products at the Fifth Expo, the eight-wheeled rickshaws at this expo are still lacking in improvements, and incomplete technology still persists."

(1907 Tokyo Industrial Expo)

"Except for one or two aspects, rickshaws are undertaken by handicraftsmen. Many of them are made by craftsmen. Without ambitious plans, they are fonder of insignificant aspects such as color, while little attention is paid to design, structure and production technology of rickshaws."

(Tokyo Taisho Expo 1916)

As these experts pointed out, the technical improvement in rickshaws focus on low-tech aspects such as improvement of appearance and novelty shape. Under these conditions, rickshaws cannot hold a candle to other modes of transportation such as bicycles and cars, and as a result, rickshaws inevitably became a thing of the past.

Section 4 Concluding remarks

The following conclusions can be drawn from the investigations in this chapter. First, the development and decline of the rickshaw sector are determined by both demand and supply, with demand playing a greater role. As in many other traditional industries, this was caused by Japan's consumption structure and supply capacity in the infancy of industrialization. Rickshaws were invented and popularized in response to the needs of the populace. The growth of the rickshaw sector was also the result of rising demand. The overseas market is also an aspect that cannot be overlooked.

Second, from the perspective of supply, the rickshaw sector saw a wealth of producers in a short time due to the existence of a great many carpenters who had specialized in making carts. This resulted in the formation of an industry which developed for a long time. Many people were skilled craftsmen, including Osuke Akiha, who made technical improvements to rickshaws. Moreover, the rickshaw industry adopted a division of labor system in the early stage, resulting in higher productivity and spurring the development of the contracting system.

Third, there are limitations to the improvement in traditional technology. The technological improvements of the rickshaw industry faced two problems. First, excellent craftsmen such as Osuke Akiha could not meet the requirements of the times through experience and hard work alone, despite their great skills. Second, modern means of transportation including bicycles and automobiles appeared almost simultaneously with rickshaws, but had technical superiority. This limited the development of rickshaws.

Fourth, rickshaws also played an important role, in industrial development and employment, foreign exchange earnings, and offering a convenient life for citizens. Not only was it a transitional innovation product, it also was the product of an era.

Notes

1 Guan Quan (1996, 1998, 2001) discussed these three industries at length.
2 Interestingly, sewing machines were the largest export in the 1950s after World War II, showing the relationship between the complexity of mechanical technology and production.
3 There are few similar industries. If there are any, the safety match may be one of them. It existed for less than 200 years from its emergence (early nineteenth century) to its basic demise (late twentieth century). While some countries and regions produce and use this, it is basically nonexistent as an industry. Interestingly, the invention and use of safety matches as well as the formation of the industry are roughly similar to that of bicycles. Bicycles are still a sound mode of transport and have not been completely replaced by cars because of the difference in functions between the two. Matches are basically been replaced by lighters.

4 On the discussion of traditional and modern industries in Japan, see Chapter 2 of this book and Guan Quan (1997, 2003).
5 On the traffic conditions before the Meiji period, see Saitou (1992).
6 On the history of the invention and development of rickshaws, see Saitou (1979).
7 As regards the number of rickshaws owned, two types of statistics are available. One is the *Japanese Statistical Yearbook*, and the other is the *List of Requisitioned Items*. Regarding the latter, Mataji Umemura, Nobukiyo Takamatsu, and Shigeru Ito made a new estimation (1983). There are also records of the number of car manufacturers.
8 *The Provincial and County Tables of Products in the 7th Year of the Meiji Period* was published by the Meiji Documentation Society (1959). In 1874, it covered three urban prefectures and 60 rural prefectures. For the number of prefectures that were later merged, see Saito (1979), pp. 153–154.
9 For more details, see Saito (1979), pp. 110–125.
10 For more details, see Shihiko Saitoto (1979) pp. 101–103.
11 The figures used here are from the year 1887. At the time, there were other modes of transport, such as skis. However, this was only used in regions with snow, so the data is not used here. There are also figures on horses as a means of transport, but these is excluded here due to different analysis purposes.
12 As regards expenses at that time, the national average fee was Qian 5.9 for rickshaws, 4.6 for carriages, and 13.9 for sedan chairs.
13 Due to lack of space, the figure for 1898 is not shown here. In addition, data on urban population before 1889 is not available. It is impossible to judge the situation before that date.
14 This view also applies to bicycles.
15 It is impossible to judge how this ratio has changed since then, as there is no production data classified by prefecture. However, the ratios of ownership are 33.1% (1889), 32.4 (1898), and 29.9 (1909). The data is relatively stable, with a slight decline, indicating that other cities were developing.
16 On the evolution of technology of rickshaws, see Saito (1979).
17 See Saito (1979) pp. 203–212.
18 On the development of the Japanese bicycle industry, see Chapter 9 of this book and Guan Quan (1996, 2003).
19 See Saito (1992) pp. 178–179
20 Wu Baoshan (1947).
21 Yang Ruiliu, Hou Houpei (1931) p. 11 records the number of vehicles. The original data is "Customs Statistics."
22 The introduction below is from Saito (1979).
23 See Japan Rubber Manufacturers Association (1969).
24 Originally, various modes of transport had different functions, and should not be compared in terms of quantity alone. However, the comparison between bicycles and rickshaws, and c between cars and carriages does not present a big problem.
25 Bicycles are rarely used for transporting passengers. In this sense, they cannot replace rickshaws. The increase in bicycle ownership is generally an increase in new owners. People who used to travel by rickshaw used bicycles instead, indicating that there were two types of people among bicycle owners. Moreover, rickshaws were, in part, replaced by cars because cars can be used to carry passengers (taxi).

Moreover, many people who pulled rickshaws now drove taxis. See Saito (1992) pp. 237–244.

26 On the number of rickshaws, see Japan's Patent Office (1958). On specific inventors and name of inventions, see the *Detailed List of Inventions* by Japan's Patent Office.

27 There is a developmental type of rickshaw that combines the functions of bicycles, namely tricycles. This was used before and after World War II, and is still widely popular in China and Southeast Asia today.

28 The data cited comes from the part on expos in the *Data on the History of the Development of Industry in the Early Stage of the Meiji Period* by Meiji Documentation Society.

9 Intermediate industry

The development of the bicycle industry

Section 1 Introduction

Today, a bicycle is an established, familiar mode of transport. In any country with certain economic development, people of all ages own a bicycle, However, bicycles were still considered a luxury just a few decades ago, at least in China. At that time, it was one of the big four items (watch, sewing machine, bicycle, radio).[1] Before the founding of the People's Republic of China, bicycles were only owned by the upper class. The most famous is a rumor of the last emperor riding a bicycle in the imperial city. At that time, China was able to produce bicycles, but only a few factories could make them.[2]

The bicycle sector is a type of transplanted sector, but from the perspective of its production structure and technical system, it is similar to a traditional industry. When the bicycle was exported to Japan in the second half of the nineteenth century, bicycles were still in a state of development. In this sense, it is appropriate to analyze the bicycle industry as an intermediate industry.[3] Of course, there are a great many intermediate industries. The bicycle industry has been chosen for two reasons. First, the bicycle industry began to take shape from the end of the nineteenth century to the early twentieth century, and then apace rapidly in the 1930s and became an important sector of the machinery sector. In other words, from import to import substitution to export, the entire process is the flying goose paradigm before World War II.[4] Second, it is representative to a certain degree in terms of the digestion and absorption of imported technology. The development of the bicycle industry in Japan was made possible thanks to the sustained efforts of many enterprising entrepreneurs and craftsmen. Since enterprises in the bicycle industry were mostly SMEs, an industry with SMEs as the mainstay gradually took shape and evolved into one of the most important machinery industries.

Studies on the Japanese bicycle industry before World War II are few and far between. For example, research was conducted by Tsuneyoshi Takeuti (1980, 1984) from the historical perspective, by Masaaki Kawamura (1994) from the perspective of parts, and by Tsutomu Demizu (1990) from the perspective of industrial history. However, these studies are limited to a certain period, area or aspect, and do not look at the long-term development of the

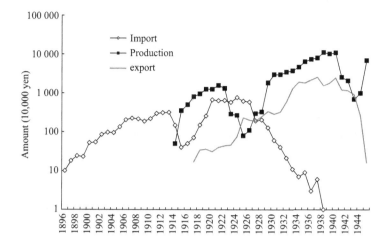

Figure 9.1 Production and import/export of bicycles.
Source: Imports and Exports: *Japan's Chronology of Foreign Statistics*; production volume: Japan Bicycle Promotion Institute (1973).

bicycle sector as a whole. This chapter chiefly examines the development process and characteristics of the bicycle sector from the perspective of technological development, especially technological innovation.

The bicycle sector in Japan probably began toward the end of the nineteenth century and the early twentieth century. Full popularization was realized by the first half of the twentieth century. Figure 9.1 shows the production and import and export of Japanese bicycles in the early twentieth century. In general, it is the process of import, reproduction (import substitution), and export. The import of bicycles was first recorded in 1896, with a value of merely 100,000 yen. This increased year by year, falling slightly during World War I, but increasing after the war. The market value reached 7.68 million yen in 1924, a record high, before World War II. After that, it plunged rapidly and ended completely around 1938.

No official statistical data are available on domestic production from about 1899, when the bicycle sector took shape, to World War I. Thus, it is difficult to give an accurate description. However, Mitayaseisakujyo, a representative company produced 1,000 bicycles per month (1909). According to this calculation, it can be estimated that a rapid increase took place after the Russo-Japanese War. Production volume soared from 460,000 yen in 1914 to 12.56 million yen in 1919, a 26-fold increase in five years. Thereafter, there was a temporary decrease due to the 1923 Great Kantō earthquake, but it developed rapidly again in the Showa era (1926–1988), reaching 100 million yen in 1938.

In terms of exports, Mitayaseisakujyo exported several bicycles to China in 1908, and the market increased year-on-year until the Taisho period (1912–1925). The official statistics began in 1917, which showed the market volume as 170,000 yen. In 1927, the volume reached 1.88 million yen. In that year, exports surpassed imports, and reached 6 million yen in 1932. In 1937, bicycles became the top export product in the machinery and appliances sector. From this, it can be seen that the Japanese bicycle sector belongs to the typical "flying goose paradigm" from its import, independent production (import substitution), to exports. This is wholly different from the rickshaw sector.[5]

Section 2 From Technology import to technological innovation

I. Technology import

The bicycle was invented by the German Baron C.F. Drais in 1813 (patented in France in 1818). At that time, bicycles were crude, and made from wood. Many people have made improvements to bicycles since then. In 1839, the British blacksmith K. Macmillan invented a device in which a rider drove the rear wheels using their feet, so that the bicycle acted as a vehicle. More parts were invented from 1860 to 1880, and bicycles changed from a dangerous recreational tool into a safe mode of transport. The main components invented in this period were the flywheel, foot brakes, spokes, chains, inner tubes, fenders, triangular brackets, pneumatic tires, and transmissions, among others.

Bicycles were exported to Japan at a time when this technology had seen great improvements. The first bicycle exported to Japan was developed by the Frenchman P. Michaux from 1860 to 1863. As this model is simple, people copied and produced a similar product for rent soon afterwards. In 1870 or so, the common bicycle which was developed by the Frenchman and modified by the Briton James Starley called the "father of bicycles" was imported by Japan. This type of bicycle was quickly copied by Japanese craftsmen. For example, Jinnosuke Kajino from Yokohama who copied it in 1877.[6] According to records, his factory "originally imported raw materials from the U.S., and performed processes such as welding, as well as assembly. Through great efforts, it could produce parts such as wheels and handlebars." The earliest domestic bicycles were called "Gold Japan" and "Silver Japan."

In 1879, the Englishman H.J. Lauson invented a safer bicycle which used a chain to drive the rear wheel. J.K. Starley subsequently completed the prototype of the safe bicycle. This was copied by Japan's Mitayaseisakujyo in 1890. According to the *70-Year History of Mitayaseisakujyo*,

> The steel pipe for the frame is made in the same way as that of guns. The round steel rod is perforated vertically, and the parts such as steel balls, seat, spokes, and chains are all self-made. It takes six craftsmen one month to produce.[7]

Bicycles developed in Europe and the U.S. were copied by Japan which had a weak industrial foundation, indicating that Japanese craftsmen only had the ability to copy during the Meiji period. It is said that in 1868 (the first year of the Meiji period), Hisashige Tanaka, hailed as the ancestor of modern industrial technology in Japan, invented the bicycle. If this was the case, there was a gap of about 50 years between Japan and Western Europe. Therefore, this period can be regarded as a period of trial and error, laying the groundwork for regular production.[8] Moreover, from the perspective of technology transfer, imitative production is a type of introduction with the best independent production. This achievement shows that the gap between Japan and Western Europe was small as far as this technical system is concerned.

However, imitation in this period is just the acts of individuals, rather than the formation of the bicycle sector. At this time, there were only three commercial enterprises : the Kajino Bicycle Factory, the Miyata Corporation, and the Imperial Bicycle Factory. There was not yet a part production system with decisive significance for the assembly-type bicycle sector. Mitayaseisakujyo manufactured guns in the early days, and attempted to produce bicycles in 1890. In 1899, Mitayaseisakujyo resumed production of bicycles, along with the Okamoto Iron Works in Nagoya. Many bicycle-part manufacturers sprang up in Sakai (city) in the Osaka area. These marked the course of the Japanese bicycle industry. Sakai is historically a region noted for making guns. Many people who were blacksmiths had the ability to process metals. As not many guns were produced during this period, some craftsmen set about making bicycles and parts.[9]

The characteristics of this period can be summarized in three points: First, legions of complete bicycle factories and parts factories emerged. In 1909, factories producing complete bicycles included Mitayaseisakujyo (Tokyo), Okamoto Iron Works (Nagoya), Tokyo Bicycle Factory (Tokyo), Kosakakojo (Osaka), Okawa Bicycle Factory(Okayama), and Usiyama Second Factory (Kumamoto), among others. Parts factories were widely distributed in such regions as Tokyo, Osaka, Kyoto, Hyogo, Fukushima, Ishikawa, Fukuoka, Okayama, and Kumamoto.[10] For example, in 1899, Kiyoyoshi Kitagawa and Kozaburo Saito founded Sorin Shokai to produce racks. Yasutaro Majima, Yoshikiti Maeda, Watanabe Yoshinosuke, Asaiti Makino, Yoshiiti Kondo, Kitaro Oizumi, and Ititaro Kosaka, who studied at Mitayaseisakujyo, began to produce parts such as handlebars, saddles, spokes, and axles. Moreover, Kotaro Takagi and Tsunejiro Tanaka began to make rims; Zenshiti Handa and Yoshihira Sakaue adopted electroplating; Itaro Yamamoto and Tomisaburo Fukuse began producing flywheels; Shigezo Wada and Kotaro Takagi began producing chains; and Tokutaro Yamashita began producing gears.[11]

Second, bicycles were officially imported by importers rather than brought in by foreigners, as had previously been the case. At that time, famous importers include Sumishokai, Sorin Shokai, Ishikawashokai, and Japan-U.S. Store. Sumishokai in 1895, Sorin Shokai in 1899, and Ishikawashokai and Japan-U.S. Store in 1900 began to import bicycles. In 1909, up to 18 bicycle importers placed advertisements in the *Current Affairs News*, and many of these importers began producing bicycles thereafter.[12]

Third, machinery and equipment were purchased for mass production rather than simple improvement and imitation. After the Russo-Japanese War, Mitayaseisakujyo purchased equipment such as lathes, punches, and pneumatic hammers. It had only thirty-five employees in 1902, eighty-eight in 1909, and up to 175 in 1916. The power of factory also soared from 10 horsepower in 1902 to 70 horsepower in 1916.[13]

According to statistics, there were thirty-six bicycle factories in Japan (with 596 employees) in 1909, most of whom (22 factories, 475 employees) were concentrated in Tokyo, Osaka, and Aichi. Factories with fewer than ten employees accounted for two-thirds. Nearly half of the factories had no power.[14] This shows that the bicycle sector had a weak foundation in this period.

II. Technology popularization

Nevertheless, bicycles and the production technology of bicycles soon began to catch on throughout Japan, and achieved full penetration in fifteen years or so from 1914. During this period, the number of bicycles owned, the number of production and sales staff, and technological innovation activities saw rapid growth. Bicycles grew at a fast clip from around 1914 to around 1929, especially around 1924. Nationwide, the number of bicycles owned jumped from one bicycle per 182 persons to one bicycle per twenty-five persons. The speed of penetration further accelerated from 1924 to 1929, with an average of one bicycle for two to three families nationwide or one to two families in developed regions.

Behind the popularization of bicycles are two factors of supply and demand. We first take a look at the supply factor. During this period, the number of bicycle sellers and manufacturers mushroomed. A great many sellers at the time could repair bicycles and even process some parts. First of all, from the perspective of the distribution of bicycle operators (producers and sellers) in this period, like the penetration of bicycles, the number of bicycle operators on average increased from thirty-three to 199 from 1910 to 1919. This is consistent with population size and economic development level in various regions. At that time, bicycle operators were basically retailers who repaired bicycles. They popularized bicycles by teaching the populace how to use, maintain, and repair them. The correlation coefficient between the number of bicycle operators and the number of bicycles owned in various regions soared from 0.784 in 1914 to 0.906 in 1919.[15]

The following records describe the producers in this period. *Factory Overview* only recorded factories with more than ten employees. This is not favorable for the bicycle industry which features mostly SMEs, because a great many bicycle companies employed fewer than ten people at the time. Nevertheless, the number of factories soared from 67 in seven regions in 1916 to 150 in fourteen regions in 1919. The number of employees jumped from

3,186 to 6,466. The horsepower increased from 1,391 to 2,351, which nearly doubled in three years. However, the average number of employees per factory did not see much change, indicating that the industry is generally suited to small-scale enterprises. According to the *Statistics Table of Factories* of 1929, there were 385 factories with more than five employees (including 190 factories with more than ten employees), totaling 8,089 employees (6,878 employees in factories with more than ten employees). Factories with more than ten employees increased by ten compared to that in 1919, while the number of employees saw little or no increase. In other words, small-scale bicycle factories actually sprang up throughout the 1920s.[16]

This tendency can also be seen in the parts production field in Sakai. In 1912, there were nineteen factories, with 156 employees and an actual production volume of 59,000 yuan. In 1926, those figures increased to 128, 788 and 2.577 million yuan, respectively. However, the average number of employees in factories was 8.2 in 1912, but fell to 6.2 in 1926, indicating that enterprises became smaller during this period.[17] Of course, this downsizing does not indicate the decline of the industry. In 1923, the average number of employees in factories was at its lowest, but the labor productivity at its highest, up to 6,542 yen. This could be attributed to the popular electric motors in this period. Due to the penetration of electric power and electric motors, SMEs could install small motors, and corresponding mechanical equipment, resulting in greater labor productivity.[18] In 1909, the motorization rate in bicycle factories with more than five employees (the proportion of power-driven enterprises to all enterprises) averaged at 28.2% in the manufacturing industry, 49.7% in the machinery industry, and 56% in the bicycle industry. The rate in the bicycle industry was higher than that of the manufacturing industry as a whole, and also higher than the machinery industry as a whole. By 1929, the figure was 82.5% in the manufacturing industry, 89% in the machinery industry, and 91% in the bicycle industry, which was still higher than the whole. Factories with more than ten people accounted for 90% = as early as 1919.[19] At this time, the motorization and electrification rate (the proportion of electric motors in power equipment) achieved full penetration in Japan.

Another key feature of this period was the gradual technological innovation activities. Generally speaking, the more active the technological innovation (especially engineering innovation), the lower the production costs, and the higher the productivity. Moreover, the more popular the bicycle-related knowledge, the more active the technological innovation activities. This mutual relationship greatly spurred the popularization and improvement of bicycle technology. Figure 9.2 shows the penetration of bicycle-related inventions in various regions. It can be seen that there were two periods of increase: From 1888 to 1897, it skyrocketed from 1% to 20%; after that there is a buffer period. There was not much progress from around 1905, but the penetration accelerated thereafter. Penetration was achieved in almost all regions by 1930.

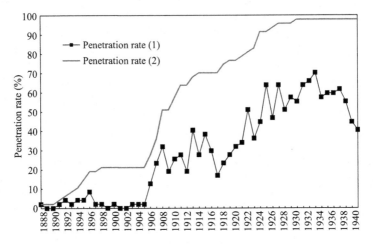

Figure 9.2 Popularization of bicycle-related inventions.

Source: *Details of Inventory* by (Japan) Patent Office.

Notes:
1 Penetration rate = number of regions (prefectures) with invention registration ÷ 47
   × 100%.
2 Penetration rate (1) = inventions in the current year.
3 Penetration rate (2) = Including previous inventions.

III. *Technological innovation*

The review report of the "Revitalization Tokyo Expo" held in 1928 states that: "Bicycles nearly drive out foreign products. Some are exported, and become an important product made in Japan."[20] In the 1930s, the bicycle sector saw accelerated development, mainly due to technological advances. This might be called the period of technological innovation. The bicycle industry in this period was quite mature. From the perspective of ownership and production volume in the late 1920s, Japan had become a global power in terms of bicycle manufacture, ranking behind France and Britain in terms of ownership, and just behind Germany in terms of production volume.[21] There were 385 factories with 8,089 employees in 1929, and 847 factories with 19,169 employees in 1937. This is obviously industry on a large scale.[22]

In the early days, the top task in the bicycle industry was to copy production skills in advanced countries, and mass produce them to meet domestic demand. This changed in the 1930s. For starters, the penetration of bicycles was basically complete, and domestic demand was close to saturation. How to tap foreign countries became an important goal. However, foreign exports were sure to hit competition from Europe and the U.S. It was impossible to rely on low prices alone. Second, after thirty years of development, the bicycle sector had the right conditions for R&D as the improvement and updating of parts was

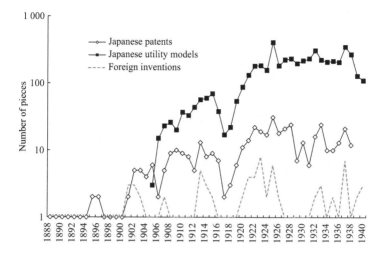

Figure 9.3 Bicycle-related inventions.
Source: *Detailed List of Inventions* by (Japan) Patent Office.

finally part of the routine work. From the establishment of the patent system in 1885 to the end of World War II in 1945, about 5,000 inventions related to the bicycle accounted for 90% of the parts and components.[23]

Figure 9.3 shows bicycle-related inventions. There were only thirteen from 1888 to 1899. From the early twentieth century to the mid-1920s, the number of invention patents basically rose, except for the period from the Russo-Japanese War to World War I. It decreased every year after this, but still maintained a level of about 10 patents per year. The *Utility Model Act* became effective in 1905, showing a strong momentum of growth from the outset. By the mid-1920s, it had been growing rapidly except during World War I, with 200 patents per year. Moreover, foreigners obtained 91 invention patents and utility models, mostly invention patents with only six utility models, indicating high-level inventions by foreigners. The following two points can be seen from the trends of the patents. First, from the early twentieth century to the mid-1920s, bicycle-related technological innovation activities gradually became active. Second, there were far more utility models than invention patents in this period, indicating that the technological innovation of bicycles mainly lay in copying foreign technology, as well as the improvement and development of auxiliary technology. Utility models are inventions at a lower level than patents, namely minor inventions or small improvements or simple inventions.[24] As bicycle technology was not complicated, small improvements and amendments became mainstream.

In this period, exports saw a rapid increase, and investment was also made in China. In 1936, Mitayaseisakujyo established Manchuria Mitayaseisakujyo in Shenyang, China to make aircraft parts and bicycles. By the end of the war, the factory had 483 employees, 362 pieces of aircraft-related equipment, 69 pieces of bicycle-making equipment, as well as other production equipment.[25] Moreover, Setsusaburo Kojima set up the Changhe Works to produce bicycles in Shenyang in 1936, Tianjin in 1938, and Shanghai in 1940, respectively. These factories became the principal bicycle manufacturers in China after the war.[26]

Section 3 Catalysts for technological innovation

I. Human resources

Eisuke Miyata (Kitamura), the second director of Mitayaseisakujyo, studied under gun-making masters for five years, and helped the first Eisuke Miyata make guns. Since 1888, Mitayaseisakujyo had produced new products such as telephones and lamps in addition to Murata rifles. In 1887, Kitamura gained new knowledge and access to first-class technology while working at Osaka's Artillery Plant and Hisashige Tanaka's Plant. After being commissioned by a foreigner to repair bicycles in 1889, he set about producing bicycles. Cognizant of the prospects, he began to officially produce bicycles in 1899.[27]

In 1900, the second Eisuke Miyata took the helm of the works and introduced equipment to improve production technology. In 1909, in order to adopt common parts production methods, he set up an inspection class and introduced the performance evaluation system. He also sent apprentices to study at tutorial schools and reformed labor management. In 1926, the individual business became a company, and the duties, responsibilities, and powers of positions were laid down, as well as the benefits and wages of employees.

In addition to improving the management and organizational structure, Eisuke Miyata, a master of technology, was also enthusiastic about technological innovation. In the era of gun making, he invented the No. 12 Miyatagun and obtained invention patents (Nos. 1476, 3558, and 3681). He later studied the carbon evaporation method through the empirical study of guns. The metal surface was specially treated and applied to the manufacture of bicycle parts with great results. Inspired by a professional magazine, he developed foot brakes (patent Nos. 14388 and 17132), handlebar pillars (patent No. 14889), frame fixings (utility model No. 10124), rickshaw wheels (utility model No. 15921), and other new technologies. Coupled with the sixteen inventions by Youtaro Niji, he had a total of twenty-two invention patents and utility models. He was awarded the Green Ribbon Medal in 1924.[28]

Matsuzo Okamoto, another key figure in the bicycle sector, was born in Nara, and was apprenticed to a blacksmith to produce agricultural implements. After working at Tanaka Iron Works for a period of time, he set up his own business. In 1899, he founded Okamoto Iron Works and began to repair bicycles and produce parts. Production of bicycles began in 1901; 1,000 bicycles were produced in 1905, and numbers rose to 6,200 by 1910. The factory size grew from twenty employees in 1909 to 290 in 1916, and the horsepower soared from four to 125. His bicycles won the third prize at the

Competitive Exhibition in 1910. Since then, he learned production technology in Germany and Britain and purchased machinery and equipment. In the same year, some parts were outsourced to promote rational production. In 1919, Okamoto Iron Works was reorganized into a joint stock company, and began to produce aircraft parts. It became the designated factory for the Army Ministry in 1920 and the Navy Ministry in 1924. In the early Showa era (late 1920s), Okamoto began making small cars, and, during the Pacific War period, produced aircraft landing gear and wheels. He received the Green Ribbon Medal in 1928, and the Meritorious Award from Japan Invention Association in 1933. He was credited with ten inventions including No. 32863 utility model.[29] The government commendation states that: "The present invention concerns the improvement in bicycle frame, brake boom, wheel disc axle, safety pedal, handlebar plug, frame joint, pedal joint, container, handle, and others, so that excellent bikes can be made."[30]

Many other people also made important contributions to the bicycle sector, such as Kyujiro Okazaki, Kousaku Matsushita, Kumakiti Arayaku, and Shozaburo Shimano. They are early practitioners of the bicycle sector, aggregators and participants who promoted the industry to new heights. For example, Shimano Industry, founded by Shimano, became Japan's largest bicycle manufacturer, and developed many new technologies. It is still an important Japanese manufacturer, with businesses in other fields.

II. Technical conditions

Several conditions must be satisfied for technology transfer from an advanced country to a developing country. One of the most important conditions is whether related technologies exist in the importing country. If they do, it is easy to achieve the learning effect. Otherwise, it is hard to make a success of introduction. Bicycle technology is not complicated, but it requires considerable metal processing technology, because the main parts of bicycles are made of metal. Japan had the technology to produce guns in pre-modern times, and had could easily digest and absorb these new technologies. Of course, this did not apply to all bicycle technologies. Therefore, some parts were produced in different periods.

In Europe, iron pipes were actually applied to industry after the industrial revolution in the eighteenth century. After steam engines were invented, iron pipes were needed to transfer steam, but the technology at that time was immature, and these were all made by drilling machines. Later, the smoke tube boiler was invented (1830) and demand grew. For the welding technology, the lost-wax process was replaced by metal arc welding (1892) and gas welding (1901). As steel technology advanced, forged steel pipes were created (1825). The inclined roller rolling process was invented in 1885, and the frame could be easily processed.[31] In 1890, Mitayaseisakujyo made bicycle frames using gun-making technology. Matsuzo Okamoto also made frames using the plate rolling method. Mitayaseisakujyo used imported materials from Britain until 1918.

Rims were locally made in the early stages. The rim supports the bicycle's weight, the rider's weight, friction and impact on the ground, and the contact with driving force and braking force through spokes, tires, inner tubes, etc. It is therefore easily damaged, and requires high-strength materials and technology. The initial rims were made of wood, surrounded by metal bars. In 1869, wheels with iron rims and needle-shaped spokes were developed. The periphery of the rim adopted solid rubber to prevent shocks and vibration. An inflatable tire was developed in 1888. The initial production of Japanese rims also used wood. Kumakiti Arayaku, a woodwork craftsman, hired a rim-making craftsman from Osaka in 1903 who began to produce rims. By 1906, it had a production capacity of 7,000 and provided rims for bicycle manufacturers including Mitayaseisakujyo, and Matsuzo Okamoto. Since then, the rim have been made of iron. Kumakiti Arayaku went to Europe with his eldest son to purchase equipment such as rolling machines to produce rims.[32]

The car chain was locally made in Japan at a later stage. The bicycle review report of the Tokyo Taisho Expo in 1913 states: "There are to date no producers of balls, spokes, and chains. It is a pity that we rely on the achievements of other countries."[33] Chains were made of metal rings and have long been used for lifting and pulling. Attempts were made to use chains to drive bicycles around 1869. In 1883, Morgan invented the short-loop chain and obtained a patent. Thereafter, block-type chain was developed. Japan originally imported these products and began to make its own at the beginning of World War I. Mitayaseisakujyo produced a block-type chain in 1916. Moreover, other companies such as Tsubakimoto made many attempts but to no avail. Due to the poor quality of strip steel used as a raw material at the outset, imported iron bars were used. Even these were superior to domestically made products. The rollers were made of wires processed by lathes but not treated by heat. The chains often broke and were ironically nicknamed "killer chains." Kumakiti Arayaku bought specialist chain-making machinery from Britain in 1915. Production was launched the next year, but it failed. The equipment was sold to Japanese Bicycle. In 1933, large enterprises including Mitayaseisakujyo, Kumakiti Arayaku, and Maruishi jointly founded Kokuekito carry out research and development.[34]

As a product composed of many parts, a bicycle is an assembled and processed product. The technical requirements and difficulty are different for the various parts, which were developed in Europe during different periods. Japan learned and copied these production skills. Figure 9.4 shows the relationship between the development of fourteen types of bicycle parts in Europe and the U.S. and their localization in Japan. The horizontal axis represents the time of development in Europe and the U.S., and the vertical axis the time of localization in Japan. At first glance, there seems to be no relationship between the two. There are actually three kinds of relationships: (1) The parts on the left (wooden rims, handlebars, pedals, saddles, gear) were developed in Europe before 1860, and localized in Japan from 1900 to 1910. Due to simple technology, localization was achieved earlier. (2) The two parts below (axles and inner tubes) were developed in Europe and the U.S. from 1860 to

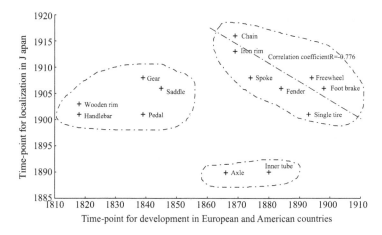

Figure 9.4 Development and localization of bicycle parts.
Source: Rokuya Takagi (1981–1986), Yuji Sano (1980).

1880, and in Japan in 1890. The production of the two parts can be directly applied to the existing traditional technology in Japan. (3) There is an obvious negative correlation relationship among those on the right (correlation coefficient = -0.776). Most of these are new technologies developed in Europe and the U.S. after the 1860s. In other words, the sooner these were developed in Europe and the U.S., the later these were used in Japan. The later these were developed in Europe and the U.S., the earlier they were localized in Japan. This demonstrates Japan's improving technology.[35]

III. Market conditions

In addition to these technical conditions, the penetration of products and technologies also requires market conditions, namely market size and market structure. The former promotes the penetration of bicycles as a demand, while the latter specifies the quantity and characteristics of technological innovation. The bicycle is a kind of consumer durable, and its popularity required the people's support. The higher the income, the stronger their spending power, and the faster the penetration of bicycles. Judging by the correlation relationship between regional industrial production volume per capita (as a proxy variable for per capita income) and bicycle ownership, the correlation coefficient was 0.695 in 1914 and 0.737 in 1929. From the perspective of market structure, from 1929 to 1937, small companies with five to fourteen employees accounted for 60–70%, while large enterprises with over 200 employees accounted for merely 0.8–1.2%. It shows that the bicycle sector had a fully competitive market structure. Although the figures alone cannot prove the relationship between regional industrial production volume per capita and technological innovation in the sector, it explains that the penetration of bicycles depends to a certain extent on people's income.

It is not easy to examine the market structure of bicycles due to the limited data, but we know that the sector was mainly comprised of SMEs, rather than monopolized by large enterprises. It should have been a fiercely competitive market. What is important is that technological innovation activities in this competitive market are highly active, at least on a par with those in monopolistic industries. From 1929 to 1937, small businesses with five to fourteen employees accounted for 60–70%, while enterprises with over 200 employees accounted for 0.8–1.2%. It can be said that the bicycle sector is a typical competitive industry. While the relationship with technological innovation cannot be directly asserted, there were up to 5,000 bicycle-related invention patents and utility models before World War II, and the vast majority of these were individual inventions by SMEs.

IV. Organization and policy conditions

Technological innovation also calls for organizational and policy conditions. For industries with a great many SMEs, industry organization has greater importance, especially for technological innovation. Technological innovation requires a wealth of funding, information, and professionals, but these are often lacking in SMEs. To survive in this competitive market, SMEs had to overcome these deficiencies. This called for organization. The bicycle sector was not an industry with immense financial and social influence. It had to survive in intense competition. Nevertheless, the practitioners entered into the industry groups[36] in Tokyo in 1903, in Osaka in 1904, and in Kobe in 1908. In 1918, the Tokyo Bicycle Association came into being, composed of 147 manufacturers, 137 wholesalers, and 3,930 retailers.[37] The association was set up to prevent disputes in business. Later, it was required to carry out the inspection of products and uniform specifications, commend meritorious personnel, participate in expos and Competitive Exhibitions, and reward inventions.

Moreover, the government policy on technology played a crucial role in nurturing and protecting industries, a fostering technological innovation. In terms of industrial policy, expos and local-level Competitive Exhibitions promoted by the state during the Meiji period provided opportunities for people to appraise and promote the development of various industries. Many enterprises were rewarded during these events, which benefited their innovation activities.[38] At the 2nd Domestic Industrial Expo (1881), Mitsumoto Suzuki, Tyotaro Saito, and Kiyonoshin Sakaguchi from the Fukushima prefecture debuted a tricycle. Afterwards, Jinnosuke Kajino displayed a bicycle at the third (1890), fourth (1895, third prize), and fifth (1903) Industrial Expo. Mitayaseisakujyo displayed products at the 4th Industrial Expo in 1895, the 5th Industrial Expo in 1903 (third prize), and Tokyo Industrial Expo in 1907 (first prize). These exhibitions provided the opportunity for peers to engage in reasonable competition, which helped enhance quality and improve production methods. For example, Matsuzo Okamoto won the third prize at the Competitive Exhibition held in Nagoya in 1910. Goaded by his rival Mitayaseisakujyo, who won first prize, he went to Europe and purchased machinery and equipment from Germany and Britain.

In addition to their supplementary role, these expos had a substitute role, namely the patent system established in 1885. Technical information is of the nature of public goods, and requires the protection of policies to a degree. The patent system is part of this policy. While offering the monopoly right for inventors within a certain period of time, it also requires the inventor to disclose the content of his invention. In other words, inventors are protected within a certain period of time so they can recoup the funds and time invested in R&D, foster new R&D, and make available the degree and content of technological advance to R&D personnel to spur new competition. This is a basic function of the patent system. Given the level of inventions and the nature of the patent system, the degree of possibility and the initiative of inventors vary. Japan enacted the *Utility Model Act* in 1905 before World War II, which greatly facilitated minor technological innovations in bicycles and technological innovations in industries. This can be seen from utility models which accounted for 90% of over 5,000 inventions.

Section 4 Concluding remarks

Bicycles were imported from Europe, but the bicycle industry in Japan achieved a quantum leap because its technical system was not complicated and its improvements were ongoing. Moreover, Japan had traditional technologies suited to the development of this industry. This heralded a glorious period for the industry. In 1937, bicycles became the top sector among the machinery and appliance industries.

The following points can be made about the development of the bicycle industry in Japan: First, the bicycle sector underwent the so-called "flying geese paradigm" process in the pre-war period: From import to production and import substitution, and to export. At the same time, three stages of industry emergence, establishment, and maturity were achieved in Japan. Second, the development of the bicycle sector required support in terms of supply and demand. The demand was created by an increase in people's income and expectations for a better means of transport. Supply was created by cost reduction brought about by technological advances and the tireless efforts of producers and sales personnel. In addition, supply played a greater role in the early stages in the new industry from introduction to development, and the role of demand increased in the later stages. Third, the bicycle industry was a typical industry chiefly composed of SMEs, entrepreneurship was indispensable. Not content with previous technologies, they always challenged new technologies, including organizational and institutional innovation. Fourth, the government's technology policy indirectly played a positive role in the sector's development. In addition to the patent system, expositions and Competitive Exhibitions, as well as policies on encouraging and rewarding inventions played different roles during different periods.

Notes

1 Four new items (TV sets, washing machines, refrigerators, and sound recorders) appeared after the reform and opening up.
2 On the situation of China's bicycle industry before the founding of the People's Republic of China, see China Bicycle Association (1991).
3 The "intermediate industry" herein means that products and technologies are imported from Western Europe, which is not particularly complicated and can be manufactured if there is a certain technical basis.
4 On the details of the development of the flying geese paradigm, see Chapter 11.
5 For discussions on the "flying geese paradigm," see Kaname Akamatsu (1956) and Ryoushin Minami (1981, 2002).
6 Jinnosuke Kajino, born in Tsukui, Kanagawa Prefecture, was engaged in the manufacture of soy sauce. He founded a bicycle factory in Yokohama in 1879, which became Japan's first bicycle factory. The factory had forty employees in 1907 but was later closed down. For more information, see Japan Bicycle Press (1959).
7 MIYATA MFG CO., LTD (1959) p. 11.
8 Japanese Bicycle Promotion Institute (1973) 80–83.
9 On the invention of bicycles and their spread and production in Japan, see Japan Bicycle Promotion Institute (1973), Yuji Sano (1985).
10 The Works Bureau of the Ministry of Agriculture and Commerce (1911) recorded a list of bicycle-related enterprises in the machinery and appliance sector and the metal sector.
11 See Eitaro Terai (1939) and Sakai Economic Bureau (1985) pp. 13–18.
12 Fuji Bicycle (1982) p. 16.
13 MIYATA MFG CO., LTD (1959).
14 Works Bureau of the Ministry of Agriculture and Commerce (1911).
15 The year for the number of bicycles owned here is 1914 and the number of operators is 1910. Moreover, the data on the number of operators is based on *Bicycle Magazine Press* (1912, 1919).
16 Relevant years on the *Statistics Table of Agriculture and Commerce* by Ministry of Agriculture and Commerce and the *Statistics Table of Factories* by Ministry of Commerce and Industry.
17 Sakai City Hall (1971) pp 25, 331.
18 On the effect of electricity penetration, see Ryoushin Minami (1976).
19 *General Overview of Factories* (1909), *Statistics Table of Factories* (1929).
20 Tokyo Expo (1929).
21 Osaka City Hall (1933).
22 MIYATA MFG CO., LTD (1959).
23 Detailed List of Inventions by Japan's Patent Office.
24 On this view, see Chapter 7 of this book, Guan (2001), Guan Quan (2011b).
25 MIYATA MFG CO., LTD (1959).
26 For details, see China Bicycle Association (1991).

27 The father-son inheritance is adopted in Japan. The son inherits his father's name, and he is also called Eisuke Miyata.

28 See MIYATA MFG CO., LTD (1959).

29 On the deeds of Matsuzo Okamoto, see NORITSU (1983).

30 Shigetaro Nara (1930) (Vol. 2) pp. 613–623.

31 Yaroku Takagi (1981–1986).

32 Daido Kogyo (1984).

33 Japan Bicycle Promotion Institute (1973) pp. 219–221.

34 On the evolution of bicycle production technology in Japan, see Rokuya Takagi (1981–1986).

35 The comparative method for the evolution process of foreign technology after being introduced to the technology importing country refers to Minami (1987). His research is on power technology in Japan.

36 A combination is a cooperative or chamber of commerce.

37 Japan Bicycle Promotion Institute (1973).

38 On the significance of Japanese Association of Modern Industries and Competitive Exhibition, see Yukihiko Kiyokawa (1995).

10 Modern industry

The rise of the automotive industry

Section 1 Introduction

Japan's automobile industry is at the forefront in the world, and Japan, naturally, has become a major power in automobile manufacturing. Although these achievements came in the wake of the rapid growth after World War II and the resulting technological advance and innovation, a good foundation was laid before World War II. For example, the major manufacturers after the war, including Toyota, Nissan, Isuzu, Daihatsu, Mazda, and Mitsubishi, had all made great contribution before the war. In particular, trucks were the principal products before the war, and also laid the foundation for the subsequent development of the automobile sector. Compared to these two industries, the automobile sector is obviously a modern industry with a more complicated technology system, and its development processes and conditions vary. As this sector features high capital and technology intensity, the support of government policies is also required. This sets automobiles apart from bicycles and rickshaws.

As the automobile sector is the most representative of today's Japan, a wealth of research has been conducted in this regard, but research on the pre-war period is sparse. This makes sense, because Japan's automobile industry was still in an immature, at least not a prominent, stage before the war. In view of this, research on the pre-war period has mainly been focused on business management and policy, while economics research, especially on technological advances and technological innovation, is rare.[1] This chapter chiefly studies the development process of the Japanese automobile sector from the perspective of technological advances and technological innovation before World War II, and compares it with the bicycle industry.

As we know, the automobile sector is one of the most comprehensive machinery industries, and its technological level stands for the industry of a country as a whole. The development of this sector differs from that of traditional industries (such as rickshaws) and intermediate industries (such as bicycles). Put simply, it is a capital-intensive and technology-intensive industry, while the previous two are basically labor-intensive industries. In a

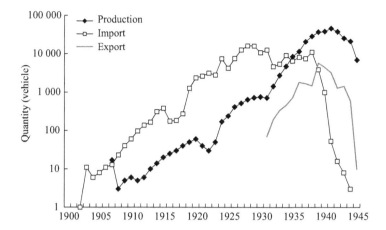

Figure 10.1 Changes in the production volume and import/export of automobiles.
Source: Simano Takao (1980).

developing country, this requires the strong support of the government for its development. Of course, efforts by private enterprises are indispensable and should play a leading role. The automobile industry is, after all, not a natural monopolistic industry.[2]

Figure 10.1 shows the changes in the production volume and import/ export of automobiles. Imports gradually increased from the early twentieth century. Except during World War I (1914–1918), it increased until the late 1920s. Thereafter, it declined to a certain extent until 1937, but still remained at a high level before a further decline. In terms of domestic production, the first car was manufactured by Tokyo Automobile Works in 1907. Thereafter, a great many enterprises made an attempt but with little success. Only the three companies, Tokyo Gas Electric, Ishikawajima Shipbuilding, and Dart Motor continued into the late 1920s until the Great Kantō earthquake (1923). The annual output was less than 100 cars. After the great earthquake, Ford Motor of Japan was founded in 1925 and General Motors of Japan in 1926, and they began to assemble vehicles.[3]

In the 1930s, automobile production got on track with strong government support, and kept growing until the outbreak of the Pacific War (1941). During the Pacific War, the production of automobiles declined somewhat due to the need to step up the production of aircraft. The Japanese auto sector took advantage of the "September 18 Incident" to penetrate the market in mainland China. Of course, it fell rapidly due to the impact of the wars. While the Japanese automobile sector scored some success in the alternative production in Japan, it did not achieve large-scale exports. The automobile industry faced a large gap compared to the bicycle industry in this regard.

Section 2 The process of technological innovation

I. Technology import

In general, for the technological development of modern industries in a developing country, it is necessary to first import technology from advanced countries, digest and absorb it, and finally develop new technologies independently. This is a long process, because the more complicated the technology, the longer this takes. Even if progress is made in a certain technical field, it will be hard to achieve success if other relevant fields lag behind. Technologically, it is a process of import, penetration and innovation. Automobile technology was imported in two ways: One was to imitate imported cars, the other was to forge cooperation with foreign enterprises. Generally, the former was suited to SMEs or industries with simple technical systems, while the latter was more suited to industries with complex technology and a wealth of capital.

(1) Imitative manufacturing

The import of technology in the automotive sector started when managers of SMEs and craftsmen imitated foreign vehicles. Forty vehicles were produced from the late nineteenth century to the 1920s (from the late Meiji period to the Taisho period).[4] The early automobiles were either steam-driven or driven by internal combustion engines. These were imitated by Japanese enthusiasts, including Torao Yamaba from Okayama Prefecture and Shintaro Yoshida, Komanosuke Utiyama, Yonetaro Yamada, Goro Haga, and Totaro Sakurai from Tokyo. The bicycle manufacturer, Mitayaseisakujyo, also made vehicles on a trial basis. The closest thing to a practical vehicle was achieved by Masujiro Hashimoto, who founded Kwaishinsha in 1911.

The earliest steam-powered vehicle was produced by Torao Yamaba from Okayama Prefecture. He had learned the rudiments of electrical engineering at the Yokosuka Naval Shipyard, and later gained knowledge on the electrical components of mine vessels at Onohamazosen join Kobe. He also conducted research at Teishinshō Electric Laboratory.[5] Thanks to this experience, he founded Yamahadenkikojo, which covered 20 square meters, and had two pole lathes, one lathe operator, one apprentice, and one assistant. Casting parts were produced by professional casting masters in the city. Due to a lack of welding technology, boilers were fastened with bolts, while water pipes and gears were self-made. The rims of wheels were made of processed iron plates. No. 8 wire was used for the spokes and frame while the body was made of beech. Trial production was completed in May 1904. The tires malfunctioned during the trail operation. It ran for about 10 kilometers non-stop.

Shintaro Yoshida of Sorin Shokai, a bicycle importer in Ginza, Tokyo, bought one horizontal gasoline-powered vehicle with two cylinders and 12 horsepower from the US in 1902. Komanosuke Utiyama, a 21-year-old technician from Sorin Shokai, manually produced a car chassis and installed a simple body for trail production of the first car. At the age of 14, Yamanouchi Kanosuke worked at a machine plant in Vladivostok, Russia, where he studied the structure and operation of cars. After returning to Japan, he worked at Teishinshō for a period of time. He was commissioned by Yoshida to assemble the first car using two to three automotive technology books and advertisements. Yoshida was pleased to see the vehicle made by Komanosuke Utiyama, and founded Tokyo Automobile Works in 1904, which mainly repaired imported cars to begin with. By 1907, he could made fuel-powered cars except for some parts.

Others also tried to produce cars on a trial basis. For example, Yonetaro Yamada of Tokyo Tsukiji Yamada Iron Works produced a car body and guards for Yoshida. Based on this, he set about making cars in 1911, and shrank the engine to one-half the size of American-made engine. Moreover, Mitayaseisakujyo, a bicycle maker, hired Prof. Masaiti Negishi from the Tokyo Vocational School (later the Tokyo Institute of Technology) as a consultant in 1909 for the trial production of a two-seater sedan with a water-cooled engine. Goro Shiga of Shiba Automobile Works Co., Ltd. in 1908, and Totaro Sakurai of Madarame Iron Works Office in 1911 also produced sedans, buses, and trucks.[6] Following these attempts, in 1911, the Kwaishinsha Automobile Factory, funded by Masujiro Hashimoto, began to engage in car manufacturing. Masujiro Hashimoto designed a V-type, 2-cylinder engine with 15 horsepower in 1914.[7]

(2) Technical cooperation

Ishikawa Shipyard adopted this method to produce automobiles at an early stage. This company was an established shipbuilding enterprise founded in 1853. Ishikawa Shipyard had been founded in 1889. Great gains were achieved during World War I. The automotive industry began to spread and develop worldwide in this period. Cognizant of this prospect, Ishikawa Shipyard purchased a Fiat car from Italy for study in 1916, and signed joint cooperation agreements with Fiat and a British company. In 1918, it signed a contract with a British company for the right to sell and manufacture two types of sedans and one type of truck in the Toyo region for 10 years for a consideration of £80,000. In 1922, a type A9 sedan was well received on the market. In 1924, it produced military protective cars. In 1926, the partnership with the foreign investor was terminated. In 1929, an independent auto department – IHI Automobile Works – was founded to produce domestic cars (Smida).

There were very few car makers during this period. According to the *Factory Overview*, in 1916 there were just three car makers. This figure had increased to fourteen in 1919, but they were all small enterprises whose t main business was car repairs.[8] In other words, some pioneers (entrepreneurs and craftsmen) attempted to make cars during the technology import period, but an industry still failed to emerge. However, such private-sector efforts were of great significance for the technological penetration and technological innovation in the later stages, and deserve to be commended.

II. Technology popularization

Following World War I, and especially the Great Kanto Earthquake (1923), demand for automobiles increased. The number of cars owned stood at 1,066 in 1914, but had increased to 4,533 in 1918, 24,300 in 1924, and 88,700 in 1930.[9] Aware of the penetration rate of Japanese cars, American car makers began to enter the Japanese market. Ford Motor and General Motors in 1926 set up subsidiaries in Japan in 1925 and 1926. Existing Japanese companies also made continual efforts. There were a great many new entrants, especially SMEs who produced auto parts.

Figure 10.2 shows the penetration of automobile plants. As can be seen from the figure, areas where there were automobile plants accounted for merely 40% before the Great Kanto Earthquake, but reached 70% in 1931 and surpassed 90% in 1936. These factories produced parts or repaired automobiles, indicating that auto production technology became popular in a short period of time. Few information exists on automobile factories in this

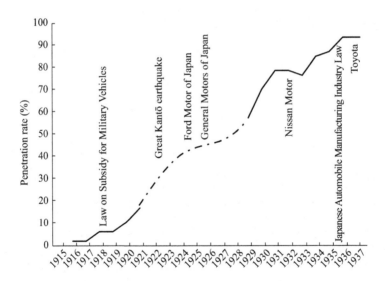

Figure 10.2 Popularization of automobile factories.

Source: 1916–1919 from the *Factory Overview* of the Ministry of Agriculture and Commerce, and 1929–1937 from the *Statistics Table of Factories* by the Ministry of Commerce and Industry.

Notes:
1 Factory with over 10 employees from 1916 to 1919, and factory with over 5 employees from 1929 to 1937.
2 Penetration rate = Number of regions with factories ÷ 47 × 100%.
3 The dotted line is the imaginary linking line assumed by the author.

period. In 1924, there were only twenty-three automobile factories in Tokyo, but the figure had reached forty seven by the next year. The large plants were IHI Automobile (295 employees) and Hakuyosha (124 employees). Compared to Tokyo, factories in Osaka were smaller in size. In 1926, there were seventeen factories there, most of which were small with five to ten employees. Dart Auto, the largest factory, had seventy employees.[10]

What exactly is the state of production technology in this period? For starters, we take a look at the review report of the Peace Memorial Fair held in 1922, which marked the beginning of this period. It states:

> Cars at this fair are significant improvements on those at the Taisho Expo. The immensely practical cars are on a par with foreign products. This is gratifying achievement. However, it is a pity that many aspects including shape and structure are the imitation of foreign cars.[11]

Moreover, the review report of the Tokyo Expo in 1928, at the end of this period, states that:

> From another perspective, however, the products reach such a level due to the special protection of the Army. These are significantly inferior to foreign products in either price and output, and the aspects such as design and technology leave a lot to be desired. While this is the current status in Japan, nothing can be done to make improvement. It's a pity.[12]

The above evaluation can be regarded as a comprehensive judgment of the technology level of Japanese automobiles at that time. It also objectively reflects the overall technology level of Japanese industry. However, it can be seen that it is nearly impossible for the automobile sector, a product of modern industries, to achieve rapid development in a country with a weak industrial base, because this required a long period of time and a huge investment in human and material resources.

The technology was still immature. However, in order to meet the rapidly growing demand, the supply system was gradually taking shape. This system had roughly the following three characteristics: a wealth of SMEs, a small number of foreign-funded enterprises, and the government's protection policy with the army at its center. Government policies will be discussed below.

III. Technological innovation

As automobile technology became popular in the 1920s, the automobile industry also began to take shape, and an independent industry gradually came into being in the 1930s. As this industry became established, progress was made in automobile production technology, including a great many inventions and improvements. Generally speaking, technological innovation would follow the technology penetration period. In other words, improvements and innovations of popularized technologies emerged. Figure 10.3 shows

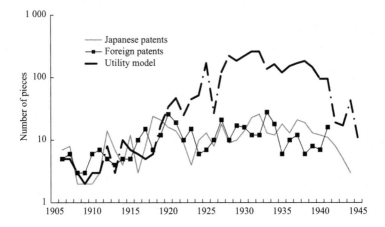

Figure 10.3 Changes in automobile-related inventions.

Source: *Detailed List of Inventions* by (Japan) Patent Office.

Notes:
1 The patents for some years are missing.
2 Utility models contain data on those by foreigners.

the changes in inventions related to automobiles. Three aspects can be seen from this: First, there were few patented inventions during the entire period (910 inventions), mostly twenty to thirty inventions per year, which rarely exceeded fifty. These also included inventions by foreigners. The vast majority of Japanese inventions were simple technological improvements, with no significant inventions. For example, regarding the automobile fenders that were not invented by foreigners, Japanese inventions accounted for 35% of all inventions from the Meiji period to the Taisho period. This shows that automobile technology was complex, and Japan was hard-pressed to make important inventions at that time.

Second, the number of utility models (3,101) is 2.4 times greater than patents, indicating that most of the inventions related to cars are improved technologies. This, of course, is nothing out of the ordinary. From this standpoint, it is different from the bicycle sector. From the perspective of the overall level of inventions, the two sometimes share similarities. For the technical innovation of bicycles, utility models outnumber invention patents by five times. In other words, given the limited overall technology and industry in Japan at that time, it was hard to produce important inventions for cars or bicycles.

Third, both patents and utility models saw considerable increase before the 1930s, but there was no marked increase during the 1930s. That is to say, there were fewer technological innovation in the 1930s – a period of technological innovation. The reasons should be manifold: First, the industrial technology level was not high. Second, the war may have resulted in the transfer of the industrial focus: the aircraft industry was more important at the time, while little attention was paid to the automotive industry. However, it is puzzling that the *Japanese Automobile Manufacturing Industry Law of 1936* should produce a good effect, but it was not manifested in technological innovation.

The sluggish technological innovation activities are also manifested in the production structure of the automobile sector. It improved compared to the capital-labor ratio throughout the 1930s, but per capita production volume fell. In 1929, the capital-labor ratio reached 0.84. In the ensuing decade, it was not lower than 1.0 except in 1932 and 1935.[13] In other words, the increase in capital investment surpassed the increase in labor investment. By contrast, per capita production volume decreased from 16,200 yen in 1929 to 7,300 yen in 1934, and then 3,900 yen[14] in 1939. This indicates that the increase in actual production volume was lower than that of the growth rate of employees. From 1934 to 1939, the number of employees jumped from 17,000 to 58,000, an increase of 2.4 times, while the actual production volume increased by 1.8 times. It is in contrast to the bicycle sector in this regard.[15]

Section 3 Catalysts for technological innovation

The course of technological development, as described in the preceding section, was the result of the sustained efforts of a great many people. Like the rickshaw and bicycle sectors, these efforts include human resources, market conditions, and government policies. However, the manifestation and role of various conditions are different as the characteristics of each sector are not the same. For example, technological innovation in the bicycle sector is intimately related to the government's technological policies, especially the convening of expos, although this is an indirect effect. Expos are geared to the entire industry rather than the bicycle industry alone. This is different in the automobile industry, because its development is directly related to the government to a certain extent, including the enactment of laws. Moreover, the significance of zaibatsu and foreign capital in this sector is absent in the bicycle sector. Furthermore, the early technology of bicycles can be applied to traditional gun-making techniques. However, this correlation is very low in the automobile sector, except for certain correlations in aspects such as casting. These technologies were chiefly imported from Western Europe in modern times.[16]

I. Human resources

Pioneers in the automotive sector such as Torao Yamaba, Shintaro Yoshida, and Komanosuke Utiyama have been introduced above. They are craftsmen-turned-managers and are hereafter called the first type. They have craftsmanship and entrepreneurship, which made possible the import of successful technology and the subsequent popularization of the automotive industry. There are managers who were technical personnel with regular schooling, who are hereinafter called the second type. Masujiro Hashimoto (Tokyo Institute of Technology) and Kiichiro Toyoda (Tokyo Imperial University) belong to this category. Nevertheless, they are the same as the first type in terms of entrepreneurship and craftsmanship. This is of great value for research. A great many Japanese business managers, technicians, and workers are possessed of this spirit. This tendency even existed after World War II, when economy and technology reached a higher level of development. This, we think, may be a characteristic of Japanese culture.[17]

Masujiro Hashimoto was born in Nukata-gun, Aichi Prefecture (present-day Okazaki City) in 1875. He graduated from the Machinery Department of Tokyo Institute of Technology in 1895 and joined the army in the following year. He worked at Sumitomo Beisi Metal Mining Co., Ltd. in 1900. In 1902, he went to the US as an intern of the Ministry of Agriculture and Commerce. After three-year internship at a gas tank manufacturing firm in New York, he returned to Japan and worked as a technician at Etchūjima Eki Iron Works in Tokyo. This company went bankrupt soon afterwards. After working for three years at Sakito Mining Institute in Kyushu, he founded the Kwaishinsha Automobile Factory in 1911. In the early days of entrepreneurship, he often visited a Japanese automobile joint venture under the Ohkura Zaibatsu system to pick the brains of technicians and Kihatiro Okura. Since it was not suitable for making cars in this period, he started with importing, assembling, and selling automobiles. The first "Dart" vehicle was produced in 1914 and won the bronze medal at the Taisho Expo. Following the trial production of several automobiles, he founded Kwaishinsha in 1918 and purchased from the US more than 20 pieces of machinery and equipment including state-of-the-art automotive working machines such as crankshaft grinding discs, camshaft grinding discs, circular grinding discs, and gear teeth abrasive discs. The model 41 sedan was awarded the gold medal at the Peace Memorial Expo held in 1922. In 1924, it qualified as a protected vehicle for military use and received government and military funding under the *Law on Subsidy for Military Vehicles*. Nevertheless, Japanese cars were not widely recognized as the expanded vehicle market caused by the Great Kanto Earthquake was dominated by imported cars and the subsidiaries of American Ford and General Motors enterprises in Japan. In 1926, it merged with the Utility Car Manufacturing Company in Osaka to form Dart Automobile Manufacturer, and continued to produce protected cars for military purposes.

II. Market conditions

Granted that the aforesaid entrepreneurship and craftsmanship are important, market conditions cannot be ignored. They cover two aspects: market size, and market structure. The former is "demand-pull" while the latter is related to the Schumpeter hypothesis.[18] The *Statistical Yearbook of Japan* recorded the number of automobiles owned as early as 1912. There were only 535 vehicles, including 304 in Tokyo, 85 in Kanagawa, 21 in Kyoto, and 20 in Osaka. All these were large cities. More importantly, there are no records of cars at all in up to 19 counties. It is not until 1924 that there were cars in all the regions. As mentioned earlier, the automobile industry gradually took shape

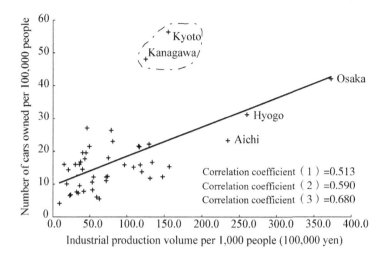

Figure 10.4 Relationship between income level and penetration of automobiles (1924).

Source: Population and number of cars: *Statistical Yearbook of Japan*; industrial production volume: Minister's Secretariat Statistics Department, Ministry of
International Trade and Industry (1961).

Notes:
1 Tokyo is excluded here, but the correlation coefficient is calculated.
2 Correlation coefficient (1) includes Tokyo; correlation coefficient (2) excludes Tokyo;
  correlation coefficient (3) excludes Tokyo, Kyoto, and Kanagawa.

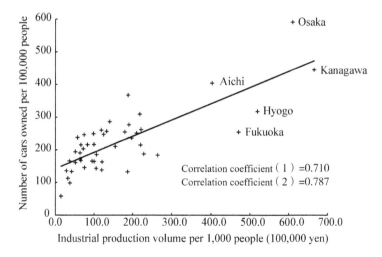

Figure 10.5 Relationship between income level and penetration of automobiles (1937).

Source: Population and number of cars: *Statistical Yearbook of Japan*; industrial production volume: Minister's Secretariat Statistics Department, Ministry of
International Trade and Industry (1961).

Notes:
1 Tokyo is excluded here, but the correlation coefficient is calculated.
2 Correlation coefficient (1) includes Tokyo; correlation coefficient (2) excludes Tokyo.

from this time to the 1930s. For example, the average number of cars in each county was 314 in 1924, but this had reached 4,579 in 1937, a rapid increase in just dozens of years. The role of demand cannot be underestimated.

Figures 10.4 and 10.5 show the penetration of automobiles throughout Japan in 1924 and 1937. While not all regions had cars in 1924, the regions where there were vehicles showed a highly positive correlation between per capita income (industrial output per 1,000 people) and the number of cars owned (correlation coefficient = 0.5–0.7). This relationship became stronger in 1937 (correlation coefficient = 0.7–0.8). In other words, the penetration of automobiles depends, in large measure, on incomes. An increase in income not only results in more cars owned, but also improves their quality. In brief, technological innovation which takes place in response to market demand is called "demand-pull" innovation. An emerging industry at the time, the automotive sector is also a typical capital-intensive and technology-intensive sector. However, technological innovation in Japan at the time was still demand-pull, as evidenced by the overwhelming majority of utility models (Figure 10.3).

The automobile market should have a dual structure. Specifically, on the one hand, a few large enterprises chiefly produce vehicles to form a monopoly market; on the other hand, many SMEs are involved in the competitive parts market. In 1929 and 1937, the number of factories with fewer than 30 employees accounted for 85.3% and 86.7% of the total, and the number of employees accounted for 27.1% and 22.2%, respectively. The proportion of factories with over 100 employees accounted for 3.0% and 4.1%, and the number of employees accounted for 51.8% and 64.9%, respectively. Further, there was only one factory with over 1,000 employees in 1929, and the number of employees accounted for 19.8%. In 1937, this figure reached five, and the number of employees accounted for 43.7%. In terms of production volume, in 1929, factories with fewer than 30 employees accounted for 5.4%, the number (4) of factories with over 200 employees accounted for up to 90.5%, and the number of factories with over 1,000 employees accounted for 64.7%.[19] As regards technological innovation activities, utility models developed by individuals and SMEs far outnumbered invention patents by legal persons or large enterprises. This corresponds to the dual structure of the market.

III. Government policies

Compared to rickshaws and bicycles, the government has always supported the automobile sector by enacting the *Law on Subsidy for Military Vehicles* and the *Japanese Automobile Manufacturing Industry Law*. Manufacturers could obtain a subsidy under these laws.[20] The former was enacted in 1918 whereby the state provided financial support to related companies if it requisitioned ordinary cars for military use. This also revitalized the domestic automobile sector and increased the number of cars owned.[21] To this end, the Army invested heavily in the R&D of automobiles. For example, the Army's automobile R&D expenses were 150,000 yen in 1917 and 480,000 yen in 1924. The automobile award fee increased from 40,000 yen in 1919 to 200,000–300,000 yen in the early 1920s, and later to 500,000–800,000 yen.[22]

The *Japanese Automobile Manufacturing Industry Law* was promulgated in 1936 based on the *Outline of the Automobile Industry* (enacted in 1935). This law was enacted when the government realized that the Japanese automobile market had been dominated by foreign companies from the late 1920s to the early 1930s. The *Japanese Automobile Manufacturing Industry Law* stipulated that the manufacturing and assembly of over a certain number of vehicles required government permission, so that military vehicles could be localized. Under this law, Ford and General Motors who had already invested in the Japanese market ended car assembly and quit the Japanese market after 1939. At the same time, three companies, namely Toyota Automatic Loom Works which targeted models for the popular market, Nissan who had begun to produce small cars, and the Internal Combustion Engine Automobile Industry who had scored some achievements with chariots and tractors, were designated by the government as paramilitary car manufacturing companies to produce vehicles under the supervision of the government.

In addition to these legal means, the government also supported the automobile sector in other forms. For example, in order to solve technical problems, the Ministry of Commerce and Industry established the "Automobile Technical Committee" in August 1939 for research on problems related to automotive production technology such as saving fuel, studying alternative fuels, and manufacturing of vehicles using alternative fuel. In November of the same year, in response to the Military's "bill for improvement of quality and performance of Japanese automobiles," research institutes were set up in Nissan and Toyota. In other words, unified standards were formulated and were reviewed and adopted and trial production commenced in 1941. Moreover, the Ministry of Commerce and Industry set up an automobile department for the comprehensive R&D of automobiles under the Machinery Test Institute in 1942. It had Japan's first regular test track with a total length of 2 kilometers and parts inspection plant.

IV. Zaibatsu and foreign capital

It is worth mentioning the role of zaibatsu. Given the technical complexity and capital intensity in the automobile industry, government support and the involvement of huge capital forces were indispensable. However, zaibatsu at that time did not value the automobile industry. Hidemasa Morikawa holds that this is one of the reasons for the developing technology in the automobile industry.[23] For example, Mitsubishi Heavy Industries began developing cars in 1917, and Kobe Shipyard under its affiliation began studying a of an Italian Fiat, producing their first car in 1918. This vehicle, called Mitsubishi Model A, was manufactured by the company except for some parts such as ball bearings. With a self-made engine, chassis, and body, it is one of the few cars that was recognized for practicality. In 1918, the *Law on Subsidy for Military Vehicles* came into effect. Mitsubishi trial-produced four military trucks which were completed in 1920. However, Mitsubishi withdrew from the automobile sector in 1921, probably afraid that it had incurred immense costs for vehicles for which there was no market. However, some enterprises much smaller and less powerful than Mitsubishi persisted, such as Kwaishinsha and Hakuyosha. Nissan, Isuzu, and Toyota also came through against overwhelming difficulties.

As mentioned earlier, Ford had set up Japan Ford in Yokohama in 1925, and GM had set up Japan General Motors in Osaka in 1926. Entering the Japanese market in the form of assembly was a type of complete vehicle import. This became the mainstream type of automotive market supply in Japan before the mid-1930s. The following points can be made about the impact of foreign capital on the Japanese market. First, as Ford and General Motors entered the Japanese market, their mass production and sales systems were adopted in Japan. In particular, Ford's production modes and management modes were used as the model for production, sales and management in the automobile industry in a developing country. Second, the two enterprises purchased a wealth of parts made in Japan, which spurred the development of the parts industry that had long impeded the development of the automotive sector. The third is the negative impact. In other words, the emerging Japanese automobile sector could not resist the price and quality of this assembly mode, and as a result, developed at a slower pace.

Section 4 Concluding remarks

The automobile sector is the most archetypical machinery sector in modern times. Today, countries the world over are making technological innovations and improvements. For example, electric and hybrid cars are being produced, and there are more possibilities for other technological advances going forward. This industry in Japan has seen a century of development and is now leading the world. This is the result of long-term investment. Japan has also experienced hardships and difficulties, as well as the tireless efforts of entrepreneurs, market demand, and national policies.

This chapter has studied the relationship between the development of the Japanese automobile sector and technological innovation before World War II, and several conclusions can be drawn. First, the Japanese automobile sector before the war basically developed thanks to the efforts of the private sector. In particular, craftsmen-turned-entrepreneurs and technician-turned-managers made important contributions. In other words, craftsmanship and entrepreneurship made possible the development of the automotive sector. Of course, there is no denying the role of the government, because the automobile sector requires a great deal of capital, investment, and technology, and sometimes policy protection, unlike bicycles and rickshaws.

Second, there was a lack of technological advance and technological innovation in the automotive sector, which was mainly caused by the following factors. First, the heavy chemical industry had not yet developed, and the raw materials and technologies required for many parts and components industries were scarce. Second, Japan possessed little technical knowledge of the automotive industry, and could hardly produce products that could compete with European and U.S. products. Third, despite their strength, old zaibatsu was relatively conservative, and did give its support to the developing industry. Of course, low income levels indicated a limited market demand. The government later transferred industrial policies to the aircraft industry (Pacific War). All these had a negative impact on the development of the automotive sector.

Third, nevertheless, the expanding market made a positive contribution to the development of the automotive sector. After the 1920s, technological penetration and technological innovation in the automotive industry received great support from the market ("demand-pull"). Further, the market structure of the automotive sector also cramped technological innovation. The complete vehicle factories composed of a few large enterprises and the parts factories composed of the majority of SMEs constituted the "dual structure." This structure corresponded to the results of technological innovation; large enterprises had more invention patents, while SMEs had more utility models.

Fourth, compared to emerging zaibatsu, the most influential and powerful old zaibatsu at the time adopted a negative attitude toward the automotive sector, which was another reason for the sluggish development of the Japanese auto sector. Foreign investment in Japan had both positive and negative effects, despite its short duration. The positive effect is that it brought many new production and management methods to Japan; the negative effect is that the development of local Japanese enterprises was delayed to some extent.

Notes

1 Shigeki Yamaoka (1988) has produced research on the history of technology from an engineering perspective. Research on small-scale cars includes that by No Inman (1999).
2 Natural monopoly industries generally refer to urban public sectors such as water supply, gas supply, etc.
3 On the development course of Japan's automobile industry, see the Society of Bicycle Industry History (1965–1969).
4 See the Society of Automobile Industry History (1965).
5 Namely, the Ministry of Posts, a government body in charge of communication.
6 See the Society of Automobile Industry History (1965).
7 Kwaishinsha will be discussed later.
8 *General Overview of Factories* covers factories with more than ten people. Moreover, these factories have a scale of 10–100 people. Yanase Shokai had the largest automobile factory with about 200 people. Nearly all these factories adopted power equipment.

9 Nissan Motor (1965) p. 13. Statistics on car ownership during this period are not necessarily accurate. For example, Takao Shimano (1980) recorded only 791 cars in 1914, 3,869 in 1918, and 20,587 in 1924. The figures stated here for 1924 differ from those in *Japan Statistical Yearbook*.

10 Data on Tokyo is obtained from Tokyo City Hall's *Factory Overview* of *Tokyo* (1924, 1925), and data on Osaka from Osaka City Hall's *List of Factories in Osaka* (1926).

11 Peace Memorial Expo (1923), pp. 1009–1015.

12 Tokyo Expo (1929), pp. 481–482.

13 As there is no data on capital stock, the horsepower of prime motors is used here.

14 The production volume is adjusted using the index of the machinery industry as a whole; see Miyohe Shinohara (1972).

15 The output per capita of the bicycle industry was 2,400 yen in 1929, 2,800 yen in 1934, and 2,900 yen in 1939.

16 For details, see Nissan Motor (1965), Toyota Motor (1967), and Suzuki Motor (1970).

17 However, specific and detailed demonstration is required here.

18 On the issue of demand-pull and technology-push, and Schumpeter's hypothesis, see Chapter 3 or Guan (2000).

19 *Statistical Table of Factories* by the Ministry of Commerce and Industry (1929, 1937).

20 Soon after the law was adopted, three companies, Tokyo Gas Electric, IHI Motor Works and Dart Motors, were identified as the recipients of subsidies.

21 Soon after the law was enacted, Tokyo Gas Electric, IHI Motor Works and Dart Motors were designated as the recipients of subsidies.

22 *Statistical Yearbook of the Ministry of the Army* over the years by the Minister of the Army.

23 For details, see Hidemasa Morikawa (1980).

Part V

Concluding remarks and implications

11 Concluding remarks and implications

Section 1 Introduction

As mentioned earlier, this book primarily studies the relationship between technological innovation and economic development in modern Japan, using patent data as a valid indicator of technological innovation. Valuable conclusions and inspiration were obtained from the quantitative analysis of economic activity-related data. This will be discussed below. We will first discuss several issues relating to economic development and technological innovation in modern Japan. First, when economic growth began in modern Japan, it lagged significantly behind Western European countries in terms of technology, as well as in political, social, and cultural aspects.[1] Japan was the first non-Western or American country to realize modern economic growth, and there was innovation in many aspects, although these were not advanced compared to those in Western Europe. For a country wholly different from European and U.S. cultures to achieve such rapid development in a short period of time, requires a strong government, and also a good foundation in the private sector. This is thanks, in part, to the accumulation in pre-modern times and in part to the efforts in modern times.[2] The establishment of the patent system, as studied in this book, and the emergence of a number of inventions illustrate the contribution of technological advances and the role of society in economic development in modern Japan. Second, it is hard for a non-European country to take the lead in achieving economic development, because Western European countries shared consistent cultural and social foundations, and similar development levels. These advantages were not available in Japan. For a country steeped in history, it is hard to fully look at the advanced Western European countries, and also be willing to learn from them. In fact, there was heated debate among politicians and the private sector in modern Japan (especially in the Meiji period (1868–1912)) over whether to achieve full westernization. China would see similar disputes in the second half of the nineteenth century. The insightful people of the Westernization School proposed "Chinese (learning as the) essence and Western (learning for its) utility." This view was not conservative at the time. It at least has a positive and pioneering significance. However, the Westernization school did not become mainstream in China, and their ideas were not applied or promoted. Under the leadership of the government, Japan began to learn from Western Europe, and advanced the three slogans of Bunmei Kaika, Fukoku Kyōhei, and Shokusan Kōgyō, which translate as "Civilization and Enlightenment," "Enrich the Nation; Strengthen the Army," and "Encourage Industry." The slogans were implemented to good effect. Third, in response to the call and promotion by the government, the private sector set up businesses, spread education, and introduced modern science and technology. Japanese society witnessed tremendous changes. This is an important symbol of modernization in a country. Many developing countries often invigorate the economy by introducing some of the market principles, while preserving other aspects of their own characteristics, including their political systems. This is often doomed to failure, because modern society is an organic whole. The market economy reflects the subjective willingness of individuals and requires private ownership as a guarantee. This calls for the protection of law. Otherwise, individuals are unwilling to engage in economic activities, much less technological innovation activities, because the results of their own technological innovation activities are easily used for free and copied by others. The same is true in politics. In a market economy, agents are required to speak for different people. This requires different parties to be involved in politics through competition, in which winners make decisions, and losers adjust their stance. Notwithstanding, the fact that modern Japan did not fully implement the strict "separation of the three powers" system, was reflected to a great extent. This system also yielded positive results, laying a strong foundation for democratization after World War II.[3]

Section 2 Concluding remarks

I. Industrial development theory

In the early days of economic development in modern Japan, traditional industries played a bigger role than modern industries, and their development was a precondition for the subsequent development of modern industries. In general, the economy of a backward country is composed of existing traditional sectors and modern sectors imported from developed countries, namely the "dual structure." Economic development is achieved through competition and adjustment in these two sectors. However, this development is not necessarily balanced, but varies with change. From the perspective of the dual structure, it is inevitable that the focus shifts from the traditional sector to the modern. The equation of economic development to industrialization can be said to be the shrinking of traditional sectors and the expansion of modern sectors. However, the expansion of the modern sector takes time, because they generally require a high-level of technology and abundant capital. It is impossible to create these two types of resources in the short term. Even if they are available, they may not be used properly, because in a developing country there is a shortage of entrepreneurs, technicians, and skilled labor because of a poor education system and lack of experience in industrialization. In view of this, traditional industries can maintain the momentum of economic development, and also help to amasses capital, technology, and talent, laying a foundation for the development of more modern industries.[4]

The importance of traditional industries can be construed from the following points. First, before modern industries emerged, economic growth largely depended on the development of traditional industries. This was the case in Japan before World War II. The traditional industries, such as textiles and food, contributed greatly to economic growth.[5] Second, traditional industries were generally labor-intensive, and generated more jobs, which is of great significance for social stability. The manufacturing sector in modern Japan still employed over half its employees from 1909 to 1940, even after a certain level of industrialization had been achieved.[6] According to estimates based on this figure, traditional industries should have had a higher proportion of employees in the early stage of economic development, before 1909. Third, some traditional industries belonged to the export industry, and played an important role in the valuable foreign exchange required for modern industries, such as raw silk, green tea and other primary products and primary industrial products, as well as products in traditional industries during the mid-Meiji period. At that time, the rickshaw, invented by the Japanese in the early Meiji period was the only export among mechanical products.

However, the development of traditional industries alone was not enough. Industrialization could not be achieved without the development of modern industries. In modern Japan, traditional and modern industries developed synergistically. As industrialization intensified, the proportion of modern industries gradually expanded as modern industries grew faster than traditional industries. This is the inevitable result of industrialization. The principal reason is the difference in productivity. Modern industries depend on state-of-the-art machinery and well-trained labor, with better productivity than traditional industries. For example, from 1909–1940, the actual output per capita in modern industries was nearly double that of traditional industries. However, traditional industries would not be completely replaced by modern industries, as they are rooted in Japan's unique culture. This is even the case in modern Japan when European and U.S. culture has a considerable level of penetration. For example, while the dietary culture in modern Japan is wholly different from that in early modern times, foods such as miso soup, soy sauce, and seafood have not completely vanished. Instead, demand for these foods has continued to expand, because, as levels of income increase, there is higher demand for the basic necessities of life. Of course, the production methods and technologies for a great many traditional products have seen tremendous changes..

A slew of factors promotes industrial development, such as increased demand in the developed market, increased supply capacity due to technological innovation, as well as the government's industrial policies. All of these are significant. The focus is now on technological innovation and the discussion of its role in traditional and modern industries. The development of traditional and modern industries requires the support of technological innovation. In modern Japan, traditional industries play a bigger role. Prior to World War II, Japan's industry developed thanks to technological innovation. Although not comparable to that in Western European countries, technological innovation was rare and valuable in a backward country. In particular, the many low-level technological innovations in traditional industries, greatly supported the development of traditional industries in the early days of industrialization. This can be called the "prime power."

The technological innovation of traditional industries is more important, because they have an advantage in terms of quantity, and the development of grassroots technologies is highly supported.[7] The so-called advantage in terms of quantity means a greater contribution to industrial development. This can be explained in two ways. First, if technological innovation is applied to production activities, it will spur economic development through an increase in productivity. This can be seen from the comparison of technological innovations based on industries in Japan before World War II. In other words, the greater the number of technological innovations, the greater the output in an industry. Second, the emergence of a slew of technological innovations creates new R&D capabilities. In other words, a wealth of people could engage in R&D in traditional industries and could develop new technologies by gaining experience and carrying out sustained research. Together with entrepreneurs, they were vital for Japan's technological and industrial development at that time.

However, modern industries had a great many high-level technological innovations that were not available in traditional industries. Many of these copied imported technologies, but were of great value to Japan at that time and contributed greatly to industrial development. However, given the small number of these technologies, they did not make as great a contribution to the Japanese economy as those of traditional industries. Of course, this is limited to quantity only. If quality and development prospects are considered, there is more potential for technological innovation in modern industries. As the economy developed, the technological innovation in modern industries increasingly showed its importance and value.

II. Technological innovation theory

Before World War II, Japan saw a wealth of highly practical technological innovations. This is also a salient feature of technological innovation in Japan during this period, and was the driving force behind Japan's economic development. As a matter of fact, Japan's gradual development as a technological powerhouse was, to a large extent, due to a gradual accumulation of these innovations. This was originally a feature of technological innovation in traditional industries. As traditional industries had an advantage in terms of quantity at that time, these also represented the characteristics of Japan as a whole. In fact, the technological innovation of traditional and modern industries varied in many ways. For example, technological innovation in traditional industries was usually carried out by individuals, mostly based on work experience. These technologies developed and improved. At the same time, due to the low level of technology, many people with such technical know-how could carry out R&D, thus making it competitive. Moreover, while there were quite a few engineering innovations, product innovations were few and far between, because the products in traditional industries were simple, and it was not easy to develop new products.

By contrast, innovation in modern industries had an organizational nature, as evidenced by the majority of on-the-job inventions. Given the scientific nature of modern industries, technological innovation generally requires a host of equipment. Of course, since modern industrial ideas were mostly imported from Western Europe, innovations were chiefly copies of imported technologies. As there were usually only a few large companies in modern industries, once they mastered a technology, they quickly became monopolistic. Finally, there were new products from the innovation efforts in modern industries, because they were still in the process of development, and the market and consumers required constant improvement. Modern industries had diversity and development potential from a technical perspective. Some technologies can lead to a host of new products.

There are other differences in technological innovation between traditional and modern industries. For example, technological innovation had different sources. The technological innovation in traditional industries is "demand-pull," while it is "technology-push" in modern industries because the market already exists and there is already huge demand. The market for modern industries developed through new products, and these depended on technology. Like industrial development, there are other diverse factors which spurred technological innovation. This book focused on human resources, market conditions, and government policy, and also studied their respective contributions to traditional and modern industries.

For starters, there are entrepreneurs or business managers, technicians, employees and craftsmen, but not all of these engaged in technological innovation activities. From the perspective of technological innovation, they performed different roles in traditional and modern industries. For example, there were more craftsman-turned-managers in traditional industries, who were also major participants in technological innovation. In comparison, technical personnel who received a specialized education are the mainstay of modern industries. Craftsmen improved technology in traditional industries by dint of their experience and dedication. Technicians conducted imitative R&D on imported technologies using their theoretical knowledge. Judging by the results, there were more innovations with a low technological level, such as utility models in traditional industries, and more innovations with high technological level, such as invention patents in modern industries. For the overall technological level in Japan, invention patents were great innovations, but were not necessarily the best technology for Western Europe and even the world as a whole.

These human resources are in one sense, a symbol of "social competence."[8] An improvement in quantity and quality means an improvement in the technological level of the entire society. Therefore, training is vital. In modern Japan, there is a balance between the demand for talent due to industrial development and the supply of talent spurred by education and development. At the same time, the equilibrium point is moving to the right. In other words, qualified personnel are being continuously trained to meet the needs of industrial development. This is a salient feature of the development of education in Japan before World War II.

The second factor is market conditions. There are two issues related to technological innovation. One is the level of market development, and the other is the market structure. The level of market development refers to the market size: the more developed the market, the larger its size. Traditional industries generally had a large market size, because products in traditional industries were used in everyday life and were related to life's basic necessities. As far as technological innovation is concerned, a large market size means there is a greater chance of sparking off innovation based on market demand. If the market size is small and there is not much demand, it is necessary to tap the market through new products. The former is called "demand-pull" market, and the latter "technology-push" market. The traditional industries market in modern Japan was relatively large, so there was more demand-induced innovation. Modern industries had a smaller market size, so technological innovation was chiefly achieved through the stimulus of new inventions.

As regards the relationship between market structure and technological innovation, there was some debate over the famous Schumpeter hypothesis, but no agreement was achieved. As we know, there was a difference in technological innovation between traditional and modern industries in Japan, and one of the important differences was the market structure. In other words, the market in traditional industries was generally competitive, and the market in modern industries was monopolistic. Therefore, as mentioned earlier, technological innovation in the two industries had significantly different characteristics, which showed two different markets. Specifically, technological innovation in competitive markets featured practical petty innovations, while monopolistic markets had more underlying and high-level innovation.

The third factor was the role of government. Two points were made here. The first dealt with technical policies, including the enactment of a patent system, a commendation system, a subsidy system, the convening of Expos, and the establishment of national research institutions, among others. These measures performed different roles at different times depending on the stage of industrial development. The convening of Expos and the commendation system played a bigger role in the early stages of economic development, while the patent system and national research institutions were more important later on. The facts in Japan before World War II prove that some policies had contradictory parts, but if these were used properly, they could play an appropriate role. Expos were held to popularize new technological knowledge and promote new products. The patent system granted monopoly rights to inventors. Essentially, the two were incompatible, but different strategies adopted at different times were commendable. Second, while education was not necessarily directly related to technological innovation, its development was indispensable for training technological innovation talents. Strategies for developing education were legion. From the perspective of technological innovation, the following two points were noteworthy in Japan before World War II. One was the drawing up of education policies according to the needs of industrial development and economic development, and the other was the importance attached to industrial education. Regarding the former, there was high input in primary education and higher education in the early days of economic development, because more people were required to be involved. At the same time, in order to import advanced foreign technology, professionals who understand modern scientific knowledge and technology were required. Therefore, it was essential to build a few institutes of higher education. After the penetration of primary education, the focus gradually shifted to secondary education, because as the economy developed, more skilled workers were needed, and the industrial upgrading created higher demands for workers who needed to master intermediate-level scientific knowledge and technology. As a consequence, primary education, higher education, and secondary education developed to have their respective divisions of labor. This was consistent with the course of industry development. Traditional industries were in the majority in the early days, but the focus then shifted to modern industries. Heavy chemical industrialization commenced after World War II. The number and quality of talents required at each stage varies. Moreover, in Japan before World War II, continuation and industrial education were developed, in addition to regular education. Most of these establishments belonged to secondary education. Workers attended night schools or various industrial schools, such as agricultural and forestry schools or vocational schools, in their spare time.

III. Flying geese paradigm theory

The process of technology development in Japan before World War II was divided into three stages according to the path of technology import→ technology penetration→ technological innovation. The author analyzed the technological development model in Japan as a backward country during this period. As far as the conclusions were concerned, technological development in a backward country was similar to industrial development. In general, this was achieved through technology import→ penetration and innovation → technology transfer and export. This is highly similar to the flying geese paradigm for industrial development in a backward country. Although the scope of study in this book does not cover technology transfer to foreign countries after digestion and absorption, it is based on the following reasons. First, at the time, Japan's technology transfer to other countries and regions was rare, except its investment in several colonies, such as Taiwan, the Korean Peninsula, and Northeast China, occupied by Japan at the time, as well as North China following the all-out aggression against China.[9] Second, under the influence of the first point, there is little research on Japan's technology transfer overseas before World War II compared to technology import and penetration. Third, many people have insufficient recognition of technology transfer as a component of technological development, just like insufficient attention to technological innovation.[10]

Before World War II, Japan's economic development was equal to industrialization. In fact, it was closely related to overseas countries. This can be considered from two aspects. First, industries imported from Western Europe (modern industries) chiefly experienced the process from import → import substitution (domestic production) → export. This process is called the "flying geese paradigm." Second, in traditional industries, advanced technology imported from Western Europe was used to improve the existing technical system to improve the quality and production volume of products. Many of these industries became export industries. The above two models achieved a great deal of success. The former belonged to the "flying geese paradigm theory" while the latter belonged to the "product life cycle theory." The discussion was carried out by the former from the perspective of a backward country, and by the latter from the perspective of a developed country. The two have their respective values.

As we know, a great many goods in modern Japan were gradually exported after undergoing the process of import and domestic production. The process from import to production (import substitution) to export is similar to the posture of a group of flying geese if it is painted on paper. Professor Kaname Akamatsu of Hitotsubashi University called it the "flying geese paradigm." This argument about industrial development was later discussed by Kiyoshi Kojima and others, and was widely accepted. Ippe Yamazawa expanded this change into five stages: import → import substitution → export → maturity → reverse export.[11]

If we say the flying geese paradigm discusses how backward countries learn from advanced countries to achieve development and catch up, then product life-cycle theory studies the process of how to develop new products by learning from advanced countries, standardizing products throughout the market, and their replacement by middle-sized countries.[12] From the standpoint of advanced countries to backward countries, there is a fundamental difference with the flying geese paradigm. However, if we focus on the second part of the product life cycle theory, it is highly similar to the viewpoint of flying geese paradigm. We believe that the two can be discussed together at this stage.

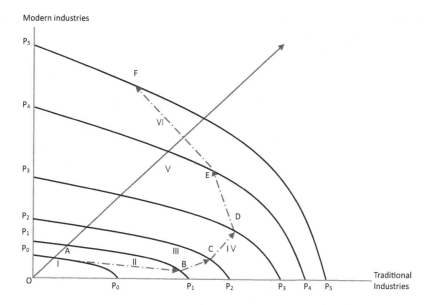

Figure 11.1 Forms of industrial development in modern Japan.
Note: Changes in consumption are omitted here.

Below is the summary and induction based on these two development models. Figure 11.1 shows the changes and development in the Japanese economy (referring to the manufacturing sector). This is represented by the production possibility curve (PPC), which comprises traditional and modern industries. In the first period, two products were produced and consumed at point A as no international trade was carried out. Consumer goods were related to the basic necessities of life produced by traditional industries, while capital goods such as machinery, steel, and chemicals were produced by modern industries. During this period, as trade was liberalized, the production factors of products concentrated in traditional industries grew quickly, resulting in the shift of the PCC from P_0P_0 to P_1P_1. If the relative price remains unchanged, the Rybczynski line will tilt to the lower right, and the new production equilibrium point is point B.[13] This means that more products from traditional industries were exported and more products from modern industries were imported. In the second period, traditional industries continued to grow, and modern industries also begin to grow, but not as quickly. At this time, the PPC moves from P_1P_1 to P_2P_2, the Rybczynski line will tilt to the upper right, and point C becomes the new production point. As the economy develops, the PPC may move from P_2P_2 to P_3P_3. At this time, traditional and modern industries see synchronized growth, and the Rybczynski line will see a neutral change. In other words, it will move to the upper right corner along the 45-degree line, and the new production point is point D. In the fourth and fifth periods, the economy continues to develop, the PPC will move toward P_4P_4 and P_5P_5 near the vertical axis, and the economy as a whole sees a shift from traditional to modern industries. In the sixth period, this relationship will be reversed. In other words, the share of traditional industries shrinks and plays a secondary role, while modern industries have a growing share and occupy a dominant position. About four periods were completed in modern Japan (1868–1945), while the latter two periods were completed after World War II.

This form of technological development is highly similar to that of industrial development. The chart of the product life cycle theory is used for illustration. Figure 11.2 shows the form of technological development in backward countries. The case industries, namely the rickshaw, bicycle, and car industries, are used for illustration. First, the changes in the rickshaw industry as a representative of traditional industries were observed. In the early days of economic development (as shown in the first period in the figure), technology developed rapidly, but ownership was at a low level. However, as rickshaw technology developed, Japan had comparative advantage, and began to spread the technology to neighboring countries. Rickshaws were the most common means of transportation in major cities during the Republic of China. This is also the case in many countries in South and Southeast Asia. Rickshaws in these countries were first imported from Japan, but some countries eventually began to self-produce. In the second period, the technology ownership and domestic demand reached its highest point, and then began to fall, while technology export reached its highest level, and then began to decline. In the third period, technology ownership, demand, and exports plunged rapidly, but imports took their place.[14]

We looked at the industries where localization can be more easily achieved. The bicycle industry is an intermediate industry here. In the first period, both the technology ownership and demand were low, but would slowly increase. More demand than ownership indicates import from abroad. In the second period, both the technology ownership and demand grew, but ownership increased faster than demand, and as a result, the amount of technologies imported from developed countries began to fall. In the third period, the technology ownership gradually overtook the demand and exports began. Moreover, as a whole, the absolute level is a continual increase in the process, namely a growing quantity.[15] As mentioned earlier, the bicycle industry in Japan began to take shape at the end of the nineteenth century, and, by 1937, had became the top machinery and appliance export. Bicycle technology also began to be exported at this time. In 1936, Mitayaseisakujyo set up a factory in Shenyang. The merchant Setsusaburo Kojima also established a factory in Shenyang in the same year, a factory in Tianjin in 1938, and a factory in Shanghai in 1940. The factories later became the forerunners in the Chinese bicycle industry.[16]

Finally, we looked at the car industry, which has more complex technology and the localization of which was more complicated. In the first period,

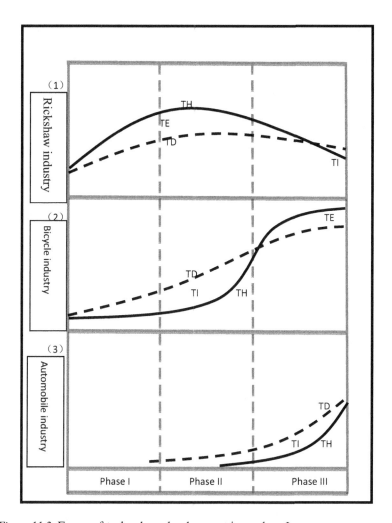

Figure 11.2 Forms of technology development in modern Japan.

Note: TH is technology ownership, TD is technology demand, TI is technology import, TE is technology output.

there was a low demand for technology, without technology ownership, and imports were required, albeit in a small quantity. In the second period, technology ownership increased slightly, and Japan began to produce cars, albeit at a very low level. The demand did not increase rapidly, because the domestic consumption level was not high at this time, as few people could afford to buy cars. In the third period, both demand and ownership increased rapidly. Although imports were still required, the rate of increase in ownership outstripped that of demand and imports began to decrease. According to the preceding chapters, a few forerunners in Japan began to attempt to produce cars in around the early twentieth century, but with little success. There was a slight improvement in the 1920s, but it was still sluggish.[17] In the mid-1930s, the industry was gradually on the right track following the establishment of car makers such as Toyota, Nissan, and Isuzu.

As mentioned above, before World War II, Japan had seen a pattern of continuous technological development from traditional industries, to transplantation industries that could be easily localized, to transplantation industries the localization of which were difficult. The international transfer of this technology was achieved thanks to the huge population in the neighboring countries which provided a market for the export of Japanese products and technologies. In this way, an entire supply chain was formed. As the first Asian country to undertake modern economic growth, Japan could import a slew of advanced technologies from Western Europe. After these had been digested and absorbed, Japan could also export technologies to neighboring countries in addition to meeting its domestic demand. It should be noted that, at that time, Taiwan of China, the Korean Peninsula, Northeast China, and other regions, were Japanese colonies and provided a huge market for Japanese exports and technology transfer.

Section 3 Implications

I. Industrial development

The pattern of industrial development from traditional to modern industries in modern Japan also applies to many other developing countries. In general, similar to modern Japan, developing countries have many traditional industries such as agriculture, handicrafts, and commerce, and modern industries imported from developed countries such as machinery, chemicals, and metallurgy. However, in the early days of economic development, traditional industries had an overwhelming advantage as modern industries were not mature enough. It is well-known that modern industries require a wealth of capital and technology for development, and it takes time. The technology system of modern industries is complicated, making it harder to digest and absorb in a short time. By comparison, traditional industries are generally labor-intensive, and are more important than modern industries for generating jobs. Given the reality of surplus labor in developing countries, the development of traditional industries is indispensable in the early stages for the development of modern industries. In fact, the development of traditional industries in modern Japan was faster than that in the pre-modern period. This is attributable to the transplantation of modern industries. It can be said that this is good cooperation because of the mutual promotion of the two industries.

However, today's developing countries tend to strive for rapid industrialization. To this end, modern industries are vigorously transplanted without due regard to the actual situation, while traditional industries are not well developed, making it hard to achieve good results. China implemented a planned economy after 1949. To catch up with developed countries, China gave priority to the development of heavy industry, with scant regard to its light industry or agriculture. This laid a significant industrial foundation during this period, and facilitated the rapid development in the subsequent reform and opening up period, but at enormous cost, including low efficiency, waste of resources, and slow improvement in the well-being of its people.[18]

II. Technical innovation

As mentioned earlier, small-scale technological innovations, such as the improvement (including penetration) of traditional technologies, are of great significance for the economy in the early days of development. As shown above, traditional industries occupied an overwhelming market share in the early days of economic development. Whether traditional industries can develop has a great influence on the economy as a whole. In Japan, the development of traditional industries meant an increase in quantity and quality improvement, which comes chiefly in the wake of technological advance. Like utility models, minor technological innovations were more in line with the reality in backward countries, because small technological innovations could generally be developed and used without much funding. Therefore, small technological innovations can produce great economic benefit overall.

After 1949, the Chinese government greatly encouraged small-scale technological innovations. From the 1950s to the reform and opening up, great efforts were made to encourage minor inventions and improvements. Nevertheless, the economic effect was not significant due to the market system at the time. On the one hand, the factories were state- or collective-owned, and technical personnel and laborers were not enthusiastic about production and technological innovation due to a lack of incentive. At the same time, there were no legal and policy systems that rewarded technological innovation, and the *Patent Law* was not enacted until 1985.

III. The role of government

The government had a greater role in technological innovation than in other fields, because technology is of the nature of public goods and it is not easy to corner the market. In the absence of some legal and policy support, others can easily use the outcomes of technological innovation for free. The upshot is the diminishing technological innovation activities, which severely compromises long-term technological development. Therefore, a great many countries issued policies to protect technology, especially the establishment of patent system. In this sense, technological innovation is intimately related to government policy on technology. The degree and level of technological innovation activities varies according to the dynamics and scope of laws and policies. For example, China enacted the *Patent Law* in 1985. Thereafter, technological innovation activities such as invention patents and utility models yielded fruitful results. In the twenty-first century, China's development has flourished, and it has become the country with the greatest number of patent applications worldwide.

The government also plays a role in the training of talent. Technological innovation necessitates a wealth of professionals with scientific knowledge and know-how. Of course, these professionals must be produced via a good education system. As mentioned earlier, technological innovation in traditional industries in the early stages of modern Japan was chiefly made by grassroots craftsmen and entrepreneurs, who carried out innovation through the accumulation of experience and routine improvements. However, to develop its economy, a country needs to shift from traditional to modern industries, and technological innovation in modern industries requires high-level professional knowledge. Education policies in modern Japan facilitated the cultivation of these professionals. It has been observed that there was "dual structure" in the early days of education development in modern Japan, namely prioritizing the development of primary education and higher education. The compulsory education implemented earlier promoted public education, which is not easy to in a backward country, due to a shortage of talents and funding. It is not easy to achieve comprehensive development in the short term, and so it needs to be made a priority. It is important that primary education can open the minds of the populace, so that as many people as possible are literate and can understand government policy. Many developing countries today find it hard to promote industrialization due to the poor literacy levels. Because of a low level of schooling. Funds and manpower are needed to develop education, so the education and economic development actually promote each other. They are two sides of the same coin. Another lesson to be learned from Japan is the importance of industrial education. The Japanese government promoted this early on, which produced a wealth of applied talent for the development of traditional industries and modern industries.

Although much later than Japan, China adopted a similar development approach for education. During the planned economy period, China mainly developed primary education, and higher education. Secondary industrial education basically developed after the reform and opening up. Except during the Cultural Revolution, technician training schools, vocational and agricultural schools as well as many tutoring classes have always existed. Moreover, China also launched several nationwide "anti-illiteracy campaigns," which played a positive role in spreading the most basic knowledge among its people. More famous are the nationwide movements in the 1950s, in the early days of reform and opening up. In the 1950s, shortly after the founding of the People's Republic of China, there was a severe shortage of talent. The vast majority of the population were illiterate. Overall, it was the same as, or even worse than, Japan in the Meiji period.[19] In the early days of reform and opening up, due to the impact of the Cultural Revolution, the education system was in tatters.

In a sense, it was highly similar to the situation in the 1950s. In particular, at the beginning of the Cultural Revolution, school students became the "Red Guards" and later were sent to the countryside for work. Many of them did not complete middle school or high school studies. In the early 1980s, the government produced policies to help these people attend literacy courses and obtain diplomas. With greater investment in higher education and a lower threshold for admissions, a variety of higher education approaches were adopted, such as TV University, workers' university, part-time university, day-student schools, and self-study which has helped to solve the shortage of qualified professionals.

Section 4 Subsequent topics

These are the main conclusions of this book. Although these conclusions are limited, we believe that these are of important for Japan's economic development and technological advancement after World War II, and will provide inspiration for economic development in other countries. Many developing countries today still fail to launch modern economic growth or achieve its smooth development, largely due to a lack of economic, political, and social conditions, which were available to modern Japan. These conditions are the result of gradual improvement. Politically, it requires a strong government. Many former colonies countries that become independent after World War II have not set up modern political systems, and lack competent governments. Some leaders of the independence and liberation movements have instead become new dictators. Instead of building a progressive country, they regard it as their own private property. In many countries, factions juggle for power, wreaking great havoc on the people. There is no economic development to speak of. Some countries want to develop their economies, but fail to achieve this due to a weak social basis and a dearth of human resources. A lack of stable policies, coupled with the intervention of other bigger countries, prevents the normal development of the economy.

China, a big country steeped in history, has no shortage of natural resources. In modern times, many people with high ideals have been committed to the development of the country. However, the rule of the feudal dynasty in the second half of the nineteenth century, meant it was difficult to really launch modern economic growth in China. Despite tremendous efforts by a great many enlightened people, China did not see normal economic development such as that in modern Japan. During the Republic of China period (1912–1949), a wealth of private enterprises emerged, and progress was made in such sectors as textile, flour, papermaking, tobacco, matchsticks, hardware, machinery, chemicals, cement, power, and coal. Some enterprises achieved considerable development, and some headway was made in technology. However, this development trend came to a hall due to political turmoil and aggression by foreign countries, especially the Japanese occupation of

Northeast China in 1931 and the all-out invasion of China in 1937. This dealt a hammer blow to China's hard-won development momentum. The author defines economic development in this period as a "failed takeoff."[20]

The government committed itself to developing the economy after 1949, but resource utilization and mechanisms lacked flexibility due to the implementation of the planned economy. As a result, it became inefficient and the economy grew slowly. In 1978, the reform and opening-up policy was initiated, whereby market regulation was implemented, and large-scale foreign investment was introduced. Coupled with the foundation laid during the planned economy period, the Chinese economy began to see rapid growth and achieved tremendous results during the next forty years. Although China still lags far behind Japan, it has a promising future. Even if the growth rate slows down, China has at least reached the level of middle income. Development will continue as long as no major problems occur.

Notes

1 Japanese scholars hold that Japan initiated modern economic growth in around 1886, see Ryoushin Minami (1981).
2 Japanese scholars hold that Japan had a good economy during the Edo period; see Ryoushin Minami (1981).
3 Japan set up the cabinet in 1885, enacted the constitution in 1889, and convened a Diet congress in 1890.
4 It is noteworthy that the importance of traditional industries, as emphasized here, is inconsistent with the views of some advocates of traditional industries. They chiefly study traditional industries without paying attention to the development of modern industries. In terms of time, they focused more on pre-modern times, such as the Edo period. This makes sense, because that period was dominated by traditional industries. They concluded that traditional industries could only represent pre-modern times. The development of traditional industries in this book refers to more modern times. One important difference is that modern industries were gradually imported from Western Europe.
5 See Ryoushin Minami (1981).
6 For example, in 1902, the state-owned railway had 24,000 employees, while there were 191,000 rickshaw runners.
7 Technological innovation in traditional industries accounted for two-thirds of the total. Utility models were concentrated in traditional industries, while most of invention patents belonged to modern industries.
8 The term social competence is a concept advanced by Kuznets for Japan, chiefly referring to the overall competence required for economic development in a country. Japan had such competence; see Kuznets (1968), Ryoushin Minami (1981).
9 On Japanese investment in Northeast China and North China before World War II, see the relevant chapters by Guan Quan (2018).
10 Many studies exist on technology transfer. Generally, there are a wealth of studies from the perspectives of international trade, international investment, and multinational corporations. Sueo Sekiguchi (1988) studied the relationship between direct investment and technology transfer.

11 For the flying geese paradigm, see Kaname Akamatsu (1956), Kiyoshi Kojima (1966, 1973), and Ippe Yamazawa (1984).
12 See Vernon (1966).
13 According to theory of international trade, the production point and consumption point is separated after the opening up of trade.
14 However, imports of rickshaws were almost non-existent, because modes of urban transport in Japan were gradually replaced by bicycles and cars.
15 Of course, the quality is also improving, but it is not displayed here.
16 On the development of China's bicycle industry, see Guan Quan (2000a, 2000b, 2018).
17 American car giants, Ford and General Motors, established factories in Japan in 1925 and 1926, respectively, but were expelled, with government support, as Japan developed its own car sector.
18 On the general situation of industrial development in China after 1949, see Guan Quan (2019).
19 According to research, 43% of men and 10% of women were literate and could use an abacus in the early Meiji period in Japan. See Ryoushin Minami (1981). By contrast, according to China's census data, in 1964, 233.27 million or 33.58% of the population was illiterate; in 1982, this was 229.96 million or 22.81%; in 1990 this was 180.03 million, or 15.88%; and in 2000, the illiterate population was 85.07 million or 6.72%. See *China's Statistical Yearbook 2001*.
20 See Guan Quan (2018).

References

I. Literature

1. Japanese Literature

Abe, T. (1989). *Development of the Cotton-Weaving Industry in Late-Meiji Japan.* Tokyo: University of Tokyo Press.

Abe, T. and Kikkawa. T. (1987). The Transition of Motive Power in Japanese Small- and Medium-sized Factories: In the Case of the Cotton Weaving Industry. *Socio-Economic History, 53*(2): 135–158.

Abe, T. and Sawai, M., Eds (1996). *Entrepreneurship and Development in Modern Japan.* Osaka: Osaka University Press.

Akamatsu, K. (1956) The Flying Geese Pattern of the Industrial Development of Our Country – The Case of Machine and Tool-making Industries. *The Hitotsubashi Review, 36*(5): 68–80.

Arashi, K. (1957). *History of Plows in Modern Japan.* Rural Culture Association.

Business History Society of Japan (1985). *A 20-year of Business History Society of Japan: Retrospect and Prospect.* Tokyo: University of Tokyo Press.

Demizu, T. (1990). Technological Innovation in the Bicycle Parts Industry. (Nakaoka, T. Ed.). *An International Comparison of Technology Formation.* Tokyo: Chikuma Syobo.

Doi, N. (1977). Firm Size, Market Power, and Research and Development. *Keizaigaku Ronkyu, 31*(2): 99–123.

Doi, N. (1993). R & D and Firm Size: A Further Examination from Japanese Manufacturing Firm. *Keizaigaku Ronkyu, 46*(4): 1–31.

Doi, T. (1983). Economic Analysis of the Seri Cultural Industry in Japan. The Nokei Ronson: *The Review of Agricultural Economics Hokkaido University, 39*: 245–328.

Fujino, S., Fujino, Sirou., and Ono A. (1979). *Textile Industries.* Tokyo: Toyo Keizai.

Furukawa, T. (1966). *A History of Industries. III.* (Japanese History Series12) Tokyo: Yamakawa Shuppan-sha.

Guan, Q. (1995). Technological Innovation and Industrial Development in Pre-War Japan: Analysis of Patent Data. *The Gizyutu to Bunmei. Journal of the Japan Society for the History of Industrial Technology, 9*(2): 49–65.

Guan, Q. (1996). The Developments of the Bicycle Industry and Technological Absorption in Pre-war Japan. *Socio-Economic History, 62*(5): 1–31.

Guan, Q. (1997a). The Change in Industrial Structure of Modern Industry and Traditional Industry: An Analysis on Statistic Chart of Manufacturing Plants during 1909–1940 (製造業における近代産業と在来産業の構造変化：1909–40年(工場統計表)による分析). *Economy and Economics* (経済と経済学) *82*: 7–29.

Guan, Q. (1997b). Estimation and Analysis of Locality of Power Revolution (動力革命の地域性：推計と分析). *Economy and Economics* (経済と経済学) *84*: 23–56.

Guan, Q. (1998). The Meaning and Limit of Technical Improvement of Traditional Industry: The Rise and Fall of the Rickshaw Industry (在来産業における技術改良の意義と限界：人力車工業盛衰記). *Economy and Economics*(経済と経済学) *87*: 49–65.

Guan, Q. (2000a). Technological Innovations and Inventors in Prewar Japan. *The Economic Review*, *51*(3): 232–42.

Guan, Q. (2000b). The Unbalanced Development of the Chinese Bicycle Industry. *The Hitotsubashi Review*, *123*(5): 12–34.

Guan, Q. (2000c). Development and Innovation in the Chinese Bicycle Industry. *The Hitotsubashi Review*, *124*(5): 16–32.

Guan, Q. (2003). *The Innovation of Modern Japan: Patent and Economic Development* (近代日本のイノベーション：特許と経済発展). Tokyo: Fukosha.

Hara, Y. (1996). *Development Economics*. Tokyo: Iwanami Shoten.

Hashimoto, J. (1994). Technical Policies in Prewar Japan. *Journal of Social Science*, *46*(3): 233–55.

Hatsumeikyoukai. (1974). *Japan Institute of Invention and Innovation*. The 70-Year History of Japan Institute of Invention and Innovation Tokyo: Sobunsha

Hatsumeikyoukai. (1995). *Development Economics*. Tokyo: Sobunsha.

Hiroshige, T. (1973). *The Social History of Science: Scientific Research Systems in Modern Japan* Nature and Science Series). Tokyo: Chuokoronsha.

Holding Company Liquidity Committee. (1950). *Japanese Zaibatsu and its Dissolution* (Material) (日本財閥とその解体(資料)).

Holding Company Liquidity Committee. (1983). *Japanese Zaibatsu and its Dissolution* (日本財閥とその解体).

Hondai, S. (1992). *Simultaneous Growth of Big and Small Business: An Analysis on Specialization* (大企業と中小企業の同時成長：企業間分業の分析). Tokyo: Dobunkan.

Ichikawa, K. (1965). *Japanese Patent Law*. Tokyo: Nihon Hatsumei Shinbunsha.

Imai, K., Murakami, Y. and Tsukui, J. (1970). Information, Technology, Firm size：Outlook and Some Demonstration（情報・技術・企業規模：展望と若干の実証）. *Economic Analysis on Information and Technology*. (Research Report No. 24). Japan Center for Economic Research.

Imai, K., Uzawa, H., Komiya, R., Negishi T. and Murakami Y. (1972). *Elements of Price Theory III*. Tokyo: Iwanami Shoten, Publishers.

Imatsu, K. (1989). *Technological Conditions in Modern Japan* (近代日本の技術的条件). Kyoto: Yanagihara Shote.

Industry Department of Osaka City Hall. (1933). *Bicycle Industry in Osaka* (大阪の自転車工業).

Industry Sector of Economic Affairs Bureau of Sakai City. (1985). *Traditional Industries in Sakai City*.

Institute of Innovation Research, Hitotsubashi University. (Ed.) (2001). *Introduction to Innovation Management*. Tokyo: Nihon Keizai Shinbunsha.

Institution of History of Suzuki Motor Corp. (1970). *A 50-Year History* (50年史).

Institution of History of Toyota Motor Corp. (1967). *A 30-Year History of Toyota Motors*.

Ishii, T. (1979). *Sakichi Toyoda and Development of Loom Technology* (豊田佐吉と織機技術の発展) (1–6) Hatsumei, *76*(1)–(6).

Ishii, T. (1979–80). *Communication Technology and Invention in Modern Japan* (近代日本の通信技術と発明) (1)–(6). *Hatsumei, 76*(9)–*77*(6).

Ishii, T. (1980–82). Industrial Technology in Pre-War Japan based on Patent Statistics (1–40). *Patent News,* 5460–5863.

Ishii, T. (1983). Industrial Growth and Patents in Pre-War Japan. (Yu Saito, Ed.). *The Economics of Invention and Patents.* Tokyo: Japan Institute of Invention and Innovation.

Ishii, T. (1986). *Development Process of Textile Machinery Technology.* (Nakaoka Ishii and Utsida, Eds) Chapter 2.

Ishii, T. (1987). *Development of Power Loom Manufacturing Technology.* (Minami and Kiyokawa Eds). Chapter 7.

Ishii, T. and Makino, F. (1982). Factors for Diffusion of Technology—Case Study of Power Loom. *The Economic Review, 33*(4) 334–359.

Iwautsi, R. (1973). The Rise and Development of Modern Engineers in Japan. *Japan Business History Review, 7*(3): 32–63.

Iwautsi, R. (1977). The Rise and Development of Engineers. (Hazama, H., Ed.). *Japanese Company and Society.* (Japanese Business History 6). Tokyo: Nihon Keizai Shinbunsha.

Japanese Battery and Appliance Industries Association. (1960). *The History of Japan Battery Industry.*

Japanese Bicycle Promotion Institute. (1973). *A Century of the Bicycle* (自転車の一世紀).

Japan Institute of Invention and Innovation. (1974). 70 Year-history of JIII.

Japanese Patent Office. (1950). List of Inventions and Utility Models (発明及び実用新案の分類表). Tokyo: Gihodo.

Japanese Patent Office. (1955). *A 70-Year History of Patent Law.* Tokyo: Gihodo.

Japanese Patent Office. (1958). The Classification Table of Patents (特許分類別目録). Tokyo: Gihodo.

Japanese Patent Office. (1958). *The Classification Table of Utility Models* (実用新案分類別目録). Tokyo: Gihodo.

Japanese Patent Office. (1984–85). *A 100-Year of History of Industrial Property Rights* (1). Tokyo: Gihodo.

Japanese Radio History Edition Association (日本無線史編纂委員会). (1950–51). *The History of Japanese Radio* (日本無線史) (1–3). Radio Regulatory Commission (電波監理委員会).

Kako, T. (1986). Development and Diffusion of the Appropriate Technology in Agriculture—The Case of the Walking Tractor. *The Economic Review, 37*(3): 193–207.

Kami, T. (1984). *Technology Innovation and Patent Economic Theory.* Tokyo: Taga Shupan.

Kanbayashi, T. (1943). The History of Japanese Industrial Electrification (日本工業電化発達史). (Koyama, H., Kanbayashi, T. and Kitahara, M., Ed.). *Research on Japanese Industrial Organization* (日本産業機構研究). Tokyo: Ito Books.

Kankoukai , MBS. (1959). National Statistic Table of 1874 (7th year of Meiji) (明治7年府県物産表). *Historical Material of Industrial Development in the Early Meiji Period* (明治前期産業発達史資料), 1.

Kawamura, M. (1994). The Condition of the Bicycle Industry in Sakai in Meiji・ Taisho Japan （明治・ 大正期における堺の自転車工業の状況について). *Historical Review of Transport and Communications, 34.*

Kiyokawa, Y. (1973). On the Technology of Cotton Industry: Ante-Bellum Japanese Case (1). *The Economic Review, 24*(2): 117–137.

Kiyokawa, Y. (1974). On the the Japanese-owned Cotton Mills as a Transfered Technology to China. *The Economic Review, 25*(3): 238–263.

Kiyokawa, Y. (1975). The Technology Gap and Establishment Process of Introduction Technology: Focusing on the Textile Industry (技術格差と導入技術の定着過程：繊維産業の経験を中心に). (Okawa, K and Minami, R., Eds). *The Economic Development of Modern Japan.* Tokyo: Toyo Keizai.

Kiyokawa, Y. (1984). Issues about Acceptance of Western Technologies (欧米技術の受容をめぐる諸問題). (Socio-Economic History Society). *Studies in Socio-Economic History* (The 50th Anniversary of the E stablishment of Socio-Economic History). Tokyo: Yuhikaku Publishing

Kiyokawa, Y. (1985). Choice of Technique in the Japanese Cotton Spinning Industry— The Case of the Ring Frame. *The Economic Review, 36*(3): 214–227.

Kiyokawa, Y. (1995). *Technology Diffusion and Economic Development in Japan.* Tokyo: Toyo Keizai.

Kiyokawa, Y. (Ed.). (1987). *Industrialization and Technological Progress in Japan.* Tokyo: Toyo Keizai.

Kobayashi, M. (1977). *Industrialization and Transfer of State Enterprises to Private Ownership in Japan.* Tokyo: Toyo Keizai.

Kojima, K. (1966). *The Trade and Economic Development of Japan* (日本貿易と経済発展). Tokyo: Kunimoto Syobo.

Kojima, K. (1973). *International Trade and Multinational Enterprises* (世界貿易と多国籍企業). Tokyo: Sobunsha.

Kuznets. (1973). Summary and Criticism (総括と批判)（Part 2. (Okawa, K. and Hayami, Y., Eds). *Long-Term Analysis of the Japanese Economy: Development, Structure and Fluctuation* (日本経済の長期分析：成長・ 構造・ 波動). Tokyo: Nihon Keizai Shinbunsha.

Makino, F. (1987). Power Selection of the Silk-Spinning Industry (製糸業における動力選択). *Bulletin of Tokyo Gakugei University: Part 3: Social Science, 39*: 31–45.

Makino, F. (1996). *The Invited Prometheus – Technological Development in Prewar Japan.* Tokyo: Fukosha.

Matsuda, Y., Sato, M. and Arita, F. (1984). Factory Manufacturing in Later Meiji Period. *The Hitotsubashi Review, 29*(3): 279–302.

Matsumoto, T. (1993). Functions of Local Trade Associations and the Local Manufacturing Insustry in Interwar Japan. *Socio-Economic History, 58*(5): 609–639.

Minami, R. (1965). *Railway Transportation and Electricity* (鉄道と電力). Tokyo: Toyo Keizai.

Minami, R. (1973). Economic Growth and Dual Labor Market Theory (経済成長と二重構造). (Okawa, K and Hayami, Y., Ed.). *Long-Term Analysis of the Japanese Economy: Development, Structure and Fluctuation* (日本経済の長期分析：成長・ 構造・ 波動). Tokyo: Nihon Keizai Shinbunsha.

Minami, R. (1974). The Introduction of Electric Power and Its Impact on the Manufacturing Industries: With Special Reference to Smaller Scale Plants. *The Hitotsubashi review, 71*(4): 77–105.

Minami, R. (1976). *The Power Revolution and Technological Developments*. Tokyo: Toyo Keizai.

Minami, R. (1981). *Economic Development in Japan*. Toyo Keizai.

Minami, R. (1987). *The Technological Development in Japan: Overview of Pre-war Period*(日本の技術発展：戦前期の概観) (Minami and Kiyokawa, Ed.), Chapter 1.

Minami, R. (1996). *Economic Development and Income Distribution in Japan*. Tokyo: Iwanami Shoten.

Minami, R. (2002). *Economic Development in Japan* (3rd edn). Tokyo: Toyo Keizai.

Minami, R. (Ed.). (1975). *Economic Development in Modern Japan*. Tokyo: Toyo Keizai.

Minami, R. and Kiyokawa, Y. (Eds). (1987). *The Nature and Meaning of Technological Development in Japan* (日本の技術発展：その特質と含意). (Minami and Kiyokawa, Eds). Chapter 14.

Minami, R. and Makino, F. (1983). Choice of Technology—An Analysis of Cotton Weaving Industry. *The Economic Review*, *34*(3): 216–230.

Minami, R. and Makino, F. (1986). Power Revolution in the Lumbering Industry—An Economic Analysis. *The Economic Review*, *37*(3): 208–220.

Minami, R. and Makino, F. (1987). *Technical Choice of Silk Industry*. (Minami and Kiyokawa, Eds). Chapter 3.

Minami, R. and Makino, F. (1988). Factors of the Mechanization of the Japanese Rural Weaving Industry, 1910–20. *The Economic Review*, *39*(4): 308–315.

Minami, R. and Makino, F. (Eds). (2014). *Long-term Economics Statistics in Asian Countries 3: China*. Tokyo: Toyo Keizai.

Ministry of Education, Science and Culture. (1962). *The Growth and Education in Japan* (日本の成長と教育). Tokyo: Teikoku Chiho Gyosei Gkkai.

Ministry of International Trade and Industry. (Ed.). (1961). *A 50-Year History of Industrial Statistics* (工業統計50年史).

Ministry of International Trade and Industry. (Ed.). (1964). *The History of Business and Industrial Policy* (商工政策史), *14*. Publishing Association of History of Business and Industrial Policy.

Ministry of International Trade and Industry. (Ed.). (1979). *The History of Business and Industrial Policy* (商工政策史), *13*. Industrial Technology. Publishing Association of History of Business and Industrial Policy.

Miyata Manufacturing. (1959). *A 70-year History of Miyata Manufacturing*.

Miyazaki, K. (Ed.). (1960). *A History of the Japanese Battery Industry* (日本乾電池工業史). Japan Battery and Appliance Industries Association.

Morikawa, H. (1975). *Engineers: The Bearers of Japan Modernization* (技術者：日本近代化の担い手). Tokyo: Nihon Keizai Shinbunsha.

Morikawa, H. (1980). Historical Studies on the Management of the Zaibatsu. Tokyo: Toyo Keizai.

Murakami, N. (1986). Innovation and Evolution of Market Structure—A Study of the Postwar Japanese Textile Industry. *The Economic Review, 37*(1): 34–42.

Murakami, N. (1988). Innovation, Firm Size, and Emissions Regulation in Automobile Industry—Schumpeterian Hypothesis Reconsidered. *The Economic Review, 39*(4): 325–335.

Murashita, Y. (1989). The Transition of Motive Power in Japanese Factories, 1904–1920: Based on Kojo Tsuran. *Socio-Economic History, 54*(5): 673–699.

Murashita, Y. (1990). The Motive Power of Japanese Factories during its Early Stage: based on Kojo Tsuran (工場通覧からみた工場創業期の原動力). *The Journal of Economic Studies*. (Seikei University), *20*(2): 133–142.

Murayama, T. (Ed.). (1939). *Invention of the Internal Combustion Engine* (内燃機関の発明). Tokyo: Yokendo.

Nakakawa, K. (1981). *An Introduction of Comparative Studies of Management* (比較経営史序説). Tokyo: University of Tokyo Press.

Nakamura, K. (1944). *The 50-Year History of Invention*. Tokyo: Tokyo Shuppan.

Nakamura, T. (1976). The Size and Structure of Traditional Industry: Based on Population Census in 1920 (9th year of Taisho). (Umemura, M., Shinbo, H., Nishikawa, S. and Hayami, A. Eds). *The Development of the Japanese Economy: From Tokugawa Japan to Modern Japan* (日本経済の発展：近世から近代へ). Tokyo: Nihon Keizai Shinbunsha.

Nakamura, T. (1985). *The Economy in the Meiji-Taisho Period*. Tokyo: University of Tokyo Press.

Nakamura, T. (1993). *Japanese Economy: The Growth and Structure* (日本経済:その成長と構造). Tokyo: University of Tokyo Press.

Nakamura, T. (Ed.). (1997). *Economic Development and Traditional Industry of Japan* (日本の経済発展と在来産業). Tokyo: Yamakawa Shuppansha.

Nakamura, T. and Odaka, K. (1989). *Dual Labor Market Theory*. Odaka, K. (Ed.). Tokyo: Iwanami Shoten.

Nakaoka, T. (1992). Technology Transfer and Traditional Industry (技術移転と在来産業). *Studies in Socio-Economic History* (The 60th Anniversary of the establishment of Socio-Economic History). Tokyo: Yuhikaku Publishing.

Nakaoka, T., Ishii, T. and Uchida, H. (1986). *Technological Development in Modern Japan*. Tokyo: United Nations University.

NEC Corporation. (1972). *A 70-Year History of NEC Corporation* (日本電気株式会社70年史).

Nichibei Fuji Cycle. (1982). *A 80-Year History of the Nichibei Fuji Cycle* (日米富士自転車80年史稿).

Nishikawa, S. (1985). *A Growth History of the Japanese Economy*. Tokyo: Toyo Keizai.

Nishikawa, S. and Abe, T. (Eds). (1990). *The Era of Industrialization* (産業化の時) (Part 1) Tokyo: Iwanami Shoten.

Nissan Motor Co., Ltd. (1965). *A 30-Year History of Nissan Motors* (日産自動車30年史).

No, I. (1999). The Rise and Development of Three-wheeled Vehicle Manufacturing in Inter-war Japan. *Socio-Economic History*, 65(3): 295–314.

Noritz Bicycle (ノーリツ自転車). (1983). *Memories of Past 100 Years* (茫茫百年).

Odaka, K. (1984). *Labor Market Analysis: The Development of Dual Labor Market Theory in Japan* (労働市場分析：二重構造の日本的展開). Tokyo: Iwanami Shoten.

Odaka, K. (1989). Dual Labor Market Theory. (Nakamura, T. and Odaka, K., Eds). *Dual Labor Market Theory* (Economic History of Japan, 6). Tokyo: Iwanami Shoten.

Odaka, K. (1990). Bearer for Industry (産業の担い手). (Nishikawa, S and Abe, T., Eds). *The Era of Industrialization* (産業化の時代) (Part 1) Economic History of Japan, 4). Tokyo: Iwanami Shoten.

Odaka, K. (1993). *The World of Craftsmen and the World of Factory Men*. Tokyo: Libro Co. Ltd.

Odaka, K. (1995). Adaption of Factory System and Labor Management (工場制度の定着と労務管理). (Miyamoto, M. and Abe, T., Eds). *Innovation of Management and Industrialization* (経営革新と工業化) (Japanese Business History 2). Tokyo: Iwanami Shoten.

Odaka, K. and Saito, O. (Eds). (1996). *200 Years of the Japanese Economy* (日本経済の200年) Tokyo: Nippon Hyoron Sha.

Okawa, K. (1962). *An Analysis of the Japanese Economy*. Tokyo: Shunjusha.

Okawa, K and Hayami, Y. (1975). Employment and Wages under the Dual Labor Market Theory (二重構造下の雇用と賃金) (Okawa, K. and Minami, R. Eds). *Economic Development in Modern Japan.* Tokyo: Toyo Keizai.

Okawa, K and Hayami, Y. (Eds). (1973). *A Long-Term Analysis of the Japanese Economy: Development, Structure and Fluctuation* (日本経済の長期分析：成長・構造・波動). Tokyo: Nihon Keizai Shinbunsha.

Okawa, K. and Kohama, H. (1993). *Theory of Economic Development.* Tokyo: Toyo Keizai.

Okawa, K. and Minami, R.. (1975). Employment and Wages under the Dual Labor Market Theory (二重構造下の雇用と賃金). (Minami, R. and Okawa, K., Eds). *Economic Development in Modern Japan.* Tokyo: Toyo Keizai.

Okawa, K. and Rosovsky. H. (1966). The 100-Year Economic Growth in Japan (日本における経済成長の百年) (Lockwood, W.W. Ed.). *The State and Economic Enterprise in Japan: Essays in the Political Economy of Growth.* Tokyo: Nihon Keizai Shinbunsha.

Ono, A. (1968). Technical Progress and Types of Borrowed Technology (技術進歩と Borrowed Technology の類型). (Tsukui, J. and Murakami, Y., Eds). *The Outlook for Theory of Economic Growth* (経済成長理論の展望). Tokyo: Iwanami Shoten.

Ono, A. (1986). Borrowed Technology in Iron and Steel：Brazil, India, and Japan. (Okawa, K., Ed.). *Japan and Developing Countries.* Chapter 7. Tokyo: Keiso Shobo.

Ono, A. and Minami, R. (1973). *Economic Growth and Dual Labor Market Theory* (Okawa, K and Hayami, Y. Eds). Chapter 5.

Otsuka, K. (1987). *Development and Technology Revolution of the Cotton Industry* (綿工業の発展と技術革新). (Minami, R. and Kiyokawa, Y., Eds). Chapter 6.

Otsuka, K. (1990). *Economic Development and Choice of Technology: The Experience of Japan and Developing Countries* (経済発展と技術選択：日本の経験と発展途上国). Tokyo: Bunshindo.

Publishing Association of Automobile Industrial History (自動車工業史刊行部会). (1965). *History of Japanese Automobile Industry* (日本自動車工業史稿)(1). Tokyo: Hosokawa Kappanjo.

Publishing Association of Automobile Industrial History (自動車工業史刊行部会). (1967). *History of Japanese Automobile Industry* (日本自動車工業史稿),（２）. Tokyo: Hosokawa Kappanjo.

Publishing Association of Automobile Industrial History (自動車工業史刊行部会). (1969). *History of Japanese Automobile Industry* (日本自動車工業史稿),（３）. Tokyo: Hosokawa Kappanjo.

Sakai City Hall. (1971). *The Sequel of History of Sakai City* (堺市史続編), 2.

Saito, K. (1987). *The Study on "New Konzen" Theroy: Masatoshi Okochi and Riken Group* (新興コンツェルン理研の研究：大河内正敏と理研産業団). Tokyo: Jichosha.

Saito, O. (1985). *The Age of Proto-Industrialization.* Tokyo: Nippon Hyoron Sha.

Shinbo, H. (1978). *Price Movements and Economic Development in Tokugawa Japan.* Tokyo: Toyo Keizai.

Shinbo, H. (1995). *A Handbook of Modern Japanese Economic History.* Tokyo: Sobunsha.

Saito, T. (1979). *Rickshaw.* Aichi: Quali.

Saito, T. (1992). *Cultural History of Rut* (轍の文化史). Tokyo: Diamond.

Saitou, T. (1979). *Jinrikisha* Aichi: Quali.

Sakiura, S. (1984). *An Economic Analysis of Rice Breeding*. Tokyo: Yokendo.

Sakuma, A. (1998). *Innovation and Market Structure* (イノベーションと市場構造). Tokyo: Yuhikaku Publishing.

Sano, Y. (1980). *The History of Invention – Bicycle* (発明の歴史自転車). Tokyo: Japan Institute of Invention and Innovation.

Sano, Y. (1985). *A Cultural History of the Bicycle* (自転車の文化史). Tokyo: Bun-ichi Sogo Shuppan.

Sawai, M. (1991). Science and Technology Policies During the 2nd Sino-Japanese War. (Nihon, K. and Kai, K., Eds). *Modern Japan Research: Economic Policy and Industry* (近代日本研究経済政策と産業). Tokyo: Yamakawa Shuppansha.

Sawai, M. (1995). Heavy Industrialization and Engineers (重化学工業化と技術者). (Miyamoto, M. and Abe, T., Eds). *Business Innovation and Industrialization* (経営革新と工業化) (Japanese Business History 2). Tokyo: Iwanami Shoten.

Sekiguchi, S. (1988). *The Economics of Direct Foreign Investment and Transfer of Technology*. Tokyo: Chuo Keizai Sha.

Shimizu, H. (1953). The Spread of Western-style Plowing with Draught Animals and the Development of Tilling Technology. Association of Agricultural Development History (農業発達史調査会). *History of Japanese Agricultural Development* (日本農業発達史), 1). Tokyo: Chuokoronsha.

Shimizu, H. (1954). The Early Stages of Agricultural Machine Development (農機具発達の一段階). Association of Agricultural Development History (農業発達史調査会). *History of Japanese Agricultural Development* (日本農業発達), 4). Tokyo: Chuokoronsha.

Shintani, M. (1987). *The Choice of Technology in the Tea-processing Industry* (製茶業における技術選択). (Minami and Kiyokawa, Eds). Chapter 2.

Shinohara, M. (1972). Industrial Production. *Long-Term Economic Statistics of Japan, 10*. Tokyo: Toyo Keizai.

Shinohara, M. (1976). *The Theory of Industrial Structure* (産業構造論). (2nd edn, Economics 18). Tokyo: Chikuma Shobo .

Shionoya, Y. (1987). Two-sector Pattern of Industrialization: Criticism of Hoffmann Rules. (Yuzo Yamada, et al., Eds). *Economic Growth and Industrial Structure* (経済成長と産業構造). Tokyo: Shunjusha.

Socio-Economic History. (1979). *Energy and Economy*. Osaka: Western Japan Culture Association.

Sugihara, K. (1996). *Patterns and Development of Intra-Asian Trade*. Kyoto: Minerva Shobor.

Sugiura, Y. (1987). *Spatial Diffusion of Technology: A Case of Spread of Electric Light Company in Fukui*. (Minami and Kiyokawa, Eds). Chapter 10.

Sugiura, Y. (1988). Diffusion of Electric Motors among Silk Mills—A Case of Fukui Prefecture. *The Economic Review, 39*(4): 298–307.

The History of Science Society of Japan. (1967). *Japanese Studies in the History of Science 3: Overview of History* 3 . Tokyo: Dai-Ichi Hoki.

The Japan Bicycle News (日本輪界新聞社). (1959). *The Development of Local Cycle* (地方輪界の歩み).

The Japan Rubber Manufacturers Association. (1969). *The History of Japan Rubber Manufacturing Industry,1*. Tokyo: Toyo Keizai.

The Japan Society of Mechanical Engineers. (Ed.). (1949). *A 50-Year History of the Japanese Machine Industry* (日本機械工業50年).

Takagi, Y. (1992). *Development Economics*. Tokyo: Yuhikaku Publishing.

Takagi, Y. (1981–1986). Changes in Industrial Processing Technology of Bicycle Parts(1–15). *Technology Information of Bicycle*, 13–32.

Takahashi, K. (1936). *An Autobiography of Korekiyo Takahashi.* Tokyo: Chikura Shobo.

Takeshita, J. (1980). *Japanese Bicycle Industry in the Formative Period* (形成期のわが国自転車産業). United Nations University Project.

Takeshita, J. (1984). *Japanese Bicycle Industry in the Establishment Period* (確立期のわが国自転車産業). Bulletin of the Faculty of School Ecomonic, Hiroshima University, 5: 99–142.

Tamura, D. (1937). *The Overview of Invention of Photography.* Tokyo: Hatsumei Shuppansha.

Tamura, T. (1988–1989). History of Japanese Patent Law (1–3). *Patent Management, 38*(10). *39*(2)–(4).

Tanaka, Y. and Wakimoto, K. (1983). *Multivariate Statistical Analysis.* Tokyo: Gendai-Sugakusha.

Tanimoto, M. (1998). *The Weaving Industry in the Japanese Indigenous Economic Development.* Nagoya: The University of Nagoya Press.

Terai, E. (1939). *Bicycle in Sakai City.* Bicycle Industry Association of Sakai City.

Tokyo Exhibition for Encouragement of National Industries in Commemoration of the Ceremony of Enthronement. (1929). *The Report of Tokyo Exhibition for Encouragement of National Industries in Commemoration of the Ceremony of Enthronement* (大礼記念・ 国産振興東京博覧会審査報告) (1928).

Tokyo Industrial Research Institution. (1951). *A 50-Year History of the Tokyo Industrial Research Institution.* Tokyo.

Torii, Y. (1979). *Theory of Economic Evolution (An Introduction to Economics 10).* Tokyo: Toyo Keizai.

Tsunoyama, S. (1988). *Trading State. Japanese Information Strategy: Review Consular Report* (通商国家 日本の情報戦略： 領事報告を読む).

Tsunoyama, S. (Ed.). (1986). *A Study on Japanese Consular Reports* (日本領事報告の研究). Tokyo: Dobunkan.

Yimayi, K., Uzawa, H., Komiya, R., Negishi, T. and Murakami, Y. (1972). *Price Theory* III. Tokyo: Iwanami Shoten.

Uchida, H. (1986). *The History of Technological Policy.* Nakaoka , Ishii and Uchida (1986). Chapter 3.

Uchida, H. (1988). Growth and Distribution of Engineers for the Industrial Development 1880–1920—A Statistical Survey. *The Economic Review, 39*(4): 289–297.

Uchida, H. (1990). Transfer of Technology. Nishikawa, S. and Abe, T. (Ed.). *The Era of Industrialization* (産業化の時代) (Part 1). (Economic History of Japan 4). Tokyo: Iwanami Shoten.

Udagawa, M. (1984). *History of Conglomerates' Management•Newly-risen Conglomerates.* Tokyo: Nihon Keizai Shimbun, Inc

Uekusa, M. (1982). *Industrial Organization.* Tokyo: Chikuma Shobo.

Uekusa, M. (Ed.). (1995). *Japanese Industrial Organization.* Tokyo: Yuhikaku Publishing.

Umemura, M., Takamatsu, N. and Ito, S. (1983). Regional Economics Statistics (地域経済統計). *Long-Term Economic Statistics of Japan, 13.* Tokyo: Toyo Keizai.

Umemura, M., Takamatsu, N., Umemura, M., Akasaka, K., Minami, R., Takamatsu, N., Akira, K. and Ito, S. (1988). Labor Force. *Long-Term Economic Statistics of Japan 2.* Tokyo: Toyo Keizai.

Wakasugi, R., Tanichi, M., Wada, Y. and Toyata, F. (1996). *Technology Revolution and Economies of Scale: One Mystery* (技術革新と規模の経済：１つの謎). (Research Series 30). The Research Institute of International Trade and Industry.

Watanabe, T. (1996). *Development Economics: Economics and Modern Asia* (2nd edn). Tokyo: Nippon Hyoron Sha.

Yamaguchi, K. (1965). *Economic Analysis of Early Meiji Era* (明治前期経済の分). Tokyo: University of Tokyo Press.

Yamaguchi, K. et al. (Eds). (1966). *A 100-Year History of Japanese Industry* (日本産業百年史). Tokyo: Nihon Keizai Shinbunsha.

Yamamoto, M. (1973). *The History of Japanese Exhibitions* (日本博覧会史). Tokyo: Risosha.

Yamamoto, Y. (Ed.). (1990). *The Era of Industrialization* (産業化の時代) (Part 2). Tokyo: Iwanami Shoten.

Yamaoka, S. (1988). *Japanese Diesel Car: Technology Formation of Automobile Industry and Society* (日本のディーゼル自動車：自動車工業の技術形成と社会). Tokyo: Nihon Keizai Hyoronsha.

Yamazawa, I. (1984). *Economic Development of Japan and International Trade*. Tokyo: Toyo Keizai.

Yamazawa, I. and Yamamoto, Y. (1979). *Foreign Trade and Balance of Payments*. Tokyo: Toyo Keizai.

Yoshifuji, K. (1982). *Summary of Patent Law (6th ed.)*. Tokyo: Yuhikaku.

Yui, T. (1964). *The Historical Study on the Policies of Small- and Medium-sized Enterprises* (中小企業政策の史的研究). Tokyo: Toyo Keizai.

2. English Literature

Arrow, K. J. (1962a). Economic Welfare and the Allocation of Resources for Invention in R. Nelson (Ed.), *The Rate and Direction of Invention Activity: Economic and Social Factors*, N. B. E. R., Princeton NJ: Princeton University Press.

Arrow, K. J. (1962b). The Economic Implication of Learning by Doing. *Review of Economic Studies*, 29 (June): 153–173.

Baldwin, W. L. and J. T. Scott. (1987). *Market Structure and Technological Change*. Chichester: Harwood.

Barro, R. J. and Martin, X. S. I. (1992). Convergence. *Journal of Political Economy 100*, Apr.

Barro, R. J. and Martin, X. S. I. (1995) *Economic Growth*. New York: McGraw-Hill.

Barsby, S. L. (1969). Economic Backwardness and the Characteristics of Development. *Journal of Economic History*, 29: 449–472.

Baumol, W. J. (1986). Productivity Growth, Convergence and Welfare: What the Long-Run Data Show. *American Economic Review 76*, Dec.

Clark, C. (1940). *The Conditions of Economic Progress*.

Cohen, W. M. and Levin, R. C. (1989). Empirical Studies of Innovation and Market Structure in Schmalensee, R. and Willig, R. (Eds). *Handbook of Industrial Organization*. Amsterdam: North Holland.

Coombs, R., Saviotti, P. and Walsh, V. (1987). *Economics and Technological Change*, London: Macmillan.

David, P. A. (1975). *Technical Choice, Innovation and Economic Growth: Essays on American and British Experience in the Nineteenth Century*. Cambridge: Cambridge University Press.

Davies, S. (1979). *The Diffusion of Process Innovations*. Cambridge: Cambridge University Press.

De Long, J. B. (1988). Productivity Growth, Convergence, and Welfare: Comment. *American Economic Review 78*: 1138–1154.

Dosi, G. et al. (1988). *Technical Change and Economic Theory*. London: Pinter Books.

Freeman, C. (1982). *The Economics of Industrial Innovation*. Harmondsworth: Penguin.

Gerschenkron, A. (1962). *Economic Backwardness in Historical Perspective*. Cambridge, MA: Harvard University Press.

Guan, Q. (关权). (2000). Innovation and Market Structure in Prewar Japan. *Hitotsubashi Journal of Commerce and Management, 35*(1): 19–36.

Guan, Q. (关权). (2001). Technological Innovation and the Patent System in Prewar Japan. *Hitotsubashi Journal of Commerce and Management, 36*(1). Oct.

Hoffmann, W. G. (1958). *The Growth of Industrial Economies*. Translated by W. O. Henderson and Chaloner, W. H. Manchester.

Jewkes, J. and Sawers, D. and Stillerman, R. (1969). *The Sources of Invention* (2nd edn). London: Macmillan.

Jones, C. I. (1998). *Introduction to Economic Growth*. New York: Norton.

Kamien, M. I. and Schwartz, N. L. (1982). *Market Structure and Innovation*. Cambridge: Cambridge University Press.

Kaufer, E. (1989). *The Economics of the Patent System*. Chur: Harwood.

Kuznets, S. (1955). Economic Growth and Income Inequality. *American Economic Review, 45*(1): 1–28.

Kuznets, S. (1966). *Modern Economic Growth: Rate, Structure and Spread*, New Haven, CT and London: Yale University Press.

Kuznets, S. (1968). Notes on Japan's Economic Growth in Klein, L. and Ohkawa, K. (Eds), *Economic Growth: The Japanese Experience since the Meiji Era*. Richard D. Irwin.

Kuznets, S. (1971). *Economic Growth of Nations: Total Output and Production Structure*. Cambridge MA: Harvard University Press.

Lin, J. Y. (1995). The Needham Puzzle: Why the Industrial Revolution Did Not Originate in China. *Economic Development and Cultural Change, 43*(2): 269–292.

Machlup, F. (1958). *An Economic Review of the Patents System*, Study No.15 of Subcommittee on Patents, Trademarks and Copyrights of the Committee on the Judiciary United State Sen., 85th Cong., 2nd Sess.

Mansfield, E. (1968a). *The Economics of Technological Change*. New York: Norton.

Mansfield, E. (1968b). *Industrial Research and Technological Innovation: An Econometric Analysis*, New York: Norton.

Mankiw, N. G. and Romer, D. and Well, D. (1992). A Contribution to the Empirics of Economic Growth. *Quarterly Journal of Economics, 107*: 407–437.

Minami, R. (1987) *Pawer Revolution in the Industrialization of Japan: 1885–1940*. Kinokuniya.

Minami, R., Kwan, K S, Makino, F. and Seo, Joung-Hae (Eds). (1995). *Acquiring, Adapting and Developing Technologies: Lessons from the Japanese Experience*. London: Macmillan.

Mowery, D. and Rosenberg, N. (1979). The Influence of Market Demand upon Innovation: A Critical Review of Some Recent Empirical Studies. *Research Policy*, 8: 102–153.

Nordhaus, W. D. (1969). *Invention, Growth, and Welfare: A Theoretical Treatment of Technological Change*. Cambridge MA: MIT Press.

Ono Akira, (1986). Technical Progress in Silk Industry in Prewar Japan: The Types of Borrowed Technology. *Hitotsubashi Journal of Economics, 27*(1): 1–10.

Otsuka, K., Ranis, G. and Saxonhouse, G. (1988). *Comparative Technology Choice in Development: The Indian and Japanese Cotton Textile Industry*. London: Macmillan.

Rosovsky, H. (1961). *Capital Formation in Japan: 1868–1940*. Free Press of Glencoe.

Schmookler, J. (1957). Inventors Past and Present. *Review of Economics and Statistics, 8*.

Schmookler, J. (1966). *Invention and Economic Growth*. Cambridge MA: Harvard University Press.

Schumpeter, J. A. (1934). *The Theory of Economic Development: An Inquiry into Profits, Capital, Credit, Interest, and the Business Cycle*. Cambridge MA: Harvard University Press.

Schumpeter, J. A. (1950). *Capitalism, Socialism and Democracy* (3rd edn). New York: Harper & Row.

Solow, R. M. (1956). A Contribution to the Theory of Economic Growth. *Quarterly Journal of Economics, 70*: 65–94.

Solow, R. M. (1957). Technical Change and the Aggregate Production Function. *Review of Economics and Statistics, 39*: 312–320.

Stoneman, P. (1983). *The Economics of Technological Change*, Oxford: Oxford University Press.

Stoneman, P. (Ed.). (1995). *Handbook of the Economics of Innovation and Technological Change*. Oxford: Basil Blackwell Ltd.

Vernon, R. (1966). International Investment and International Trade in the Product Cycle. *Quarterly Journal of Economics, 3*: 190–207.

3. Chinese Literature

Chinese Bicycle Association. (1991). *A Brief History of China's Bicycle Industry*.

Guan, Q. (2011a). China's Industrial Production in the 1910s: Evaluation and Estimation of "Statistics Table of Agriculture and Commerce". *China Review of Political Economy* (Renmin University of China), 4: 121–144.

Guan, Q. (2011b). The Patent System and the Development of the Japanese Economy. *Nankai Japan Studies*, Beijing: World Affairs Press.

Guan, Q. (2013). The Cycle and Grade of Economic Take-off and Advantage of Backwardness. *Frontiers, 29*: 42–51.

Guan, Q. (2014). *Development Economics: China's Economic Development*. Beijing: Tsinghua University Press.

Guan, Q. (2015). Comparative Study of Industries in China and Japan in the 1930s. *Open Economic Review* (Renmin University of China), 5: 143–161.

Guan, Q. (2017). The Development of China's Bicycle Industry. *Research on the History of Industry and Technology* 1.

Guan, Q. (2018). *Development Economics*. Beijing: China Renmin University Press.

Guan, Q. (2019a). *China's Economic Development: Centennial Course*, Beijing: Renmin University of China Press.

Guan, Q. (2019b). China's Industrial Development over 70 Years. *Economic Theory and Business Management* (Renmin University of China), 9: 4–17.

Liu, X. L. (1993). *Economics of Technological Innovation.* Economic Press China.

United Front Work Department of the CPC Central Committee. (1992). *Socialist Transformation of Capitalist Industry and Commerce in China: Central Volume,* Beijing: CPC History Publishing House.

Wang, H. X. (1988). *Phoenix over 30 Years: 1958–1988,* Shanghai Academy of Social Sciences Press.

Wang, J. F. and Xia, S. H. (1987). *Patent Law of China.* Beijing: Masses Publishing House.

Wu, B. S. (1947). *China's National Income, 1933, 1936 and 1946, Social Science,* 9(2): 12–30.

Wu, B. S.,Wang, F. S., Zhang, J. H., Ma, L. Y., Nan, Z. W., and Bei, Y. L. (1947). *China's National Income* (1933). Shanghai: Zhonghua Book Company.

Yang, D. L. and Hou H. P. (1931). *Statistics of China's International Trade Over Sixty-five Years.* Institute of Social Sciences, Academia Sinica.

4. Translated Literature

(France) Bergère. (1994). *The Golden Age of the Chinese Bourgeoisie* (translated by Zhang Fuqiang and Xu Shifen). Shanghai: Shanghai People's Publishing House.

(Japan) Hayami, Y. (US) Ruttan, V. W. (2000). *Agricultural Development: An International Perspective.* (translated by Guo X.,zhang, J. M. wang, S. M. Zhang, J. H. Luo, H. Y. Zhang, A. Z. and Huang, J. B.). Beijing: China Social Sciences Press.

(US) Kuznets, S. (1989). *Modern Economic Growth: Rate, Structure and Spread.* (translated by Dai Rui and Yi Cheng). Beijing: Beijing College of Economics Press.

(US) Kuznets, S. (1999). *Economic Growth of Nations* (translated by Chang, X., Pan, T. S., Huang Y. T. and Lin, N. S.). Beijing: The Commercial Press.

(Britain) Maddison, A. (2009). *The World Economy: Historical Statistics* (translated by Wu, X.Y., and Shi, F.Q.). Beijing: Peking University Press.

(Japan) Minami, R. (1991). *China's economic development: comparison with Japan* (translated by Jing Wenxue). Economic Management Press.

(Britain) Mitchell, B.R. (2002). *Palgrave International Historical Statistics.* (translated by He Liping). Beijing: Economic Science Press.

(US) Rostow, W.W. (1988). *The Economics of Take-Off into Sustained Growth* (translated by He L. P., Shen, X. Li, S. J. Wang, J. M. Liu, D. H. Chen, J. Zhu, S. Q. Qin, M. R. Lu, T. Dong, Y. Chu, H. J. Shen, W. L.). Chengdu: Sichuan People's Publishing House.

(US) Rostow, W.W. (2001). *The Stages of Economic Growth: A Non-Communist Manifesto* (translated by Guo Xibao and Wang Songmao). Beijing: China Social Sciences Press.

(US) Schumpeter, J. A. (1990). *Theory of Economic Development* (translated by He, W. and Yi, J. X.) Beijing: The Commercial Press.

(US) Schumpeter, J. A. (1999). *Capitalism, Socialism and Democracy.* (translated by Wu Liangjian). Beijing: The Commercial Press.

II. Materials

Bicycle Association. (1912). *National Yearbook of Bicycles* (Revised).

Bicycle Association. (1919). *Japanese Bicycle Yearbook.*

Japanese Invention Dictionary Publication Society. (1939). *Dictionary of Japanese Inventors.*

Japanese Statistical Society. (1987). *Long-term Statistics of Japan*, 1–5.

Kobe City Hall. (1935). *Industrial Survey*.

Matsuhara, K. (1952). *Top 50 Japanese Inventors*. Tokyo: Invention Book Publication Society.

Ministry of International Trade and Industry. (1961). *Industrial Statistics in 50 Years* (Document 1).

Nagoya City Department of Industry. (1936). *Industrial Survey*. (China) National Bureau of Statistics. *China Statistical Yearbook* for each year.

Nara, S. (1930). *Japanese Inventors, 1 and 2*. Tokyo: Imperial Inventor Biography Publication Society.

Nara, S. (1957). *Tokyo Inventor Biography*. Tokyo: Gihodo.

Nara, S. (1961). *Japan Inventor Biography*. Tokyo: Chartered News Agency

Osaka Invention Association. (1936). *Record of Japanese Inventors*.

Peace Memorial Tokyo Expo. (1923). *Peace Memorial Tokyo Expo, Review Report*

Statistics of Workshops by the Ministry of Commerce and Industry for each year.

Statistics Table of Agriculture and Commerce by the Works Bureau of Ministry of Agriculture and Commerce for each year.

Statistics of Workshops by the Works Bureau of Ministry of Agriculture and Commerce for each year.

Statistical Yearbook of the Ministry of the Army by the Ministry of the Army.

Shimano, T. (1980). *Statistical Table of Commodity Production. Output and Input over the Years*, Tokyo: Aritsuneshoin.

Shitiji, I. (1924). *Report of the 3rd Invention Expo*, 3rd Invention Expo.

Tokyo City Hall. (1934). *Industrial Survey*.

Tokyo Expo Committee. (1929). *Review Report of Tokyo Expo held to promote domestic commodities to celebrate the Emperor of Japan enthroning* (大礼記念、国産振興東京博覧会審査報告)(1928).

Tokyo Prefecture. (1916). Review Report of Tokyo Taisho Expo.

Toshitaka Eto. (1932). *Report of the 4th Invention Expo*, 4th Invention Expo.

Toyo Keizai Inc. (1935). *Overview of Japanese Trade*, Tokyo: Toyo Keizai.

Ukekawa, K. (1914). *Report of the 2nd Invention Expo*. 2nd Invention Expo.

Wakabayashiseya. (1909). *Report of the Invention Expo*. Invention Expo Office

Yukuzawa, K and Maeda, S. (1978). *Long-term Statistics of Japanese Trade*. Tokyo: Publisher.

Index

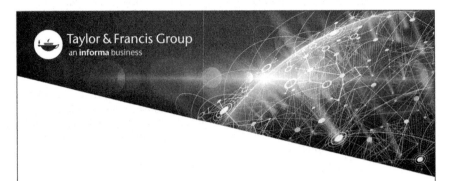